DEAD FASHION GIRL

DEAD FASHION GIRL:

A Situationist Detective Story

Fred Vermorel

For my parents, Jackie and Louis

Because I was told... warned by the [Police] Federation bloke, 'Look - mouth shut - don't say anything to anybody.' 'Cos he said 'you're walking on bloody broken glass.' And I obeyed that injunction. I kept... I made no further enquiries, I kept as far away... I had three kids to look after. I couldn't afford the push...

— *Ex-policeman on the Townsend murder investigation, interviewed for this book.*

Strange Attractor Press
BM SAP, London, WC1N 3XX, UK
www.strangeattractor.co.uk

Distributed by the MIT Press, Cambridge, Masschusetts.
And London, England
Printed and bound in Estonia by Tallinna Raamatutrükikoda

CONTENTS

PART ONE:
Dead Fashion Girl

PART TWO:
Other Connections, Other Theories

PART THREE:
Finding the Fifties: Snapshots

PART ONE:

Dead Fashion Girl

SCREENS

I'd just turned eight in September 1954, when Jean Townsend was murdered. The news swept round our junior school playground that morning like a dirty magazine, *Lilliput* or *Spick & Span*, exciting huddles of boys. My best friend Peter swore the victim had been strangled with her own silk stocking. That fitted with images of the curvy corpse ubiquitous in fifties' pulp: young women spread-eagled and splattered, with dead eyes and scarlet lips, mostly in lingerie – details of cleavage, garter and thigh lovingly picked out…

After school I ran home, got my bike out the shed and cycled to the crime scene. Jean Townsend's body was long gone, but there was a crowd still. Chattering that she was a local girl and something to do with the West End and fashion and nightclubs and film stars.

What struck me most were the screens.

General view of electoral screens around the Townsend crime scene.

Instead of tape, the police had cordoned the crime scene with polling booth screens from a nearby community hall. Then, to close gaps, they hung these screens with sacking. It looked incongruous and unsettling – like an art brut installation with Freudian undertones. As if the police were saying "don't look" – that there was something inside this huddle of screens we shouldn't see – something indecent…[1]

And of course, at the crime scene, everybody did look. Kids climbed on car bonnets, adults went on tiptoe, or lifted sacking.

When my father came home from work that evening he brought, as usual, the *Evening Standard*. The Townsend killing was front page. After dinner I spread the paper over the kitchen table looking for clues that might have eluded the police. More than half a century later I'm still looking.

---

1   The sight recalled the moveable screens often found in overcrowded post-war homes, creating polite fictions of privacy. There was a screen like that in my parents' bedroom, shielding my cot from their double bed. A folding Chinese screen – black and silky with flying herons, weeping willows and billowing clouds – through which I listened to their lovemaking.

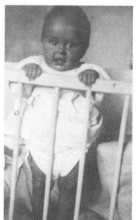

Detectives starting to put up the screens. Jean Townsend's body, covered by a tarpaulin, is arrowed. The papers described her corpse like a fashion spread: "Lovely Miss Jean Townsend, heavily made up, the fashion girl, a model, friend of stage and screen stars. Her black, gold striped scarf was still wound round her pretty neck, she wore an off-white swagger coat over a black high-necked dress with half-length sleeves, and jet earrings set with brilliants shaped in a circle with pendant beads. Her black velvet court shoes were pulled off and her legs and feet were bare showing red painted toe nails." [Composite quotation]

Tarpaulins cover spot where body was found

Police photographer

DETECTIVES EXAMINING GIRL'S SHOE

PATHOLOGIST DR. TEARE

D/SUPT. PERCY LAW SCOTLAND YARD PHOTOGRAPHIC CHIEF

W.P.C. SYLVIA THOMAS

PATHOLOGIST'S ASSISTANT MISS MARY SHIFTON

MR. LEWIS NICKOLLS SCOTLAND YARD LABORATORY

TEARE

In 1954, Donald Teare was the chief Home Office pathologist. A bit of a celebrity. Check out his smug face. But really, he didn't have much to be smug about. The year before being called to Jean Townsend's body he'd investigated the serial killer John Christie – for the second time. Teare's first investigation of Christie's victims back in 1949 had been problematic. He'd neglected to take a vaginal swab, which is basic, from one of the bodies. The result was that Christie's lodger, Timothy Evans, was wrongly accused of murder. Evans was hung. After that, Christie killed four more women, including his wife.

Anyway, here is Teare's autopsy report:

> At 1.50 p.m. [of the 15th September] I went to Uxbridge Mortuary and conducted a post-mortem examination on [Jean Townsend's] body...

> I found the deceased to be a well nourished young woman 5' 7" in height and of estimated weight between 8 and 8 1/2 stone. There were superficial abrasions on the tip of the tongue. A small blister on the left heel was covered by an adhesive dressing.

The black scarf was found to be wound round the neck three times – but was not knotted – the free ends lying at the back.

On removing the scarf an abrasion – 1/2" wide by 3/8" long was seen over the front of the throat at the level of the Adam's apple, on either side of this abrasion a pressure mark encircled the neck – varying in width from 1" to 2 1/4". In this pressure mark were seen lines of small haemorrhages corresponding to the folds of the scarf. At the back of the neck the pressure mark was particularly clearly defined, and one inch wide; its upper border was clearly marked by petechial [tiny red or purple spots] haemorrhages.

The right side of the heart was widely dilated and packed with dark blood.

The lungs were bulky and a large quantity of blood-stained froth was found in the air passages.

The stomach contained a medium sized partially digested meal in which fragments of meat – possibly liver – and vegetable matter – marrow, melon or peach – could be seen.

A careful examination of the pubic area, the vulva vagina, and anus failed to reveal any injury, nor could the presence of semen be detected with the naked eye. The vagina was rather moist, there was a little superficial erosion of the cervix, and the uterus showed changes in keeping with the end of a menstrual period.

A portion of skin on the back of the right thigh was covered with a glistening exudate - possibly slime from slugs - but was removed and handed to Superintendent Richardson.

The following samples were also removed and handed to the Superintendent:-

Head hair (plucked).
Pubic hair (plucked).
Head hair cut from the left parietal region
    where two small bruises, each ¼" in diameter
    were found in the scalp.
A smear from the vulva.
A smear from the vault of the vagina.
Heart blood.
Stomach and contents.
A piece of lacquered toe-nail.

I came to the following conclusions:–That death was due to:

Asphyxia due to strangulation by a scarf.

That death had occurred between 9.30 p.m. and 12.30 a.m. the previous night – probably round about midnight.

There was no evidence of a struggle.

While the removal of the underclothing was suggestive of an attempt at sexual interference, there were no marks on the body to confirm this suggestion.

The deceased was a perfectly healthy young woman – perfectly clean and well cared for. The "make-up" on the lips, toes and finger-nails appeared to be fresh.

Certain superficial abrasions on the body were due to the action of slugs.

The two small bruises in the scalp could have been caused by a fall onto even a soft surface.

Questioned several days later by the inquest jury, Teare repeated, "I could find no evidence that she put up a struggle in any way."

The jury foreman asked whether she had been "violated in any way."

No.

Detective Superintendent Richardson then testified:

Miss Townsend was lying on ground about two feet below the level of the footway. The ground was covered with tall grass and rough weeds. She was about 15 feet from a lamppost near the corner of Angus Drive.

Her handbag was beside her right hand and was partly open because it had no safety catch. She had long black elbow length silk gloves.

Her knickers, suspender belt, panties, stockings and right shoe were by her feet.

Coroner: Completely off her body?

Yes.

Richardson added that Jean Townsend had not been raped.

Coroner: Any signs of any violence?

The body was exceptionally neat and tidy and there were no outward signs of violence.

Coroner: Was there any sign of a struggle on the ground?

The ground was a little down trodden but nothing to indicate a serious struggle.

Richardson concluded,

In the course of our enquiries we have interviewed hundreds of people and we have not identified anyone in connection with this death.

Coroner: I take it your enquiries are still going on?

Yes, sir, and will proceed for some time to come.

The coroner summed up to the jury:

You may think there are strange factors in this case. She had this scarf around her neck but none of her clothing was disarranged except where the clothing was taken off neatly;

there was only a small [stocking] ladder which a girl coming at night could have made herself, the other shoe was found a little way away from her.

There were no signs of a struggle. She is a well-built young woman and one would have thought if anybody had assaulted her that she would have been the first person to defend herself but there is no evidence of that... The underclothing was taken off but there were no marks on her or her clothing and no marks of any violation.

The jury had already seen photos of Jean Townsend's body. They were now shown colour images of the murder scene, which they "viewed through a box lighted from the inside."

THE FASHION GIRL

Jean Mary Townsend was born on the 13th March, 1933. That very day, *Time Magazine* featured a laconic looking Adolf Hitler reclining in a garden deckchair with his dog Blondi. The week before, Radio Pictures had released the movie *King Kong*. The year also saw the publication of CG Jung's *Modern Man in Search of a Soul*: "teachings about the 'infantile-perverse-criminal' unconscious have led people to make a dangerous monster out of the unconscious, that really very natural thing."

Jean Townsend in the year she was killed, wearing the scarf she was strangled with.

Jean was an only child. Her lower middle-class parents came from the central London area of Paddington. When Jean was two-years-old the family moved 11 miles away, to 92 Bempton Drive, in the newly developed suburb of South Ruislip.

While Ruislip itself boasted a Manor Farm, a village green and a listing in the 1086 Domesday Book: a "leaping place on the river where rushes grow," South Ruislip was a drab annexe – a succession of ribbon estates developed from the 1930s.

Nevertheless, the semi-detached houses in Bempton Drive had generous back gardens, with bay windows and mock Tudor embellishments, and front gardens primly protected by dense hedges or castellated knee-high brick walls.

Plus, the area was well stocked with green spaces and municipal parks. At the bottom of Jean's street was zig zag Yeading Brook, surrounded by uncultivated shrubbery, a magnet for kids.

A short ride on the 158 bus from Jean's house was Ruislip Lido, which did for an ersatz seaside with a sandy beach, model railway, and ice-cream van.

Left. With my mother at Ruislip Lido, c.1950. Previous page. A postcard showing the Lido and high street church. A former South Ruislip resident reminisced, "In those days the Lido was a free zone – there wasn't anything organised or any activities out there. You just went up there and paddled or whatever you did." And, "There was one kid who lived almost opposite my school, Keith. He drowned in the Lido. Because in the war German bombers used to ditch a lot of their bombs around there, and some of these landed in the Lido and made quite deep bunkers under the water. This kid got trapped in one of the bunkers. He was about six."

Also a bus ride away was the extensive Ruislip Woods, wild enough to get lost in – thus congenial to lovers, truanting kids – and flashers.

In her memoir of a post-war Ruislip childhood, *What The Grown-Ups Were Doing* (2012), Michele Hanson describes being flashed by a "very rude man":

> He had on a rather shapeless brown hat, with the hat bit in a dome shape and the brim rather wavy, and he had a large, pink thumb sticking out of the front of his raincoat... but then I realised it was not a thumb... it had to be a penis.

The event and its police investigation aftermath are told in a jocular way.

"Karen" on the Ruislip Online site recalled "Naked Norman," from the same period. "He used to walk around in the woods wearing very little under his overcoat or Mac and he became the stuff of childhood scary fantasies."[2] Interviewed for this book, another female resident recalled,

> There was a man who'd run away from the American army base and was living wild in the woods. He was there for about six weeks. And the police were looking for him. They knew he was in there. They knew he was naked. He'd gone off his head. He'd made himself a sort of hidden camp. People thought he was Bigfoot. I wanted to see him so I went down to the woods all on my own. I never saw him – but I did try (laughs).[3]

Dog helps watch for 'Tarzan'

Police patrolling Park Woods at Ruislip, Middlesex, have been given a tracker dog to help hunt the "Tarzan" who scared a girl by waving a spear. The man, wearing only a loincloth, is said to have run "like the wind" when chased by a detective.

Daily Express, *June 1951*

Kids in those days were resourceful. In 1959, Veronica and Angela, two 12-year-olds, went adventuring in the woods equipped with sandwiches and a bottle of pop. A lorry driver threatened them with an airgun and attempted to molest Veronica. She smashed the bottle on his head. Then:

> We were struggling together to get the gun from the man. I started to run and got badly scratched in the bushes. I fell over and lost my shoes. He overpowered Veronica and then came for me. Eventually he made off.[4]

---

2   http://www.ruisliponline.com/lido/lidomemories.htm
3   Jackie Cliff, interview
4   *Daily Express*, April 21, 1959

———

Jean Townsend's father, Reginald, was a telephone engineer for the Post Office, an unassuming "quiet old stick." Her mother, Lilian, worked part-time for Hivac, a local radio valve factory. She also ran a "nice little industry" from her front room as a local hairdresser.

Lilian reputedly was,

> a terrible snob. People in the street used to say that. She'd never come to any community things, wouldn't go to street parties and so on. I don't know why she was such a snob. I suppose it's the same old thing – the less money you have the better you think you are.

That description is from Reg Hargrave, a friend and neighbour of the Townsends. His father had been to school with Jean Townsend's father but they lost touch. Then, unwittingly, both men, now married and with children, moved into Bempton Drive. They bumped into one another by accident one morning and renewed their friendship.

As an adult, Reg became interested in the Townsend case, and attempted to unmask what he believed was a cover-up (see below, The Carlodalatri Connection).

Another family in Bempton Drive linked the Townsends and Hargraves. This was the Sweetzers, who lived next door to the Hargraves. Reg often played with their daughter (Margaret) June Sweetzer. June was Jean Townsend's confidante and closest girlfriend. She later played a shadowy part in the original police investigation (again, see below, The Sweetzer Connection).

Reg Hargrave:

> They shared interests and had the same kind of talent. They were artistic and loved fashion. I remember June in her front room sketching pictures like in *Vogue* magazine. Women with extra-long legs – that sort of thing.

The three kids went to the same junior school, Lady Bankes. As Reg was a year younger than the girls it was their job to shepherd him, "talking over my head."

Like Lilian Townsend, the Sweetzers thought themselves above the rest of the street. Reg scoffed that the family bragged their semi,

> was a suntrap – so called. All the houses in our street had been built more or less the same way. But suntraps had white-facing on the front, so were supposedly posher.

The Sweetzers also boasted family in Culham-on-Thames, a twee Oxfordshire town where they holidayed each summer. Reg's vacations were more prosaic: "Year after bloody year we would traipse down to Eastbourne. It was a ritual."

During the war South Ruislip was bombed sporadically – it was near the military aerodrome at Northolt. Children would excavate recent bomb craters to collect the still-warm shrapnel.

Occasionally, V-bomb rockets passed overhead. Reg evoked their characteristic sound, "dum, dum, dum, dum… they had come all the way from Germany." When the sound stopped you waited for an explosion. "One afternoon one of them cut out over us and we thought that was us gone…" It exploded in nearby Dulverton Road, demolishing two houses.

The black market was rife. Another South Ruislip resident recalled that in her street (100 yards from Bempton Drive) lived a Mr Samms. "He was a black-market man. My mum said 'You must never go to see Mr Samms because he's a bad man.'

> We didn't know why Mr Samms wasn't in the war. People said he was a shirker. He was a little tiny fat man actually, wearing pebble glasses, so I don't think he would have been accepted in the army. He had a son called Terry, and Terry and me used to go out on our bikes together. But I wasn't supposed to tell mum about that because she said, 'Mr Samms, he's into black market and we think at night he goes and robs houses and

he gets all their butter and their corned beef. Bags of it –
he's got bags of it in his house. He sells it, and some nights
there's a queue.'[5]

Reg Hargrave also remembered a local butcher, Jim, "a big bloke –
always after the ladies," who did favours for local women amenable to
his "hanky panky." People joked that such women got "more than their
fair share of Jim's meat."

More hanky panky was provided by the large contingent of
American soldiers in South Ruislip. In Bempton Drive tongues
wagged when a neighbour became pregnant by a GI who married
and then left her. And:

There was a mother and daughter – both of them quite good
looking. The father, the husband, had gone off to war and these
two women – there was a regular stream of Americans. They
would turn up in uniform. People called it Bempton Drive's
'house of whores.'[6]

In those days, Reg said, Bempton Drive was, "a pretty noisy
environment. Girls used to play rounders in the street. I used to play
football. People were always shouting at us."

The street had its dramas. The Sweetzers lost one daughter, Davina, a
"blue baby" who died at seven. Another couple's daughter committed
suicide at thirty. A family at the top of the road had a "potty girl"
confined to her back garden who filled the air with "babbling and
shouting and screeching."

But the most notorious house in Bempton Drive was where the father
was sexually abusing his son and two daughters. People talked but did
nothing. It wasn't anyone's business.

---

5   Jackie Cliff, interview
6   Reg Hargrave, interview

[Reg Hargrave identified this family to me. June Sweetzer also knew about them. In the late 1990s she'd met one of the children, then working in a care home, who'd confirmed the abuse. This woman also told June that she and her siblings so hated their father they'd denounced him to the police as a suspect for Jean Townsend's killer. It's been suggested that one reason the Townsend file is closed is to protect this family. But if so, it would be simple to redact their allegation and identities. The survivors of the family declined to talk to me.]

Reg passed his 11-plus exam and progressed to grammar school. Jean and June both failed. They were sent to nearby Manor Senior.

> I think that narked Mrs Sweetzer. Every morning I'd set off in my smart new uniform and a cap. I saw less of the girls after that.

Then, aged 14, both girls unexpectedly got scholarships to study fashion at Ealing Art School.

Anti-clockwise from top. VE Day street party in Bempton Drive, 1945. Crop 1: Jean Townsend, aged 12 right and Reg Hargrave (far left, in school cap) left. Crop 2: a gap-toothed Jean Townsend, the only childhood picture of her.

MEPO 2/9623

The case files of the Metropolitan Police are kept in The National Archive, a fortress-like building in the London suburb of Kew, set in quaintly tree-lined and stuccoed suburbia. If you check the Archive web site for "Jean Townsend" you find "Unsolved murder of Jean Mary Townsend on 15th Sept. 1954 at Ruislip." The reference is MEPO 2/9623. A note explains, "This record is closed and cannot be viewed." The reason: "Contains sensitive personal information which would substantially distress or endanger a living person or his or her descendents."

Many have wondered about this. What kind of "personal information"? Who is this endangered living person? The mystery gets more intriguing when you realise the Townsend file was originally embargoed until 2058: 104 years after the murder. Unsolved murder case files are generally opened after 75 years. If there's an appeal they can be released earlier – and frequently are. An embargo for 104 years...

Murder on the way home
THE RIDDLE
OF JEAN'S
LAST WALK..

Following protests, the Met revised this embargo. The Townsend file would now be opened in 2031. But this 73-year closure was still perplexing. Especially for a stone-cold case.

In the late 1990s, as a university lecturer, I was given a research grant. I spent some of it investigating Jean Townsend's murder.

All those decades later it was a tricky event to revisit. Many witnesses had died or moved away. A folk memory of the killing lingered locally, but muddied by innuendo. Hadn't Jean Townsend been some kind of showgirl or nightclub hostess? And why was she out so late on her own that night? If not exactly a loose woman, then a woman on the loose? There was even chatter she'd been a prostitute who got unlucky. Newspaper archives offered mostly cliché and rumour. The police had no clue.

I made no progress.

Then, around 2002, I began to see that the internet and digitalised data bases might help, particularly in locating witnesses and establishing background.

MOST NIGHTS YOU'D JUST RUN

Story featuring Jackie Cliff with (right, inset) a painting of Jackie by Norman Hepple, Portrait of a Young Woman, 1953.

The first important witness I found was Jackie Cliff.

In 1954 Jackie had been a gift to tabloids covering the Townsend case. She was a local beauty, a bona fide model. The press took every opportunity to show pictures of her. They also loved her story of being stalked in Victoria Road – just like Jean.

"MODEL WAS STAND-IN AT FULL MURDER TRY-OUT. A golden-haired artist's model of 19 told the Murder Squad last night of her role as a 'stand-in' at what may have been a step-by-step rehearsal for the Ruislip murder..."

But where was Jackie now? She'd moved from Ruislip decades ago. She'd also changed her name. I eventually tracked her down to a first-floor apartment on the outskirts of Bath.

Jackie Cliff:

> I remember that day. It was a cold day, and my mum came in from Westmead shops and said, "Ooh, there's been a murder."
>
> I said, "You're joking – a murder?"
>
> I went straight out and looked and the police had put a sort of tarpaulin thing or whatever all over there.
>
> Later, some notes came through the door saying if you think you know anything at all, would you please tell the press?
>
> Then a man came knocking on the door so my mum said to me, "Did you see anything?"
>
> I said, "Well, yes I did, as a matter of fact."
>
> And funnily enough, every night I came back from the 100 Club in Oxford St, I caught the last train to South Ruislip – and then I'd run for it.
>
> In those days I used to sometimes take a short cut through the fields, and it was all boggy there. Most nights you'd just run.
>
> Well, this Jean Townsend, she was always in the same carriage as me, which was the last one. And I never saw her at the 100 Club but, wherever she went, it was regular. Anyway, we were always in the same carriage.
>
> Now I was a hippy, if you like. All scruffy old clothes, looking awful, whereas she was immaculate. She sometimes had her hair dyed red, and it looked beautiful. And she had this

strange face – I always call those faces, witchy faces. She had a hook nose and a big chin which went up.

But she was very, very attractive. She always had the most beautiful clothes on, lovely colours, and always black stockings. And she always – always, took her shoes off, in the train. Well, there was nobody in the train to see that, but us.

I thought many times of asking her if I could accompany her along Victoria Road because I was so frightened of meeting strangers there about midnight.

But we never spoke to each other. She'd see me, and I was a bit jealous of her really and I think she might have been a bit jealous of me, you know. The usual sort of thing: two girls…

Anyway, when it came to the station, we'd run for it. [Street lights were turned off at midnight.] Sometimes we took a short cut [through the fields] and sometimes we didn't. We'd run like the wind, both of us.

She always had her shoes in her hand, and they were always beautiful, velvet, pointed shoes. Not old things like I used to wear.

Everything was immaculate on her.

And when we got down to the edge where the road started, Victoria Road – 'cause there were no houses there in those days – it was just all fields – then we'd really just run for it.

I didn't know where she lived, but she used to go further on than me so I always ran behind her. I felt safe. I was never really scared if I could see her.

One night, she was in front of me and she disappeared down the road. She was faster than me.

Then a big American car came along and this American said, "Hi Baby, how about making it a twosome?" And I just kept walking on. I decided to cross over from the left-hand side of the road to the right to get rid of him.

But as I was coming up to Angus Drive he swung the car across the road and stopped it in front of me. I dashed behind it.

As I did that he put the car into reverse. I started to run really hard but he overtook me and tried the same routine up by the Westmead corner. I was petrified. I ran all the way home, using the shadows of the shops and the Dairy nearby.

Then I thought no more of it. But later I thought, "Oh, supposing that same man..."

So when this reporter knocked on our door I told him about the American.

He asked, "What did he look like?" I said, "Well he had a bit of a baby face, really."

A few hours later, I went out for some shopping.

When I came back, there were all these press men, and they broke my mum's wall in the front garden (laughs), standing on the wall, trying to get a picture of me.

I'd gone in through the back way, and when I came out the front door I went [makes gasping sound], and all these flashlights were going.

The next day there was me on the front page. It said:

THESE ARE THE EYES THAT HAVE SEEN BABY FACE, THE KILLER.

And my eyes did look funny in the pictures. But that was because of all these flashes.

They made a story out of it.

SOMETHING AMISS

As well as contacting witnesses, I explored sources like the London Metropolitan Archives (LMA). That was when I discovered that despite the Met Police embargo on the Townsend file a sample of witness statements had leaked into the public domain. These were filed at LMA with the coroner's report – accidentally not sent back to storage. No other researchers had apparently noticed their significance.[7]

Statement of Charles Henry Key, Printer, 39 years:

15th September, 1954

I left home this morning at about 6.55am and walked along Victoria road towards South Ruislip station.

As I was passing a piece of waste ground between West Mead and Angus Drive I saw something in the grass about 5 yards from the footway.

At first I thought it was two rolls of paper partly covered with black cloth. I hesitated, looked again and then saw it was a body. I went over to it and discovered it was the body of a young woman. She was lying on her back and was clothed except she had no shoes or stockings on. I saw some stockings on the grass near her feet. A handbag was lying near her hand and

---

7   LMA: Cor/mw/1954/188/01

was open. I also saw she had what appeared to be a black scarf wound round her neck.

I felt her left arm which lay straight down by her side and it was cold. I felt sure she was dead.

I then ran to the telephone box in Victoria Road and dialled the operator and told her to get the police. She put me through to Scotland Yard and I told them I had found a dead body.

Then this:

Statement of George Yates, Police Constable 792:

On Wednesday, 15 September, 1954, I was driver of 8 "X" R/T Car on 7am to 3pm duty, in company with Police Constable 764 "X" Lewis, as operator.

At 7am we received an R/T [radiotelephone] message to meet an informant in Victoria Road, South Ruislip, at the junction of Angus Drive respecting a body found.

We arrived at the scene at 7.10am where we saw Mr. Charles Henry Keys of 423 Victoria Road, South Ruislip. He pointed to a piece of waste ground on the corner of Angus Drive and said: "There's the body."

I went to the waste ground and about four yards from the footway of Victoria Road saw the body of a young woman. She was lying flat on her back. Her right arm was half raised above her head, whilst her left arm was straight down by her side. She appeared fully clothed.

One shoe and a pair of stockings lay by her feet. I noticed a black scarf was wound round her neck. Life appeared extinct.

I then noticed one shoe lying in the grass about eight feet from the body towards the footway of Victoria Road.

I then sent a message over the R/T system to Information Room requesting the immediate attention of a doctor, Duty

Officer and CID. At 7.30am Inspector Kelly arrived and at 7.50am Doctor Edmunds, Divisional Surgeon attended and pronounced life extinct. We remained at the scene until the arrival of Chief Inspector Casey.

This statement has been read over to me and is true.

PC George Yates said that in 1954. The problem is that his statement was not true at all.

His testimony is classic plodspeak, methodical, comforting and matter-of-fact: "Life appeared extinct." Yates records a well-oiled system whirring into action. Members of the investigation team arrive one by one and finally Chief Inspector Casey turns up – we imagine in a black Humber with a worried frown. A ritual familiar from crime thrillers like *Fabian of the Yard*, a series first broadcast by the BBC that very year, as a gritty portrayal of "procedure."

We have, it seems, no reason to doubt Yate's statement. It serves as the official version of how the Townsend investigation began.

But in 2009 I tracked down Yate's supposed companion in that car.

Police Constable 764 "X" turned out to be Rex Lewis. Rex had joined the force in January 1953. He retired in 1981 as a Detective Chief Superintendent. He talked to me in the spotless front room of his freshly decorated suburban house.

Rex told a different story. For a start, he denied he'd been in that car with Yates. His account also undermined Yate's timeline. Rex also painted a picture of incompetence and confusion. And a forensics calamity.

Rex Lewis:

I went in the police station that morning [adding that he was on "early turn duty" and arrived at 5.45 am] and the Sergeant said, "I've got a job for you: South Ruislip, on that patch of ground near the station."

I was the only PC on the beat that morning. At the time I was just out of probation, so I was the lowest of the low as far as experienced policemen went.

When I got there an officer was already waiting. That was a motorcyclist, Bill Knapp. He was on night duty, and anxious to get away. We were good friends. He said, "I knew you'd get here quick".

It was still quite dark. [London sunrise that September 15 began at around 6.35 am.] It was beginning to get light, but in those days they didn't have the streetlights on all night. Only at crossroads.

She was on this patch of waste ground. Just a field with fairly long, uncultivated grass. Slightly larger than a big football pitch.

Nowadays there's a petrol station near there.[8] But then they were just building it – it was foundations.

Bill and myself, we went and got a piece of tatty old tarpaulin from the forecourt to cover the body. It had a load of gravel on it. So we kind of shook most of it off. This little tatty, old, very undignified bit of tarpaulin – to cover the body from the common gaze. Later, when I lifted it off for the pathologist, I had to say the gravel was us – we'd put it there.

---

8   Currently, Vauxhall – Northern Motors, Ruislip. The station was opened shortly after the murder.

Rex's memory may have been faulty. Maybe George Yates really had been at the scene with him. After all, 53 years had passed. But this was Rex's first important assignment. "Well, it was the first murder I'd been to, so it does stick in my mind somewhat."

Rex was unlikely to forget such a dramatic car ride and R/T message as Yates reported. Unless they never happened like that. Or never happened at all.

I trust Rex's version. He was lucid and straightforward, and his account checked with other sources. It was also more believable – more human, than the self-serving drone of Yate's report. Rex's subsequent remarks about Jean Townsend's discarded tampon and other quirky details, didn't have an official or over-considered ring – rather, the curiosity of a disconcerted young policeman.

In which case Rex turned up on his own on a bicycle some time before Yates. But why would PC Yates lie?

Was his report contrived to cover up that he was [over an hour?] late for duty – which obliged the impatient-to-get-away Bill Knapp to overstay his stint, and left a rookie, Rex Lewis, in charge of a murder scene? [Rex Lewis and Bill Knapp were, apparently, not asked to give statements. Nor was the presence of Knapp at the scene mentioned in any report I've seen.]

As for that tarpaulin. Carried (dragged?) across a road and a field from a building site. Covered in gravel and cement dust and whatever else. Then draped over the victim's body. It's hard to imagine an old hand like Yates blundering in that way. Which again, suggests that Yates arrived after the crime scene had been contaminated.

Rex recalled the crime scene:

> She was lying there, on her side. Looked mature. I mean, twenty-one's not old, but she looked older than a young girl. Her hair was blonded. It was blonde. And a black skirt. The skirt was down. Clean, neatly dressed. Nicely dressed. And I couldn't see anything out of place. She looked quite

composed. As though she was just lying on the ground. As though she was asleep. Her eyes were closed.

She didn't look as though she'd put up a terrible fight or anything. Although you couldn't tell whether there'd been any scuffle 'cause it was rough old grass.

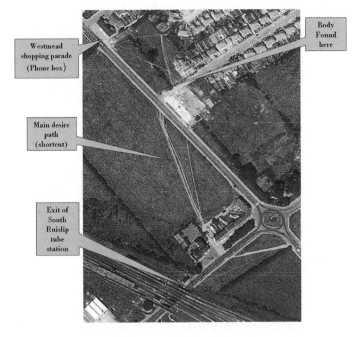

Westmead shopping parade (Phone box)

Main desire path (shortcut)

Exit of South Ruislip tube station

Body Found here

Aerial photo of crime scene taken in 1954, shortly before Jean Townsend was killed. It shows the wastelands near South Ruislip Station intersected by Victoria Road. Also, tracks (desire paths) made by people taking short cuts. This wasteland area was known locally as a place of escape, adventure, and deviance. Children played there in the day, and at night couples necked in cars parked along the road. Prostitutes down from the West End also patrolled the area for trade from the USAF servicemen stationed nearby, and some of these servicemen cruised the area in their flashy American cars looking for fun and pestering local women. These interconnected wastelands comprised several acres, an untidy interstice between housing estates and a zone of factories and warehouses.

She had a chiffon scarf round her neck, which was a bit of a fashion then. They used to knot it on the side. But somebody had put their hand in there and [does grisly sound effect] – as easy as wink. I thought to myself, "Somebody's followed her, come up behind her, got his hand inside that scarf and just twisted." And it was still round her neck. Fairly tight, because that's how they wore it. So [the killer] wouldn't have had any trouble whatsoever. And she would have just dropped. And then he held it till she uttered no more. As easy as that.

Rex was distrubed by Jean's appearance:

She was pale. A clean girl with this black chiffon scarf against the white of her skin. I couldn't see any obvious sign of damage to the body.

But I did notice a peculiar mark down her cheek. It was a sort of a funny, wiggly mark, not a scratch mark. And I did say later to a detective, "Well I noticed...." He said, "Yeah" – he told me a snail had got on her face. I didn't know they were carnivorous, but it seems they are, and this snail started chewing away at a bit of her surface skin. That was the only mark I noticed.

He described the eeriness of being alone with Jean's body:

I was alone there from early morning. There was me, there was the field and this body, and there I was. And I kept thinking that I mustn't interfere with anything, or even step close to it if I could avoid it...

At first, not a soul around. But it was a short cut to the station, and people used to use it regular to cut down to the station. So I would see a person coming: "Would you mind walking round please; this is a crime scene here." That's all I could do. And some were nosy and others were rushing to work. I was thinking, "Am I going to do anything wrong? I've got to keep people away." But I was on my own. We didn't have radios. No phones.

Then:

> Another thing – and I don't think I've ever mentioned this to anybody else. I said [to CID], "Was there any sexual thing about this?"

> Because you see, at the time she was killed, she was menstruating. And somebody had removed her sanitary device. [It was on the grass next to the body.]

> What type it was, I don't know but certainly you couldn't see anything [up her skirt]. I mean, I looked, but I wasn't in charge of the detection.

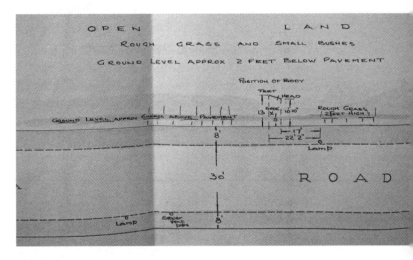

Police diagram of the body and surroundings.

> After a couple of hours I thought "Well, it's a long time for people to come!" Meaning CID.

> And then some of them started to appear. But they just had a look and then they went off. I didn't know them from Adam, because I didn't know any CID then. So, it goes through your mind: "When are these people coming to start investigating?"

You imagine from films and that, that there's like a room of CID officers, Crime Squad, all waiting for the phone call – and then they're down there with the pathologists and everything. But they take hours to assemble. They came down in dribs and drabs and eventually there was a little team and at one stage they said, "Can you get some more uniformed police?" And I said, "No, there's only me."

And they said they wanted to do a fingertip search – though they didn't call it that. They said, "Just look around." So with a couple of CID officers we kind of looked around the field. All I can remember is that it was full of snails and snail eggs. That was all there was: grass and snails. No clues. Nothing at all. Nothing at all.

Then, eventually, all the might of the CID arrived. By then it was about 10 o'clock. They said they had to wait for the pathologist, the man from the lab, and the fingerprint team and all that. No hope of fingerprints, but they still had to come. And photographers and everything.

They told me, "So you can cycle off back to the station."

ALL HELL LET LOOSE

One day, when Jean Townsend was fifteen, Reg Hargrave noticed her:

> Walking down Bempton Drive arm in arm with a very existentialist looking guy with a beard. He had curly hair – was possibly two or three years older than her. She walked with this guy as if they were engaged. It was a talking point in the street. We imagined he was from her art college.

———

I never traced the boyfriend. But I found an art school girlfriend.

Joyce Hill, nee Joyce Nunn, studied fashion at Ealing Art School with Jean Townsend and June Sweetzer. She remembered the art school and the Bempton Drive girls well.

Joyce Hill:

> The course was only for two years. That wasn't long but it kind of turned my life around. What was packed into those two years was amazing.
>
> Every morning for half a day we were taught the three R's by one particular woman teacher. The rest of the day we did all the arts.

Because it was mixed and we had boys we had to do technical drawing as well. But only the girls did fashion. We were taught embroidery, and sewing, how to make something from our own pattern, how to make a block pattern and build it up. Also things like wallpaper design. We did drawing but not life drawing.

Left. Ealing Art School *in the 1950s.*

It was very strict. We had to wear uniforms – like a pinafore thing.

And you had a tie: green. And you had a hat, like those Wrens hats they had in the war, because it wasn't long after the war. And a blazer. And you have to have everything right.

Sometimes my hat wouldn't be on straight. And the teacher used to stop her car, and say, "That girl, put your hat straight!" As far as I was concerned it was straight. But she wouldn't let it go. Fancy making a point of that! Not like now, is it?

You had to have a sports uniform too, because we had to do sports: hockey and tennis.

When we had our breaks, or if we were in the sewing room, we'd all sit round in a circle. And Anne Zouch, she reckoned she could tell fortunes, and she had this globe. So we'd sit round and have a good old laugh.

Mostly we talked about art. There was a tremendous enthusiasm for it. Well, not so much the art, but more to do with things like the Chelsea Arts Ball – it was so exciting. And the New Look. Norman Hartnell. And Dior.

I think we thought we were all very clever, because when we were in the dinner queue, when there was this threat of another world war with Russia – and it was a realistic threat – I can remember us all standing in the queue moaning about it, and saying we're not going to do that again, I'm not going through another war – Oh it's ridiculous. And going on about the adults – that they must all be mad.

But girls also talk about soppy things, they haven't changed.

―――――――

There were 16 boys and 16 girls. The boys would sit on one side of the class and the girls on the other. In breaks, if they were couples, they might sit together.

But mostly the boys would torment you. So you hated them.

The older art students were definitely apart. They sometimes had to act as chaperones, accompanying younger students to bus stops and so on. They seemed very glamorous to us.

Two of them, Pony and Jerry, were fashion models. Pony had even posed in *Vogue*. It seemed hard to believe when I saw their photos in the magazines.

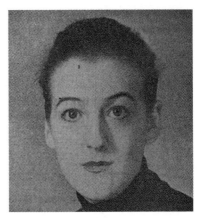

June Sweetzer and Jean Townsend: "chalk and cheese".

Jean and June – they both would arrive at college together – coming from Ruislip. And left together. They were very close – close friends.

But they were chalk and cheese. Jean was a quiet girl. A very nice girl. But June – she was more lairy.

Jean was very fastidious, very timid. I don't mean timid in the way of meeting people, but she'd say: "Oh there's a fly!" [makes a fussy noise] that sort of person. Anything would make her jump.

And she loved laughing and joking. Because June would supply her with all that. They were like a twosome.

Jean was also delicate, quite fragile. Pale rosy skin, almost an English rose type. Without make up she looked especially pale. She had an unusual face – a rather strange nose – and her eyes were round.

June looked a lot different, very high cheeks and a huge smile. Very dark hair. Lots of teeth. Very pretty. Oh yes! As I say, chalk and cheese to Jean.

Also, Jean's uniform was very precise. She couldn't have been untidy if she tried. And obviously her hair was always perfect because her mother was a hairdresser, and she was her pride and joy.

Jean was also better spoken than June. Jean spoke very precisely. She came over posh. But then she was an only child.

Jean had this aura about her. The image of someone who could be quite special. She stood out wherever she went. She would have stood out going backwards and forwards on the train.

She would have been very noticeable.

She got frightened easily. I can imagine that whatever happened to her on that night – it would have been frightening for anyone – but for her especially.

But she definitely would have made a fuss. Before anything would even have started. She would have protected herself very quickly if she felt someone was moving on to her – it would have been all hell let loose.

FV: Would she confront an attacker?

Yes. I think she could look after herself.

The Ealing Art School course lasted two years. When Jean and June turned 17, the college found both of them jobs.

June was apprenticed to a milliners, then became a fashion model.

Jean meanwhile, started work as a seamstress at M. Berman Ltd, a theatrical costumiers referred to as "Bermans", in June, 1950. By 1954 she'd been promoted to manageress of the woman's costume section for movies. This was the most glamorous department of the company. Part of Jean's job was to advise and fit visiting movie stars. She occasionally modelled garments.

We'd know more about Bermans, and Jean Townsend's role there, if its archive hadn't been destroyed after the company was taken over by its rival, Angels, in 1992. I was informed by an (admittedly embittered) ex-Bermans director that the archive was "burned" (which sounds definitive). When I told a Theatre Museum archivist he was gutted. Bermans was a unique and influential outfit.

The company began in 1900 as a military tailor. It was founded by Morris and Max Berman, Jewish émigrés from Russia. Originally based in Leicester Square, Bermans moved in 1912 round the corner to Irving Street (in those days, Green Street). Its premises were bombed in WW2 but quickly rebuilt. After the war, Max Berman's grandson, Monty, took over and expanded the business.

Bermans kept a vast stock of historical costumes. It had teams designing and making costumes to *haute couture* standard. By the 1950s, it was central to the British movie, TV, and theatre industries. It had branches in Hollywood, Rome and Paris.

When Jean worked there, Bermans was at its peak. It was considered the first destination of top ranking actors. "It was the high point in an actor's life to go to 18 Irving Street. You went to Monty to get dressed and get the character sorted out." Monty Berman also advised and befriended people in the industry. If he liked an idea he might subsidise a production with free costumes.

By 1954 Jean's social life was also flourishing. She'd become a self-assured and independent young woman, noted for her classy style and creative flair. She was active on the London nightlife scene. In particular, as an honorary member of the Londoner, a sophisticated piano bar-come-night club only two doors from Bermans, at 16 Irving Street.

This was where she spent her last night.

THE LONDONER

In 1954, murder squad detectives spent a lot of time investigating Jean's connection with the Londoner. Uniformed local police at Ruislip were bemused. They thought the perpetrator must be local.

CID thought otherwise. Rex Lewis recalled that:

> Ruislip Police Station in those days was just a converted house in the High Street and the main murder squad was at Greenford. The Ruislip canteen was tiny, with a gas stove – but the usual gossip went on. And the canteen gossip said: nightclub.

> The CID were convinced that the root cause of all her [Jean's] problems arose from this nightclub.

And:

> The CID were certain it was the seedy world she [Jean] lived in up in the West End. And – well, the CID knew more than I knew, and if they made all their enquiries in the West End, where she frequented, there's always things going on there, isn't there?

––––––––––

Jean being an honorary club member suggests a privileged status. She was also close to the Londoner club secretary, George Baron, and sometimes stayed overnight at his apartment, 7 Gerrard Mansions, 21 – 22 Gerrard Street, in Soho.

On that fateful evening, Jean had arranged a private party at the club. This was to celebrate her winning a then-fashionable gambling game called a pyramid club (see below).

Before attending, Jean travelled home to South Ruislip to glam herself up. She arrived home at her usual time, around 6pm. She had dinner with her parents. Then fixed her face and changed into party clothes, (what she was wearing that night became an issue in my investigation): black stockings, a white underslip and a black overslip, a high-necked half-sleeved black jersey dress with a black velvet belt, Spanish-heeled black suede court shoes, elbow-length black silk gloves, and an off-white swagger coat she'd recently made for herself. Finally, she wound her favourite gold-threaded black chiffon scarf three times round her neck.

Jean then picked up a black velvet handbag and left home around 8.30pm.

Around an hour later she met two girlfriends at Piccadilly Circus underground station. They all went to the Londoner.

Jean was there for around two hours. That night she decided to take the last train home to South Ruislip instead of staying in central London. She left the club with her girlfriends. All three took the tube from Leicester Square. Jean changed at Tottenham Court Road for the Central Line – her friends continued on the Northern Line.

———————

At the inquest, six days after the killing, a witness, Patricia Kemp, recalled seeing Jean on her way home.

> Coroner: Did you notice a young lady particularly in the train?
>
> Yes sir, she got on at Oxford Circus [?] I think.

Did you notice if she was wearing any make up?

Yes, sir, heavy.

Did you notice anything about her clothing?

Yes, sir, light coat and black scarf, it was speckled and dotted with gold. I noticed also, that she was wearing a black lace slip.

She had fair hair taken straight back with a comb on the left side. She was wearing ear rings and I think they were black with holes in.

What type of shoes?

Black suede.

Any gloves?

Yes, sir, black.

Anyone with her?

No sir, she was quite alone.

Edgar Phillips was the station porter at South Ruislip Station that night. He recognised Jean as a regular passenger.

Coroner: What ticket did she produce?

She had a weekly season between Strand and South Ruislip.

Phillips also reported on a group of other disembarking passengers: "They were all white, all American airmen and all had stripes. They were sober, apparently respectable and quiet." [These airmen were from the nearby South Ruislip USAF Base – they were apparently interviewed and cleared.]

The last sighting of Jean that night had been by a bank clerk, John Smith. He'd been taking American military acquaintances to the USAF Base when he saw a young woman he supposed was Jean, walking along Victoria Road near midnight. He also noticed a car with its lights on parked nearby, an "old Anglia or Prefect Ford vehicle." After dropping off the Americans he passed that way again. The car was gone.

———————

Someone heard Jean scream that night. That was Brenda Thomson, a 20-year-old factory machinist. Brenda's bedroom overlooked the wasteland where Jean's body was found. Brenda told the press:

> A few moments [after the scream] I heard the voices of two men. One I thought was rather nasal and appeared to be American. He shouted something like "Be quite!" It sounded as though he was very agitated.

In a statement to the police [one of the leaked LMA documents] she elaborated,

> My bedroom window was open. I spent about 15 minutes getting ready for bed. I then got into bed. I had only just got into bed when I heard a loud scream. It was a girl's voice and I heard her scream "Help!" The scream then sort of died away in a choking sound. The time was about 11.45 pm.

> I jumped up in bed and looked out of my bedroom window. The head of my bed is against the window. I then heard two different men's voices shouting.

> I think one was shouting at the other to be quiet – to shut up or stop it – and from the sound of the voices there were very much like Americans.

> The men's voices were raised for about two minutes and I heard no more after that.

> I looked out of the window [but] I saw no one. I stayed looking out of the window for a few seconds, just sufficient time to look up and down the road. I then got back into bed.

CLUBLAND ·

Central London in the 1950s was full of clubs. Drinking clubs, strip joints, gay clubs. They were places you went to be discreet. Or drink after hours. Many cultivated a risqué ambience and attracted bohemians, transients and outcasts.

Most clubs have left traces. You find references and descriptions in contemporary London directories, in memoirs, and in novels. They formed a network with public houses like the French House, ranging across Mayfair, Fitzrovia and Soho, with an overlapping clientele.

Many of these clubs traded in erotic allure and the promise of illicit encounters. They were often "protected" or part-owned by criminals.

The Paint Box, run by underworld "friend of the stars" and protector-lover of Diana Dors, Tommy Yeardye, was a dining club with a saucy twist. Yeardye hired "ten of London's most beautiful artist's models" to pose in the nude. Members could sketch these beauties between courses. Yeardye explained, "I want to bring art to the average man's life."

Some of the night-time drinking clubs, like the Colony Room, a scruffy top stairs dive at 41 Dean Street, became legendary, mostly due to celebrated members like the painter Francis Bacon, and the antics of its dyke manager, Muriel Belcher.

Bacon and fellow Colony Club habitués also patronised the

> notoriously sleazy, Club des Caves de France at 39 Dean Street... It was entered via a dark doorway, guarded by two

hefty bouncers who half heartedly quizzed people as to whether they were members, though proof never seemed to be required. Inside the street-level bar, where perpetual twilight reigned at any time of the day, it took a while for your eyes to adjust. It then became apparent you were in an elongated, low-ceilinged, smoke-wreathed room. Beyond the short flight of steps leading down to the tiny basement bar, there was a counter of such prodigious length it was more like a runway than a bar. Hanging above it there was a string of coloured lights. Along the facing wall, a line of drink-stained seats were positioned, the floor around them flecked with cigarette-butts. In between the seats, there was a row of wine barrels, a series of small plastic-topped tables, and a wooden dais with an upright piano on it. Each of the tables had a filthy-looking jar of pickled gherkins in the centre, the contents deliberately doused in salt so as to make the customers thirsty. Displayed on the wall behind, there was a row of elaborately framed but inept surrealist daubs, painted by an ageing, monocled sot who called himself "Baron von Schine". Despite the implausible list of international galleries where he'd supposedly exhibited, they never seemed to sell. Most days the Baron was to be seen slumped beneath them, often sound-asleep.[9]

Intersecting with such venues were the clandestine gay clubs and bars. These were used as settings in a 1961 pseudonymous novel, *The Heart in Exile*:

The Aldebaran [sic] hadn't changed much since the war, except that the walls had been repainted. It was one of the half-dozen or so queer clubs in London which those who had been excluded from it generally invested with an aura of elegance and wickedness. In reality, it was neither elegant nor

9   Paul Willetts, *Fear and Loathing in Fitzrovia*, pp244-245

wicked; it differed from the queer pubs only in the fact that its clientele was a little more expensively dressed. There was the same strain, the same expectation and disappointment, the same make believe, the same lies. It was improper without being naughty.

———————

Some newspaper reports said that Jean Townsend was a nightclub "hostess." That was untrue, but linked Jean to a fifties' emblem of notoriety.

In July, 1954, 36-year-old Hella Christofi had been murdered by her mother-in-law, Styllou Christofi. Hella was partially strangled in her house, then beaten about the head with a "blunt instrument." Her body was stripped, dragged into the garden and set alight with paraffin.[10]

---

10   A neighbour, John Byres Young, noticed the bonfire. He later testified to police:

> I noticed that the whole of the back of the building next but one was aglow, as if from the light of a fire.
> When I looked over I saw a fire in the area, and what I took to be a wax model lying on the fire. I couldn't see a head, but it should have been facing towards the French window, because the legs were towards the garden. I noticed that it was surrounded by a circle of flames. I don't remember seeing any legs from the thigh downwards. The arms were raised and bent back at the elbow. There was a very strong smell of paraffin and wax. It appeared to me that it was wearing a pair of briefs. I looked into the kitchen through the French window and saw a figure come round the table and come out into the area. There was a very bright light in the kitchen. I recognised that person as [Styllou Christofi]. I had seen her before. She came right into the area, bent over the body, and gave me the impression that she was about to stir the fire up. The fire was dying down. Having recognized the accused I thought all was in order, and I returned to my garden and then to my house. TNA: CRIM 1/2492

Styllou Christofi confessed, was tried, and hanged that December. An open and shut case.

However, rumours had emerged that Hella was connected to night-time West End venues, and so the police and press busied themselves with irrelevant details of her private life. This created an ominous and cautionary subtext. Hella, it was reported, "used to leave the quiet of Hampstead each evening and spent her nights in the clubland area of Mayfair and the West End." Neighbours affirmed, "She was gay and charming... But there was always something of a mystery about her. She liked to be known as a creative artist. She said her work took her to Mayfair at night. But we never saw any signs of her artistic creation."

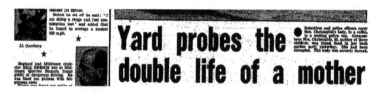

Yard probes the double life of a mother

The year after Christofi's execution, Ruth Ellis, a peroxided nude model and nightclub manager, became the last woman in Britain to be hanged after shooting her boyfriend dead. He was a public school educated cad. Ruth shot him for love.

Ellis's image as a "hostess" drew on the same pulp and soft porn stereotypes projected onto Hella Christofi – and Jean Townsend. Stock characters from pulp fiction. As in Ben Sarto's *Blood and Blondes*, (1954): "The dame was tall and blonde... She had a swell bust... violet eyes, that could sizzle any guy at a glance... Practically all her mid-section muscles moved with each step, giving a marvellous thrill of seductiveness."[11]

Such women were up to no good and therefore came to no good. In 1956 this theme was played out by a rash of hostess fatalities.

---

11   Ben Sarto, *Blood and Blondes*, 1954, pp13-14

bara Knox-Marsh, beautiful twenty-eight-year-old night club girl, died by accident after taking an overdose of a sleeping drug.

She was found dead early on Saturday morning by Mr. James McBurnie, her accountant, at whose flat in Baker-street, London, she was staying as a guest.

'Loved Life'

ing a verdict of "Accidental death," said the drug, the fall, and the breathing difficulty due to the lamp flex together caused death.

'No Evidence'

"There is no evidence before me to justify a verdict of suicide," he said.

"Life up to now for her had been one of excitement and pleasure rather than depression and eventual suicide."

Last night at the Blue Angel, the West End night club where she was until her death.

Friday night she sat in a softly-lit alcove at the club drinking lime and ginger ale.

The band was playing "Memories Are Made Of This." When the music switched to "Are You Satisfied?" she got up to dance.

Afterwards she threw a coin in the fountain pool over which a grey-blue plaster angel stands guard, and left, with a wave and a "See you tomorrow" to her friends. But her friends never saw her again.

Barbara Knox Marsh – "part owner" of The Blue Angel, a "West End 'mystery woman in black' and friend of the famous," was found dying from an overdose of Seconal in her accountant's flat. Then, Pamela Gale was found "lying in a gas filled room." Pamela had moved her two pet budgies to another room to ensure their survival. Inside another "gas filled room" witnesses found the body of Esmeralda Noel Smith. Then came Linda Justice, a "blonde... close companion of murderess Ruth Ellis." Linda was a "girl from Peckham [who] lost her way" in the temptations of clubland and died from an "overdose of sleeping pills." Finally, Janet Curtis-Bennett. She'd met a leading QC at a party. They married. Eight months later she killed herself with gin and barbiturates. Her father was suspicious: "I want to know more about why she died." The coroner interrupted questions and barred one witness statement. Three months later, her husband killed himself.

The *Daily Express* lamented that:

> There are in London now, more than 3,000 doorways to the kind of despair that lies somewhere behind these puzzling deaths. They are the doorways to those drinking clubs whose owners need only 5s [5 shillings] and 25 friends to open their doors... For here the tax dodgers, the professional gamblers, the smugglers, the confidence tricksters, the petty thieves, and the upper class flotsam of the underworld collect to drink away their leisure hours.[12]

[In the fifties, even my dad – an industrial chemist and diplomat at the French Embassy in London, was briefly involved in setting up a West

---

12   *Daily Express*, May 15, 1956

End nightclub. This was with Mr DaSilva, who ran a dry-cleaning shop near South Ruislip station. All I knew about this was that my mother got angry about it. Mr DaSilva also got angry. He came round one night and banged on our door and there was an argument. My dad said he was a cheat. My mum said my dad was a fool. Nightclubs were exciting.]

Jean Townsend's Londoner club was shadowy. In fact, practically invisible.

There are scant references in trade and entertainment directories. No one active on the club scene in those days remembered it. Nor could fifties' nightlife enthusiasts or historians offer anything.

The only newspaper references were from reports of the Townsend case. These cited the club manager as George Baron, a professional dancer. One press picture showed him inside the Londoner, stagely lamenting Jean's death.

George Baron had a flurry of press as a professional dancer in the early to mid-fifties. References in *The Stage Archive* praise his versatility and flair. By 1954, he'd become a principal dancer in the London Coliseum production of *Guys and Dolls*.

For a moment, George was trendy and news. When his son was born in 1953 he featured in picture stories with his beautiful young dancer wife, Elizabeth Baron.

Elizabeth (Liz) Baron rehearsing with an American dancer while George Baron holds their baby.

Baron's 1952 marriage certificate shows his real name was George Jones – altered to George Jones Baron. It gives his age as 23 and his father's occupation as Mining Foreman. His wife, née Elizabeth Mary Walsingham, was 22, daughter of a Surrey wine merchant.

George Baron had died in 1984. I could track his life through official certificates, phone directories and electoral registers, etc. But found no one who recalled him.

I wondered whether his wife, Elizabeth, was alive.

She'd divorced George in the 1950s and moved from London under another surname.

Eventually I found a relative of a relative. After email negotiations, I had a phone call. It was Liz Baron. [She has another name now, but I'll refer to her here as Liz Baron.]

Liz said she understood I wanted to find out about George Baron and the Londoner.

She said she couldn't help.

Then she said she could…

But she didn't want to.

And then, that her time with George had been the worst of her life.

"A nightmare."

And then she started to tell me all about George and the Londoner.

AND HORRIBLE LAUGHTER

Jackie Cliff in her prime.

Jackie Cliff, the ex-model who would chase after Jean Townsend across unlit wasteland, gave me several interviews.[13] Her biography, like that of other surviving witnesses, compensated for Jean's absent voice.

---

13   Jackie also wrote down memories and additional material in notes and letters. Her contributions were prolix and luxuriant – note pads exuding exotic scent. They were also accurate. Checking her accounts against other sources, discrepancies were rare.

Jackie and Jean were brought up in identical looking streets – Jackie's Bideford Road home being less than 300 metres from Jean's in Bempton Drive.

Socially, too, they were close. Jean's dad was a telephone engineer, Jackie's, a trained chef – so both blue collar edged with white. Both girls had mostly stay-at-home mums.

Both families had moved to South Ruislip from central London for affordable greenery and oxygen – and space. Jackie: "My mum fell in love with Ruislip the first moment she saw it. She said it was like fairyland."

They went to the same junior school, Lady Bankes – Jackie the year below Jean. So together experienced a parallel wartime schooling and coming of age. The same teachers, uncertainties and deprivations. Jackie:

> My dad came home on leave from the Navy sometimes. His kit bag was always full of apples and chocolate. Once he brought back a pineapple. I took it to school. The teachers sent it into every classroom for the children to touch and smell. It ended up in the front window of our house high up so everyone in the road could look at it.

After the war, both Jackie and Jean failed the 11 plus exam but then won art college scholarships to study fashion. Jackie at Harrow Art College; Jean at Ealing.

Jackie's story also illuminated her and Jean's situation as young women in the mid-50s. Jackie and Jean stood out as unusually independent in South Ruislip. While their career trajectories differed they were similar in one key respect – in progressing, moving up, from stuffy and safe suburbia to risky metropolis.

Both women ignored people gossiping when they came home regularly from the West End on the last train, enjoyed unusually close links with showbiz circles – getting close to the stardust most suburbans only approached through gossip columns, and both socialised with artists and bohemians. And both of them mixed with "dangerous company" in the heady and transgressive atmosphere of London's West End and Soho.

When I visited, Jackie's Bath apartment was artistically jumbled with bric-a-brac and, mementoes from her career as a model and later, striptease artist.

She spoke in bursts but sometimes her voice shook. Her quick laugh was fragile and vulnerable. She was disturbed by nightmares about her past life: predatory gangsters, threats to her independence, loss of her identity and home:

> I couldn't find the key to my London flat. Couldn't remember the phone number. Couldn't remember where the new London flat was anyway. No phone no key. It was cold and snowing. I went back to Bideford Road. Everything had gone. It was my fear in those days that this could happen...

Her nightmares about Jean Townsend were especially intense: "I still have nightmares about running at night along that road. It haunts me."

Jackie had covered her tracks, changing her name several times.

> I first changed my name when I started [nude] photography, because I didn't want my dad to ever see it. I used to think, supposing he did buy one of those magazines... I didn't want my brother or my dad to think... If they ever saw somebody like that, you know, a picture of me... I used to get scared. I thought I'd better say I was somebody else, so that's what I did. I think a lot of the girls used to do that.

Jackie was never alone for our interviews. For a start, there were her two white poodles. If I leaned forward or gestured they'd rush me from Jackie's pink settee, yapping and snarling. She'd admonish them, but fondly, reluctantly, implying that I was a guest – but this, after all, was their home. Jackie was also guarded by her boyfriend, Ted, who she'd first met in the fifties when he worked for the notorious slum landlord, Peter Rachman, as a "handyman." Ted was wiry and canny and sat in during our interviews, mostly silent but occasionally offering a thought or detail.[14]

Jackie Cliff:

> When we were young in South Ruislip and Ruislip Manor, nobody looked after us. We were just let out, and we were like gypsies really. We didn't have to come home at any particular time. Our only clock was the bats. When the bats came out, that was our clock to know we had to go home. They would go whoosh whoosh [laughs] and when they came out that was our clock.
>
> In those days the cinema was everything. Every week they had two films. An A and a B. The manager would go on the stage before the film and talk to us. There was an organ in the cinema that rose up from below.
>
> But sometimes you couldn't see the film because of all the cigarette smoke. And everyone talked or ate sandwiches and cake. Whole families would take up rows of seats, even with newborn babies crying on the knee.

---

14   Rachman let apartments to high-class hookers and their high-class clientele. He was the lover of Mandy Rice-Davis and (probably) Christine Keeler, the two women central to the Profumo Affair. Rachman died in 1962, but it's been rumoured his death was a ruse. Ted: "When he died, the weird thing is that Jane [a stripper friend of Ted's] had dinner with him two days after he had died – in Beirut (laughs). He never did die. He did a runner. Who they killed in his place I hate to think!"

Fights broke out sometimes because the person behind would put their feet on your seat. Then the manager would chuck them all out. Or, if the film was boring, other fights broke out.

Saturday morning pictures for kids was awful too. The cinema was in Eastcote and we called it the Bug Hutch. Cowboy things. And horror films. Space travel. Dan Dare. Mostly American.

The cinema was always packed and the noise of the boys at the back was deafening. We never saw the film. There was screaming and shouting all through. Most of the boys stood up all the time. They "teased the girls and made them cry."

Some kids took sandwiches and ate them in the cinema. Or threw them at each other. Jam sandwiches would go whizzing over your head. Or a foot would trip you up walking down the aisle. Sometimes even spit would stream overhead – and horrible laughter.[15]

But we went anyway. Afterwards we would go to Churchfield Gardens [park] and fights would break out, especially among the boys.

---

15   Mayhem also common in my own recollection of the 1950s. And from the *Middlesex Advertiser and County Gazette*, October 29, 1954.
MANAGER LOSES FOUR TEETH
Manager of the Savoy cinema, Hayes, Mr. Percy Martin, has recently had four front teeth knocked out by hooligans who have been causing disturbances in his cinema. The police have been called several times to turf out troublemakers.
Police called after hooligans stop Sunday film show. Staff men get escorts home.
Police were called to the Odeon Cinema, Uxbridge, on Sunday night after hooligans had let off fireworks. The show was held up for more than 10 minutes while the first six rows of the stalls were cleared. One person a few rows back said, "There was near panic for a few minutes and pandemonium broke out. The noise sounded terrific –

Once, a boy came to the cinema with a strange hand. The fingers were all joined up together. When the other boys found out they beat him up in the cinema and kicked him around. They made him show us his hand and called him "Pig's Hoof." He was crying. He was about ten years old.

And once, my whole class went to the park to stone a girl called Audrey Eliot just because she was fat. Her mother, who was also fat, tried to stop us. There were around 20 of us.

We were mostly very thin in those days. I remember going swimming at Uxbridge open air baths. You could see everybody's ribs. It would be freezing, freezing cold, and we all had to jump into the frozen water. We were sick with fear.

There was a gang – the Black Hand Gang. This was the bigger boys – and we were scared stiff of them. They used to tell us horrible stories: what they could do to us. But it was all a joke.

I can remember seeing London on fire. Even Ruislip was bombed. I can remember being in the bomb shelter all on my

---

we all wondered what was happening. Youths in the front seats were laughing out loud and shouting across the seats." [After the police arrived] about 30 people, including several women and girls, were shown out.

Two of the Odeon staff – they do not wish their names to be disclosed – have been threatened, and have had police escorts to their homes.

At this cinema on Sundays a strong-arm man has been employed to keep the young toughs out.

But a few days ago he was beaten up in an alleyway next to Burton's building by three youths who jumped him.

Another three youths grabbed and beat up the Odeon's assistant manager and left him bruised and bleeding.

own. My mother took my brother under the stairs and I was in the shelter. It was like that then. People didn't worry so much about their kids. Everybody was like that.

We had one toothbrush for all of us. It didn't have many bristles. We mostly cleaned our teeth with an apple.

We lived on mince meat, cabbage, potatoes, bread, marge and jam. Pudding was tinned fruit and the top of the milk.

Birthday parties were a big thing. Jelly, sandwiches with spam, orange drinks with a straw, and your hair washed with DRENE shampoo. Afterwards, the DRENE would smell so good for ages and it made you feel so good.

I went to Lady Bankes [junior school]. Every morning in assembly it was pummelled into us that God was looking at everything we did. He could see in through the school windows. We imagined he'd got great big eyes, with beams on. And if you were bad or naughty, or didn't do certain things, God would know, you see. No matter where you were, you knew he was watching you.

All our teachers were lady teachers because all the men were in the war. And these teachers all seemed to have really big feet, these big shoes, and they tapped out the hymns. And in assembly you could see them on this row of chairs on stage, tapping away, while we had to sing these hymns – All Things Bright and Beautiful was one of them. And then we knew that God would be looking in through the windows and would say, "Oh that's alright. That's good."

But one day I got the cane from Miss Poland, our head teacher. I got the cane and God didn't save me (laughs). He didn't. He was looking but he was tired out. He'd been doing quite a bit of other things, you know, and I never trusted him any more after that. I got whacked on the backs of my legs and all on my hands, and I never told my mum.

Miss Poland – she was horrible and she was small but she had the loudest voice – singing voice – [sings, imitating the teacher] "All things bright..." you know, really loud.

And there was a lady teacher playing the piano.

It was all women, you see.

There weren't any men around in general. I don't remember men much. Everybody in my life was all ladies. You just got used to it.

All the neighbours we had, we called them Auntie. We didn't have any uncles because they mostly were all away.

About the only man in my street, Bideford Road, in the war, was a Polish man living with one of our neighbours. We were told her husband was serving in the war. She used to come out of the house dressed with this great big shoulder-padded fur coat like Old Mother Riley. Well, all us kids, we were frightened to look at her because we just thought he might see us looking. Then one day we heard that he'd bitten off one of her titties. It was in the paper [laughs], and it said that all these Poles are all mad. And all the old mums were saying, "It serves her right." "That Pole, he's bitten one of that woman's titties off and it serves her right!"

Then came a transformation post-war:

The first man I ever really got to know was my maths teacher after the war, and I was so frightened of him that I shook when he was nearby. Just because he was a man.

A man so totally different from a woman. Do you know what I mean? He was big and tall and had a nice tweed jacket on, lots of wavy hair and horn-rimmed glasses, and he strode around the classroom.

And before that it was just these weird ladies.

When the men came back from the war, our parents used to go to the Clay Pigeon [pub] and we used to sit on the step outside.

And the ladies had powder and lipstick. And a bit of scent. And they looked like angels to me when they were made up.

And did they dress up! When they were normal, they were like nothing. They were just nothing. Then suddenly: a hat, veil – a little veil, lovely little white gloves on, and nylon stockings – and they had got it all from somewhere – and you had never known this other side of them. This side where they could go out and have a drink, and talk to men and be sociable.

Because in the war the women didn't have anything. They were just making ends meet from minute to minute. I mean, even a potato was quite a prize in a way.

So you never expected to ever see anything like a pretty lady – you just thought all ladies were like your teachers. And then suddenly, there they all were, all made up. They looked lovely, gorgeous. It was wonderful to be with them. They were animated, saying all the things that they hadn't been able to say when the men had been away.

CAREFUL WHAT YOU WISH FOR

Elizabeth Walsingham, actress. Soon to become Mrs Elizabeth Baron.

I first met Liz Baron in a pub near her retirement home. She came warily, with her daughter, to check me out. Following that, we had several private meetings at her home. Liz was generous with her time and gave me access to cuttings and photos. She was also candid. This was the first time she'd told someone outside the family about her marriage with George Baron – or about the Londoner scene – and she seemed eager to unburden herself – she ended by dubbing me her "confessor."

Liz came from a theatrical family. Her parents toured with a version of ENSA and she accompanied them.

> I wanted to be a nurse but my father said no way! – I could catch something. He always used to get *The Stage*. One day he saw they were asking for singers and dancers – and I did both. I went up to London, sang and danced, and got the job.
>
> "Liz Graham." That was my stage name.
>
> To start with I was in *The Belle of New York*, which was the original *Guys and Dolls*. Then after a while I met GB [George Baron] – which is what I shall refer to him as – in a pantomime. That was at Wyndham's [Wyndham's Theatre, Charing Cross Road], a very upper-class sort of pantomime. GB was quite established then. And for my sins, and to my shame, I saw his photograph outside the front of house.
>
> That's the photograph I fell in love with. Well, it was David Bowie, wasn't it really? Bowie and Adam Faith rolled into one.
>
> I thought "Ooh, he's gorgeous!" and I said to myself, "I'm going to marry him."
>
> Fool! Fool, I was. Careful what you wish for – you might get it...
>
> And then I started working with GB and he took me to various parties and gatherings and so on. And I don't know – I guess it was just physical attraction. Because I've always liked blonde men. God knows why.

GEORGE BARON

GB had been brought up in Pendlebury, which is on the Manchester to Bolton road.

When he was about six or seven, his mother was one side of the main road and he was the other. And he ran across and got knocked down by a lorry. And they were going to amputate his leg. But there was an American surgeon visiting Salford Royal Hospital. He said that if George's mother would agree to having muscle grafts taken from her...

Anyway, they saved his leg and he had a scar going right down and getting wider and wider, right down to his ankle.

They suggested he did a ballet class to exercise his leg, so he started to learn locally. He passed a lot of exams, and then – I don't know how or why or when – he came down to London.

I do know that he was living in London with Brian Michie. Michie was a broadcaster – well known then and he sort of – how can I put this? – took GB under his arm.[16]

And that's how George got into the West End scene.

---

16   Bryan Michie, 1906-1971, a former schoolmaster. As "Britain's favourite compere," millions heard him weekly on *In Town Tonight*, and *Housewife's Choice*. Michie also did stints at acting, for example, in a 1943 Jack and Jill panto as "a colossal and voluptuous Dame Horner." But mostly he was a producer of variety entertainment and talent shows, a showbiz Mr Fixit, who worked closely with the entertainment impresario Jack Hylton. Michie "discovered" Ernie Wise and paired him with Eric Morecambe. It was likely at a talent show that Michie met the teenaged George – and then they became lovers. Employed by the BBC for 30 years Michie went on to become controller of programs at the independent TV company TWW.

Wedding of George and Liz Baron, 1952. Liz and George are centre. George is flanked on the left by his ferocious mother. To the right of Liz are her parents. Top row, third from left is Lionel Blair, the best man. Bottom row, second from left is his sister, Joyce Blair, matron of honour. Top row fourth from right is George Baron's lover and lifetime partner, Paul Clay. Top row, extreme right, Les Wallis, the ill-fated, alleged lover of Antony Armstrong-Jones (Lord Snowdon).

We married at Caxton Hall. Lionel Blair[17] was our best man. My matron of honour was his sister, Joyce Blair. I hadn't wanted that. I wanted my best friend. But when I got to the wedding, to Caxton Hall, GB had put Joyce Blair up, who came down the steps and took my arm. I was totally taken over, you know, by him.

---

17 A well-known British actor, choreographer, tap dancer and TV presenter. Didn't respond to my request for an interview.

Two more wedding photos. Liz: [Indicating the left-hand image] "That's my father in the back, and on the right is the rather camp registrar. [Laughs] Tell me who wasn't camp in London at that time!" Right. Cake moment at the reception.

When I married him, George had another club [before the Londoner], The Festival club. That was at Two Brydges Place.[18] And we lived above it.

Do you know Brydges Place? Tiny little alleyway. It's the narrowest alleyway in London, and it's next door to the Coliseum.

---

18   This club was originally called The Hogarth, and renamed during the Festival of Britain in 1951.

Brydges Place is a relic of continuous rebuilding from the 17th-19th Century around the London Coliseum. It was formerly called Taylor's Buildings (as in the image above) – and before that, Dawson's Alley. It was renamed after the now vanished Brydges Street – so called after George Brydges, 6th Baron Chandos, whose family owned the freehold. The area had an evil reputation – Brydges Street being known as, "the abode of thieves and prostitutes, and even murderers." [Beresford, Annals of Covent Garden.*] In 1685, the dramatist John Crowne condemned Brydges Street as "strumpet Fair:" "Where higling Bawds do palm their rotten Ware." Nowadays, its remnant, Brydges Place, is a 200-yard alley, at its narrowest point only 15 inches wide. It runs from St Martin's Lane to the corner of Chandos Place and Bedfordbury, and has been gentrified as a prettily flowered backyard overspill for two pubs. 2 Brydges Place, however, is still a club – these days, eponymously named, "2 Brydges Place," an exclusive dining club for the movie industry. At far right in the image above, tucked in the alcove, is the notorious male urinal. It was demolished as a public nuisance in 1953, part of a campaign to restore dignity to*

From left. Entrance to Brydges Place from St Martin's Lane. The narrowest part of the passage, which Liz Baron would negotiate with her pram late at night. At its other end the passage widens and forms an exterior drinking area for two public houses. The suited men with pints of beer are chatting on the urinal site, a cottaging paradise handily facing The Festival.

As well as that, GB – I don't know whether he rented or owned it – but on the ground floor at Number Two, there was a sort of sandwich bar. You know, those things were just sprouting up then – coffee bars. And it was called Porgy's [After *Porgy and Bess*]. That didn't last very long. Above that was where the club was, and we lived on the top floor.

[The Festival and clubs like it] were... it wouldn't be quite correct to say they were positively gay clubs – they were theatre clubs. People would come after the show, go and have a drink there – because they had extended licenses and so on. The Festival was like the Park Lane Theatre Club where I worked [as an actress].

I actually saw Frank Sinatra and Ava Gardner from our flat window once. They came into The Festival. I only saw the tops of their heads though.

And I tell you who else used to come – though maybe you ought to scratch this out – Lord Snowdon who married Princess Margaret [then known as Antony Armstrong-Jones.] He was a member.

In fact, the Festival Club was at the beginning of the beginning of the openness about gays and everything.[19]

––––––––––

When I first went to live in Brydges Place, there was a public toilet, a men's toilet, there [just opposite the club door]. It was

––––––––––

19   The Festival is celebrated by historian Matt Houlbrook in *Queer London*, 2006:

> If you walk down St. Martin's Lane towards Trafalgar Square, just before the National Portrait Gallery comes into view you'll pass a narrow alleyway called Brydges Place on your left. Down here for decades was one of the "old-fashioned" cast-iron urinals; a noted site of sexual opportunity at London's heart. It was demolished in 1953, as part of the LCC and Met's "modernization" of the cityscape. Here, at almost exactly the same time, [was opened] the Festival, an exclusive, self-consciously respectable, members' drinking and dining club behind an unmarked door.

Continuing:

> In many ways the queer history of Brydges Place is the history of queer London. Here, we can see a movement from visibility to invisibility, from an open public sexual culture to an exclusive commercial sociability. Here we can see the relationship between

a pickup place for male prostitutes. The police were watching it all the time.

But – and I swear this to you, I'd look out of the spare bedroom window and you'd see the police coming along, running their hands along the top of the wall...

Because the whores, male, used to leave money for them. Yep.

But some mornings they used to come round with the van and round up some of the old whores.

police operations and changing geographies of queer lives. Here we can see the narrowing boundaries of masculine sexual "normality" and the increasingly rigid separation between queer and "normal." Here we can see how the privatization of queer urban culture was played out in one small alleyway. The Festival was safer than the urinal; it was certainly more comfortable. Yet it was by no means accessible to all men. Here, moreover, men were drawn from London's center into its shadows, from light into darkness, from being within the public city to being outside...

And so on. However, Houlbrook mistakenly credits the club as being founded by a Ted Rodgers Bennett. Rodgers Bennett may have taken over the club from around 1954 – or revived it later – but the Festival was the creation of George Baron and Paul Clay. The Festival was also in existence before 1953. It was named after the 1951 Festival of Britain. Houlbrook told me by email that his faulty information came "from one of the interviews conducted by Tony Dean held in the National Sound Archive."

73

A JEALOUS GOD

The Festival and its successor, the Londoner, were clandestine. They had to be. The animus against gays in the 50s was vicious. The police waged a relentless campaign. In 1953 there was a landmark case involving the film maker, Kenneth Hume. The case and its aftermath helped provoke a reform of laws against homosexuality in Britain.

The bisexual Hume was a member of both The Festival and Londoner, and well known to Liz Baron:

> He had a terrible crush on me, and GB didn't like that at all. Kenneth... I can see him now. He was rather sweet and nice, and to everybody's horror suddenly this thing broke – that scandal about Lord Montague who had that motor museum down at [his country estate at] Beaulieu. He went to prison for it.

> In fact we met Kenneth, that very evening he was going down to Beaulieu. GB and I had been to some big concert at the Albert Hall, and we decided to walk home, and we met him. And then this terrible scandal broke. He and Lord Montague had been very naughty with some Boy Scouts.

From police files in The National Archive, it's clear that gays were hunted at every opportunity.

In April, 1954, Police Constable 303 "C" was "on duty" in plain clothes, loitering in a urinal.

I saw the defendant Weston. I saw him in the public lavatory in Oxford Circus. He was in the second stall on the right opposite the water closet. I kept him under observation. He was looking at a man standing at the next stall to him on his right – the third stall. He looked towards his person [his own penis] then up at the man's face, smiled at him and said something to him, I couldn't hear what. The man then left the urinal and the defendant then turned to his left, and he looked at a man who was standing at a stall on his left – the first stall. He repeated his actions and as I passed him I heard the defendant say "It's nice isn't it?"

After following Weston for some time, the policeman arrested him for "importuning male persons for an immoral purpose."

I searched him. He had £6.19.6 in money on him. He also had one lipstick, one tin of Vaseline, three hair curlers, three hair grips, one pair of tweezers, a mirror, and correspondence of an obscene nature.

He was dressed as he is now, that is, wearing two aprons. The trouser buttons from his fly were all open apart from the top one.

Exhibit 1. Letter. [Dated June 2 1953 – the day of Elizabeth II's Coronation]

Dear Cecil,

... I have not had any engagements since you have been gone and I do miss it so much it keeps yearning for you – and you gave me such lovely thrills as you can guess...

I shall always remember the lovely feeling I had when you had it in your fingers for the first time, it was simply heavenly. I long for this again.

So Cecil see what you can do about returning here again, won't you – so that we can get together once more. Would you

like a very special drawing of Mine Ready for action will try
and send you one if you would.

Well now dear – I must close – as I am going to be so busy now
getting ready for the Coronation duties here. All love and best
wishes, hoping to hear from you soon.

Yours as ever, "R"[20]

In March 1954, a Captain H, stationed in Germany, was prosecuted by
the army for a gay orgy with German students. One student testified:

We went to a room and undressed. I then lay down on my bed,
naked. Captain H came over to me and he masturbated my
penis until it was erect. When my penis was erect, Capt H took
my penis into his mouth and sucked it. During this time he sat
on my bed. When I ejaculated, Capt H swallowed my sperm.

The testimony then turned into Samuel Beckett-like absurdism:

During this time I lay on my bed whilst K sat on a chair still
dressed. When Captain H returned he was dressed in a pair
of pants only. He then told K to sit on his (H's) bed which
he (K) did. K then undressed. Capt H then came over to me
and pushed the blanket away, he had previously touched
my penis which was erect. He then masturbated my penis;
he asked me to come to his (H's) bed which I did. Captain
H then masturbated my and K's penis. During this time I
masturbated H's penis, and at the same time with H, K's
penis. Before K and I ejaculated, Captain H alternatively
took my and K's penis into his mouth, K and I ejaculated in
H's mouth, however I am unable to state who ejaculated first.
Captain H also ejaculated as I masturbated his penis. During
this procedure we lay on Captain H's bed, but I cannot state
exactly in which position we lay. It is true that there was a

---

conversation between K and myself about buggery together with H, however the act of bugger [sic] did not occur between K and myself. It is possible that I may have lain in a position where buggery with K could have been possible. After the above mentioned incident was finished, we were all sexually satisfied and I washed myself in the room.

The file also contains a handwritten confession by Captain H detailing anguish and confusion about his sexuality. Concluding:

Last May I met a man called RH. It seems as though God had sent us together. For our problems seemed identical. For a long time both of us had hoped that there was someone else in this world who could know and understand. We pledged ourselves to each other and resolved that with mutual help we would turn our backs on all the things that worried us and that through Faith we would achieve that peace which we both so desperately wanted.

Within a month of that pledge I was posted to Austria. God intends that I shall have no love on earth. He is a jealous God and He wants all my love.[21]

In the 1950s the most celebrated policeman in Britain was the Chief Constable of Nottingham, Captain Athelstan Horn Popkess.

Popkess declared his men should take up boxing. He replaced police bicycles with "Q" cars. He announced that road hogs ought to be flogged. In 1954, Popkess wrote an article for *The Practitioner*, "Special Number on Sex and its Problems."

21　　TNA: WO 71/1222

Public lavatories are... places [like cinemas] much frequented by pests like these [homosexuals]. I am always suspicious of anybody who, with quite righteous indignation, vehemently "demands an explanation" for the Police "daring" to ask him questions, just because he happened to be in the lavatory.

Popkess concluded his article:

Finally, there is the matter of lesbianism, scarcely known in an overt form in this country before the last war. Manifestations of it are noticed occasionally by some of my officers — practiced by women who tend to congregate in such places as public houses. They favour articles of male apparel and they greet each other as opposite sexes might do. Whether they are true inverts or merely sensationalists is a matter for conjecture, as there is seldom any evidence of culpable indecency. Such behaviour as this was largely thrown up by the war and it may well be a dying cult.[22]

22　Popkess had been brought up in Southern Africa. He played rugger against England for Rhodesia in 1912. He fought in the First World War in the King's African Rifles. He wrote about his adventures in an autobiography, *Sweat in My Eyes*, 1952, where he describes being mugged by two black men:

We were so close to each other that I caught his breath. I grabbed him round his chest and he couldn't bring his arm down. I jerked my knee up into his stomach. It paralyzed him, he grunted and sagged away. I turned to deal with his friend, but he had vanished. The man I had done with started to crawl away. Should I topple him off the bridge onto the rocks below? I let him be. The Soldiers' Chorus from Faust to came into my head, and I went on home whistling it.

In 1923, Popkess married Gilbertia Lilian Popkiss [no relation], brought up in Surbiton, "a handsome woman with Titian hair." In 1935, Gilbertia rode through Nottingham dressed as Queen Boadicea, in a chariot drawn by two horses. Popkess divorced her four years later, citing a Mr Crampton. He remarried to Dorothy Rosebudd Walsh. Dorothy became mentally ill. She committed suicide with sleeping pills.

Liz Baron was less sanguine. She recalled the rampant and conspicuous prostitution then – affecting all genders and inclinations.

> There was lots of prostitution on the streets both for men and women in those days. It was all over the place. You went out the door and they were all over the place.

> There was this club – do you remember the famous Ruth Ellis? – she had a club, and GB took me there one night, and there was a prostitute going up and down the stairs all the time we were there, with different clients. All female.

Adding:

> And I'm a little maid that was born in Cornwall, dear... [in mock Cornish accent] Oh my dear soul!

DRINK IT LOVE. IT'S GOOD FOR T' BABY

Liz Baron told me that George was bisexual, but mostly gay. When she met him he was already with his long term lover Paul Clay. Indeed, Paul lived with them at 2 Brydges Place.[23]

Paul Clay, born in 1904, was 25 years older than George – he looked far younger than his age.

"One of the bright young men in the London of the twenties," Clay had a minor acting career – its highlight being on Broadway in 1929, in Noel Coward's musical, *Bitter Sweet*.

A "tall and elegant figure," Paul was exceptionally camp, and well known on the West End gay scene. When in 1951 Paul was declared bankrupt, he was described as a "club proprietor."

Paul Clay, 1952

Paul and George lived together on and off for around thirty years. They ran several clubs together. Their relationship was tense and frequently violent. This was because George was a heavy drinker, and when drunk, prone to rages. He would assault Paul. Once, he threw him through a plate glass window.

---

23   Paul had lived there since 1959. George joined him in 1951. They were veteran West End, Soho boys – George had previously lodged at 43 Broadwick Street, Paul at 41 Whitcomb Street.

Liz Baron:

> Paul was there before I came on the scene. They lived together and Paul was, I'm being a bit vulgar here, but a stately old Queen. But he was nice really. An educated, dignified man. George pushed him around dreadfully.

———————

Soon after their marriage in 1953, George Baron's rages began to be directed at his new wife, Liz.

Liz Baron:

> I suppose if you were being a Christian – which I'm not – maybe GB was a victim of his upbringing. It's not making excuses. It's finding reasons.

> It's kind of sad isn't it really? He was an only child with this very strong, North Country mother. His father was a miner but not a tough guy. He was a softy.

> GB's mother swamped him and gave him everything. Then, like any mother I guess, when he took himself down to London she was proud of him.

> One day she came to visit us [in Brydges Place] – and this was one of the bad times, when I had a black eye and everything – and GB came in the door and she said to him,

> "George, what you been doing?" and he said,

> "What you on about mother?"

> "You shouldn't hit a woman when she's pregnant." [Laughing ironically] It's alright when she's not...

But he took no notice – because they never remember you see. This is the thing about alcoholics. They actually don't remember the next day what they did.

I mean, we had furniture broken. He'd throw me across the room. And in the morning he'd act as if nothing had happened. And I was in bits, you know...

His mother was a scary woman.

I love cooking, always have done, and once I had this leg of lamb in the oven because they were coming. And I kid you not, she came in and said [imitating broad Lancashire accent], "I don't want bloody lamb" – and she was drunk – because she drank as much as GB – "I've got you a bloody chicken." And she took my lamb out and put in a chicken...

Another time she visited and said, "I've bought you some curtains love. Yours don't match the room."

And she took my curtains down and put hers up.

And GB just stood there and never said a word. I think he was scared of her in a funny sort of way. She was a scary person. Loud and drunk. I remember trying to put her to bed one night and being attacked by her with her stiletto shoes.

She used to get absolutely plastered. The sort of woman who, after a few drinks, would really embarrass you. We went to a big restaurant once, near Covent Garden. She started drinking gin and tonics, and she'd had a few. And she went [imitates accent] "Oi Luv" to the waiter, "There's no bloody gin in 'ere. Our George will tell yer..."

GB used to humour her. But the husband – his dad – was deeply embarrassed by it all.

———

And I'd never met anything like this in my life, you know.

And it was a revelation to me when GB first took me to his old home [up North] I'd never seen anything like it. I'd never met people like it.

We went to the working men's club. I'm not being a snob here... but I walked in, and in those days we wore these pencil skirts, 6 inch heels, nipped in jackets and so on, and these two Lancashire women, one said,

"Eh up. Wear that, no knickers?"

And they got me up on the stage singing and that.

But you see the women up there – the women were the stronger. The women were tough from that area: the mill workers.

I went to a mill there, just to see. Your average person like myself didn't have an opportunity to see this – this was back in the fifties in the days when they all had bare feet. And they walked up and down these huge looms. I never did work out what they were doing.

And then they'd all stop for a coffee break and go out on a metal platform that had outdoor stairs to have their cigarettes and so on.

And every night, and I mean every night, they were up at Legion [working men's drinking club]. And I'd see her sat there with about 10 bottles of stout and she used to buy me bottles of stout.

And I didn't want them.

"Drink it love. It's good for t' baby..."

It wasn't good for me!

Liz showed me a news cutting (below) of her, George Baron, and their newborn baby.

20th Aug: 1958

(of the Day

Mr. George Baron, who learnt yesterday—while he was on stage in " Guys and Dolls "—that he had become the old tured to-day with George junior and actress wife, who

He [George] had the photographers in the bedroom. This was at the flat at Brydges Place. He was on stage in *Guys and Dolls* when it happened, and they announced it to the audience. And within a couple of hours, he had photographers in the bedroom – Joyce and Lionel [Blair] as well, and I had to sit up. I'm a very lucky woman. I have babies just like that. I don't have pre-labour – I just have backache. And it's sort of gone down in the family, because I said, "Has my mascara run?"

I thought her smile in the picture looked forced. That prompted:

When you see this picture anyone would think we were happily married. No one would believe that I was back at work within a fortnight of having our baby – but I was. And the reason was: GB didn't give me any money.

He'd go off. Wouldn't see him for a day or so. And he just didn't think he had to give me any money. So I had to get money to eat, you know. He never supported me. He never helped.

I would be struggling with – you know those prams that fold up? – not a pushchair, a pram. And he would never come and help me, and there were three flights of stairs in Brydges Place, after that tiny little alleyway.

I remember us being in clubs and GB throwing the door keys across the table and saying, "Go home darling. I'm busy."

It was horrendous really.

Since I had to go out to work because he didn't give me any money, he was quite happy to let any Tom, Dick or Harry babysit. He would let anybody he knew look after the boy. But I couldn't tolerate that – that's just not me.

And I've walked home at 1 o'clock in the morning, and once I got followed down Brydges Place. I was so frightened because it's so narrow. This was about 2-3 in the morning. I only just managed to get in and shut the door...

Plus there were all the boozy bash-ups.

In 1953 I was acting in *Heaven Sent*. That was at the Park Lane Theatre Club. I was already known as Elizabeth Baron then. Pam Manson was in the show – she was a sort of comedienne.

And one day I had to get – or they, the show, got – a make-up artist in from Leichner because I couldn't even touch my face myself to cover up the bruises.

And Pam said to me,

"Liz, my husband Louis is a solicitor and if you ever need a solicitor, tell me."

And I said, "No, I'm alright. I'm alright."

Because you keep hoping that they'll change. And I know it sounds ridiculous and naive, and when I hear people say it now I think, "Oh, come on!" But it's what you do. Because you've a child and of course, in the beginning, I guess it was a bit stars in my eyes, probably because he was such a brilliant dancer.

But I did see Louis in the end.

And on the day of the divorce I got to London and it was at the big high courts. And nobody had explained to me exactly what happened. I expected to see Louis there but I got a message from a wigged barrister, who was absolutely charming, saying, "Oh, your solicitor can't attend today, and I'll be in charge."

I didn't know him from Adam, and in the hearing GB's solicitor said that Mr Baron might appear because he had accused me of sleeping with Chris Eaton, an American actor who was actually engaged to one of my best friends, Kate Sadler. Just a lie.

In fact, another thing that came up in the hearing was when GB said to me, "Why don't you find yourself a lover?"

But GB didn't turn up.

Then the judge stopped the case halfway through. That was because of the violence. After hearing that the judge stopped the case and I got my divorce.

And there was I in my 6-inch high heels, darling... jockey cap, elbow length black gloves, black suit. All dressed up for the big day.

And I went home and sat on the bed and I felt so relieved and I took my shoes off and started to laugh and laugh. I couldn't stop laughing.

Liz and George Baron on their wedding day, "Be careful what you wish for."

SEALED FILE, CLOSED ANNEX

Unlike his friends Jean Townsend and June Sweetzer, Reg Hargrave flunked higher education.

After grammar school he dithered, hanging around in Bempton Drive. He was then conscripted into the Royal Artillery:

> In September 1954, I was stationed at High Leigh, near Knutsford in Cheshire.
>
> My morning routine was, I'd to go to the cookhouse for breakfast and pick up a newspaper on the way back. On the morning of the 17th I picked up the *Mirror* and a cup of tea. I headed back to barracks. I sat on my bed and looked at the paper.
>
> And there it was on the front page of the *Mirror*.
>
> And well, I was naturally stunned.
>
> It's not every day of the year that you read a story like that on the front page.
>
> I remember standing up – I must have been in some sort of bewilderment – and saying to the man next to me, 'I know this girl.'

———

Reg therefore missed the police investigation into Jean Townsend's murder. He heard that police had "swarmed" over Bempton Drive and all around, and that several men in the street were interrogated. When Reg went home on leave, the excitement was over.

After the army, Reg began looking for a career. He settled on becoming a patents lawyer.

> And I was lucky because that proved to be a very interesting profession, and in the end I got my own business. And that gave me the wherewithal to buy a decent house and live comfortably.

———

When we met, Reg seemed the picture of a successful patents lawyer: comfortable, affable, and plump. But he had a waspish, militant side. He'd campaigned against local corruption in Ruislip and was busy pursuing his current Hampshire MP for not coming up to scratch. Reg's wife, meanwhile, was sharp-eyed, kindly, and silver-haired. She was also a professional psychic. What a very British marriage of scepticism and mysticism, I thought. Naturally, Reg and his wife had attempted to contact Jean from "the other side" – but no luck.

It was after retiring that Reg began his private investigation into the Townsend case. It had always bugged him. Jean had been his friend, a woman with a bright future cut short. Reg suspected that details of the case were being withheld. He interviewed people, collected cuttings, researched archives. And naturally, he wanted to see the closed Townsend file. His request was turned down. He appealed to the Information Commissioner.

The Appeal was held in November 2007. It was chaired by David Farrer, QC.

An interesting confrontation: Hargrave vs Farrer. Two grammar school boys with legal training – but Reg had trained at night school, whereas the QC attended Downing College, Cambridge, and qualified at Middle Temple. Both pillars of community, self-made millionaires, fans of opera and classical music. Both owning grand shire dwellings: Reg sitting in six acres of Gloucestershire at Cud Hill House; Farrer in a Leicestershire mansion with just two acres but boasting a tennis court and a two-story coach house.

Halfway through the Appeal hearing: a surprise. Detective Superintendent David Miveld, representing the Met Police, asked that the Tribunal go into closed session.

The public, Reg included, was told to leave. Thirty minutes passed. The public was readmitted. Farrer now pronounced that the Tribunal would uphold the embargo on the Townsend file. It would stay closed. This, he said, on account of information given in camera by DS Miveld.

Case dismissed. No further appeal possible.

––––––––

Some time later the Tribunal proceedings were published with "a closed annex." This annex can only be seen by judges or the police.[24]

However, intriguing facts had slipped out from the public [and published[25]] part of the hearing.

One was that despite upholding the Met embargo on the Townsend file, the Tribunal *never inspected* the file.

The Chairman, Farrer: "We have not seen the file but have been given a general account of it by Mr. Miveld."

---

24   Reg considered requesting a judicial review. But he'd need to fund this himself, at huge cost. His family dissuaded him.
25   http://foiwiki.com/foiwiki/info_tribunal/DBFiles/Decision/i134/ Hargrave.pdf,<Accessed 18/08/2014>

The point of the Tribunal was to test the police case. Its job was to balance the Met's embargo against the appellant's [Reg Hargrave's] interests and point of view. Reg was alleging the Met investigation had been incompetent. Maybe corrupt. And that information was being concealed by the Met.

That may have been the case. It may not have been the case. But the issue couldn't be judged by taking the word of the police.

In fact, by not scrutinizing the Townsend file, by blandly (naively?) accepting the Met's "general account" of what was in it, the Tribunal neglected its function.

Farrer also decided it wasn't possible to release a redacted version of the Townsend file:

> We accept that the nature of a murder investigation is not such that the file can be redacted or partially disclosed. In this case it is all or nothing.

This was disingenuous. Many once restricted files in the Public Records Office are released with redacted details.

More reasonably, Farrer wondered whether forensic advances might help in any re-investigation, even at this late stage.

He'd initially thought this unlikely. But then:

> ...we heard... evidence in the private session which clearly altered our view on this issue because it was specific to this case. It did not indicate that a future identification and prosecution of the killer was more likely than not. It did persuade us that there was a significant possibility of such a development.

So was Scotland Yard poised to knock on the door of a homicidal octogenarian?

As I write this, more than a decade later, we are still waiting for "such a development."

We will wait for ever. It seems certain that speculation about a re-investigation was a cynical ruse to keep a lock on the case file.

———————

But then, as the Bishop said to the actress: "It just popped up out of nowhere!"

And two things popped out of that Tribunal hearing. One, shameful. The other, troubling.

First, shameful.

Answering a question from Reg Hargrave, DS Miveld asserted that "one" forensic item had been retained.

This meant that eight of the nine forensic items mentioned in the autopsy report had vanished.

This wasn't picked up by Farrer. The QC was as ignorant about the autopsy report as about everything else in the file.

And while Farrer was surely right to muse that "forensic science may advance in unforeseen ways," it's unlikely such advances can resurrect lost or destroyed samples.

[Nor could it rectify that initial blunder of covering (contaminating) the body with a "tatty" old tarpaulin from a building site. Rex Lewis: "when I lifted it off for the pathologist, I had to say the gravel was us – we'd put it there."]

Forensically, the case was as dead as Jean Townsend.

———————

Now the troubling bit.

During the open session DS Miveld had let slip that "a significant number" of documents "were missing" from the Townsend file.

Missing?

The Tribunal Report reads, "A significant number [of witness statements] were missing..." Continuing, "...but [DS Miveld] did not think that their loss seriously weakened the value of the surviving material."

Why Miveld thought that is not clear. How could he assess the significance of material he'd not seen? Material that – as was later admitted – he couldn't even itemize.

———

Missing documents?

I started to make Freedom of Information requests to the Met Police and relevant government departments.

For months they bluffed and stalled.

Then the Met announced that:

> There is no information available as to when these witness statements were detached from the record. Conversely, there is no evidence that these statements had been attached to the record in the first instance.

Gnomic, or what?

I asked how, if the statements had not been in the file "in the first instance," why then did the police categorise them "missing."

No answer.

I also asked whether there was at least a listing of statements in the existing file which showed what had been – but was no longer, – contained in the file?

No answer.

Could then, the Met at least quantify Miveld's "a significant number"? Dozens? Over a hundred?

The Met had no clue.

The Met now wrote, "There is no information available as to whether the missing documents were mislaid. That they are missing should not be taken to imply that they are lost."

Well, that could suggest that the "mislaid" material had deliberately been removed from the file and then placed somewhere else, out of reach of the Met…

If so, by whom?

Such a removal could only have been done by a body that could overrule the Met.

Special Branch? MI5?

I asked whether this was the case.

No answer.

No answer either, to whether the missing statements had been arbitrarily culled – or related to one particular line of enquiry.

———

On the 12th of September, 2008 I found a 2,476 word email in my in-tray.

This was from Sarah Pallen, "Freedom of Information Policy, Research, Review Officer."

Sarah was agitated.

She accused me of being "vexatious," "obsessive" and "harassing."

WPC Sourpuss had me bang to rights!

After being ticked off by the Met, and with no response to letters to official locations, I sent a round of letters to Tribunal members at their home addresses. A letter to Farrer's residence went unanswered. A letter to Roger Creedon, one of the two lay members of the Tribunal, drew an apology that he couldn't tell me anything – as he was sure I would understand. He wished me luck.

I now began to wonder whether one (the real?) reason the Met wouldn't open the Townsend file was less because of what we – the vexatious public – might find *inside* this file, but what we might discover or deduce had been *removed* from the file...

A GOOD EYE FOR NICE THINGS

During one interview with Liz Baron this exchange happened:

> FV: I've noticed the clubs in those days had a mixture of aristocrats and gangsters, as well as...

> Liz Baron: Oh yes, the gangsters! I know the Krays were very involved in gay clubs back then. They went to all sorts of clubs, and it's an interesting thing isn't it that gangsters seem to congregate with – or to like, show business people?

Maybe that jogged her memory.

A couple of weeks later, she rang.

She'd remembered an associate of George Baron who might be of interest. He'd been the boyfriend of one of her girlfriends. She wasn't quite sure what his role in George's life had been, but he'd been around the Londoner a lot.

His name was Dennis Stafford. She described him as a gangster and said he'd done time for murder.

Stafford was indeed a notorious gangster, as well as a notable prison escapee, and self-confessed playboy. In 1967, he was given a life sentence for his part in a gangland killing, "the one armed bandit murder." His story became the basis of the 1971 movie, *Get Carter*, starring Michael Caine and Britt Ekland.

It turned out that Dennis Stafford, now released from prison, was living near Newcastle. He'd recently published a memoir, *Fun Loving Criminal: the autobiography of a gentlemen gangster* (2007).

I ordered it from Amazon.

<hr />

Right. Dennis Stafford was Britain's most notorious prison escapee. In 1957 he was arrested in Trinidad and deported back to the UK. He'd been on the run after escaping from Wormwood Scrubs the previous year. As usual with Stafford, there was a woman involved, 20-year-old, "lovely West End showgirl," Eileen Cook. Stafford had been tracked to Trinidad after Eileen sent him a spooney telegram. Distraught, Eileen turned up at Cannon Row police station to tell Stafford how sorry she was, and that she loved him. She was "dressed in a skin-tight black cocktail dress and gaily-embroidered twelve-guinea shoes." But the police wouldn't allow her to see Stafford. She pleaded, "I don't know how long it will be before we can see each other and hold hands after this miserable separation."

97

Stafford's memoir entertainingly tells of heists and burglaries, gangland friends and enemies. He dismisses the Kray brothers as dimwits. He relishes several audacious escapes from maximum security jails, scoffs at the venality of policemen and folly of judges, and exults in his conquests of beautiful women.

Chapter 10 is called "Club Life." It was an unexpected and unique description of Jean Townsend's Londoner club.

It seemed that Stafford had bankrolled and part-owned the Londoner from the start. [I also now learned the club had kept going until the mid-sixties. Stafford even claims it existed for 23 years – which makes its invisibility even more remarkable.]

Moreover, George Baron and Paul Clay were Stafford's close friends as well as business partners (and very likely his partners in crime).

Stafford wrote how he'd met George and Paul around 1952 through an American singer he was dating, Doretta Morrow. This was at the Bijou club in Mayfair, which Stafford was using to fence stolen goods.

He hit it off with the gay couple.

> They had a good eye for nice things. If I had a good mink coat I would always put it their way, without raising any suspicion as to its legitimacy. We were good friends and they trusted me.

———————

Stafford writes that George Baron asked if he'd put money in a new club he wanted to start with Paul. Stafford claims he put up £12,000 – in today's money, about £209,000.

As much as the cash, no doubt George was looking for the security of being bankrolled by an accredited gangster. In the fifties, practically all London nightclubs and strip joints were territories contested by gangs running protection rackets. The best defence from predators was to be on the books of a bigger predator.

Stafford's criminal earnings paid for the "exclusive" trimmings of the Londoner:

> There was no sign on the door, just a little brass plaque that said "The Londoner Club", and standing outside would be a commissionaire dressed Louis XIV style. The same era was reflected in the furniture, and everyone drank from Waterford crystal glasses. Throughout the place the standards were sky-high.

The self-contained top flat above the club served as Stafford's hideout and love nest, where he enjoyed women and sometimes allowed friends to stay. (Once, when the police were hunting Stafford, they raided the flat and found the Londoner pianist, Russ Conway, "in bed with two sailors.")

The Londoner was super-exclusive. Nothing that happened inside was mentioned outside.

Hence, its appeal. Hence too, the reason why until now it had remained such a well-kept secret.

Stafford writes:

> Remember that these people were breaking the law by being homosexuals. They deserved protection and that's what they got. Any one of the members or the people who worked at the

club could have rushed to the papers with news about [the indiscretions of gay members like Rock Hudson] but no one ever did. Our club was a haven and I'm proud of that.

And:

There were only one or two other gay clubs in London in the 1950s and ours was particularly exclusive. It had to be in those less liberal times, and it was all done with a nod and a wink.

———————

Stafford insisted he wasn't gay. George and Paul were just good friends. He accepted their difference and,

They accepted me as a person who was not gay but understood their world and their feelings. I even used Polari, the gay language... but the sexual side of it wasn't for me...

Having a share in the club wasn't just a very good investment. It gave me an insight into a world that was hidden from the vast majority of straight people.

Every Monday [George and Paul] would deposit my one-third of the proceeds from the club and if we had to decorate or meet other costs they would draw out my share. They were very straight about cash – to the penny.

About the clientele, Stafford boasted that over time, "All the top choreographers, singers and show business people came [to the club]."

Not all the members were gay. The club attracted a strong element of straight members who enjoyed the fine service and elegant atmosphere...

His listing of club members and visitors [confirmed by other sources] is notable. The ballet dancers and lovers, Anton Dolin and John Gilpin. The painter John Minton, legendary for drinking and promiscuity. The gangland bruiser and actor, John Bindon, famed for his party trick of balancing up to six half pint mugs of beer on his erect penis. The Queen's Surgeon Sir Arthur Porritt, later, as Baron Porrit, Governor-General of New Zealand. Then the singer, Shirley Bassey, the actress, Marlene Dietrich, and the socialite Lady Docker, notorious for flaunting gold-plated Daimler limousines.

The pop star and actress, Shani Wallis [who later starred as Nancy in *Oliver!*] lived in Irving Street, over the road from the Londoner. She, too, was a member, and became Stafford's girlfriend for a while.

Stafford recalled:

> She could never make love on an empty stomach and she definitely liked her food. She used to order three zabigliones when she was supposed to be on a diet. [Shani Wallis was also close to George Baron – Liz Baron mentioned they often went to the races together.]

And Sarah Churchill, the actress daughter of Winston. And Antony Armstrong-Jones (Lord Snowdon). And Princess Margaret…

Of Margaret, Stafford wrote,

> She was fun and told me that she thought I was a "rascal." She was a very attractive woman who liked to put it about a bit. Never in my direction, but we were friends and we did flirt and laugh together.

Stafford mentioned that Stephen Ward [of Profumo scandal notoriety] "often dropped in."

He wrote that Ward was "a ponce," but "It didn't bother me. He was a nice fellow and I liked his company." Jack Profumo was also a habitué, "before the scandal."

Then Rock Hudson, who Stafford recalls having to cover up for after a violent scene with a gay toyboy. And the pop star, Johnnie Ray…

All this was an interesting picture of the club patronised by Jean Townsend, and where she'd spent her final evening.

NOT OVER COFFEE

While researching this book I consulted journalists and academics – and two private detectives. The most helpful tec was Simon Fluendy. Simon was ex-British Army Intelligence. He worked for two major detective agencies and freelanced as an investigative reporter.

We met at a traditional spooks' hang out, the Chesterfield Hotel in Charles Street, near Shepherd Market. Simon reclined in a leather armchair and polished off two gin and tonics while I told him the story. His instinct was that given the circumstances of Jean's killing, and the secrecy over the file, this could be a matter of national security.

He said he'd look into it.

Four months passed. Simon said it was more difficult nowadays to get information. Some of his sources were dithering. Or seemed to find the issue uncomfortable.

He then suggested a back door. Richard Thomas, "a good man if somewhat dry," who had been Information Commissioner at the time of the Townsend appeal.

> Explain why you want to reach him and feel free to drop my name. Ask him about principles rather than blunt case related questions and he might well help.

I sent the now retired Thomas a letter to his home address.

Silence.

Simon was surprised. He suggested I "pester" Thomas with a follow up letter.

Silence.

By now, a year had gone by. Simon tried another tack.

> I think it's worth trying the Met's barrister [who had represented the Met Police at the Tribunal]. She won't give away names but might give some insight.

He emailed this barrister.

> Dear Jane,
>
> I write in a personal capacity.
>
> As a former investigative journalist I have been contacted by a friend-of-a-friend who is researching a book on an unsolved murder. As a favour and because of personal interest in Freedom of Information issues, I have agreed to lend some assistance.

Simon then outlined the case, and the Tribunal's refusal to open the Townsend file. Continuing:

> While I would never ask or expect you to disclose confidential information relating to the case, it would be very helpful if you could explain a little of how the Tribunal considers such cases – for example how common it is for evidence to be heard in camera and whether the length of the 'lock up' imposed on disclosure is typical. If possible it would be of assistance if you shone a little light on the meaning of some of the rather opaque statements in the judgement.
>
> I realise that you must be very busy with case work but I do hope you could meet me briefly for a coffee and at a time and place convenient to you.
>
> Many thanks
>
> Simon Fluendy

The reply was:

> Dear Mr Fluendy
>
> Thank you for your message below; I regret that I do not feel able to assist you in this matter.
>
> Yours sincerely,
>
> Jane Oldham
>
> Barrister

Jane could not enlighten Simon. Not on the issue of "opacity." Not over coffee. Not briefly.

Simon now advised me to keep digging into Jean Townsend's professional background and social circle. Especially, her clubland and nightlife connections. That self-consciously decadent zone of fifties' London codenamed "Soho."

IT WAS SOHO

After leaving school at 15, Jackie Cliff was awarded a scholarship to study fashion at Harrow Art School. Freshly enrolled, she was introduced to erotic modelling by a photographer who took her to the Spielplatz nudist camp in Hertfordshire. Around then she also began frequenting the 100 Club in Oxford Street. Jackie:

> It was Humphrey Lyttleton and George Melly – totally mad, flamboyant – and Chris Barber and the band. We loved it – all the art students would go.

> Joan Collins used to go too. She was there almost every night of the week. We used to be in the ladies together and look at each other through the glass. And she hated me. I don't know why. I think she hated everybody except herself. Jealous. Anyway, she used to dance every single dance. She had long hair, and she was quite plump actually.

Jackie then began a relationship with an Italian lawyer and moved in with him. She meanwhile continued modelling for artists, including the portraitist, Rodrigo Moynihan.

> He used to collect floors. He'd go to auctions of houses and buy a floor. He'd say, "I've got a new floor, you must come and see it." Sometimes he had them put down in his own house, but mostly he used to have them standing up against a wall. And he'd look at one and stroke it, and say, "Look at that. Look! Can't you feel the age of that? Look at it – that's a tree."

Moynihan's wife, the painter Elinor Bellingham-Smith, also employed Jackie. Jackie befriended the family, including their teenage son, John Moynihan.

As an enthusiast for the 100 Club, John Moynihan wrote in his autobiographical *Not All a Ball*, 1970.[26]

> [The 100 Club was] what the magazines had started to call the headquarters of our existentialists. First let us consider the smell which rose from the steps leading down into this cellar; a mixture of old veg, armpits, crotch sweat, artificial air, soft drink, dirty fag smoke, bad breath, boiling socks, strangled knickers, grizzled corduroy, female handbag, Brylcreem, blanco, talcum powder, brow perspiration, mottled paintwork, boiling into a cellar smell. The smell rising from this extraordinary pit made me wobble but soon I was sniffing it with avid delight, heaving it into my lungs.

Jackie, too, recalled the "artificial air":

> In that club sometimes it was so hot we couldn't breathe. All the cigarette smoke too – you just could not breathe.

> One night, it was the hottest night of the year, and some of us had got a stamp on our wrist so we could go out the back where the dustbins were: "Oh, some air! The Oxford Street air!" (Gasps.)

> I sat on a dustbin. And then the police raided the club. They were everywhere. We didn't know what had happened – they were coming through with truncheons and everything. And they went into this back bit.

> It turned out they were looking for a man who'd escaped from prison. He was called "Rubber Bones." That was his name.

---

26 Moynihan later became a sports journalist and author. He died in 2012.

And he'd escaped from every prison. They couldn't keep him in prison. He was so rubbery he used to slither out.

Anyway, he'd slithered into 100 Oxford Street somehow, and got into the crowd. Then he slithered out and got into a dustbin.

And I think I was sitting on him that night! (laughs)

They found him in the dustbin, poor thing.

" Rubber Bones " and escort (left) on the way to Wandsworth Gaol

Through the Moynihans Jackie met her next boyfriend,

> This gorgeous young man called Keith Critchlow. He was a student at the Royal College of Art. I was so nervous of him, because he was in the in-crowd.[27]

Critchlow's family was,

---

27 Professor Keith Critchlow is nowadays an eminent artist, architect and author, and president of the Prince of Wales endorsed Temenos Academy.

All smiles and culture. Books were talked of – art – and going abroad for holidays, especially France.

Then we had coffee and more polite talk.

I was so scared because I was so silly. I had nothing except I was very pretty.

And I thought what kind of people am I living with now? Because it was all so amazing to me. It was like a dream.

Whenever I went back home to Bideford Road [South Ruislip] it was a culture shock. To see my dad – he'd say (Northern accent) "Eh, what? Eh?" (laughs). My mother was deaf, and my brother was hardly ever there.

I didn't know how to cope with this new world. It was so different. I'd never spoken to hardly anybody, you know, before I'd met these artists, and they were so sophisticated. They were sort of "Oh, the latest book" and, "Have you been to the latest opera?" I'd hardly ever even been to the pictures in those days.

For art students and bohemians in those days, the New Year's Eve Chelsea Arts Balls were indispensable entertainment.

These riotous fancy dress carnivals began with a procession of floats through the streets from Chelsea Art College, and ended inside the Albert Hall. Here, the elaborate and expensive effigies and floats, designed by artists like John Minton (and Jean Townsend's boss at Bermans, Michael Whittaker), were ritually destroyed at midnight. These events became increasingly unruly and were banned in 1958. John Moynihan described attending one with Keith Critchlow:

And then it was the midnight hour and the crowd swept back by the stewards awaited a new year with a ravenous, knock-kneed lust for destruction, the stewards throwing a rope across the bellies of the front ranks and holding them back with linked arms.

Everything seemed to happen at once, the bells of Big Ben chiming midnight, the cheers of the mob, the skirl of pipes, "Auld Lang Syne", the crowd merging, locking together, lips pressed on lips, the arrival of the absurd floats rolling awkwardly into the hall, the crowds breaking the barriers, fists exploding against jaws and stewards rugby-tackling giggling drunks, squalls of anger, women screaming, the floats being smashed, a nude art student held aloft suddenly falling into a twisted mass of fighting bodies, screaming, her breasts losing their protective covering of twinkling beads, rolling as she fell awkwardly into the mass, screams and shouts, the crowd coming on towards Father Neptune. A steward raced after a youth, caught him by the trousers, tearing them almost off, lay on top of him bashing him. The noise was hellish, the hall almost torn apart; people surged into people, wood splintered, floats were ripped up and the wreckage dragged across the floor, destruction took top priority. Skulls smashed against skulls...

"Happy New Year," I said to Keith. We shook hands.

Jackie recalled how:

I was put in a sort of a seat and lifted up on a pulley and pushed on a swing, all the way across the Albert Hall. I was only young and we were so happy, and everything was fun. You never think of frightening things when you're young.

ART STUDENTS THROW A BALL

American art students have an annual get-together, and at their League Ball in New York this year Deborah Kerr made her appearance as Queen of the Ball. After gallantly making the rounds, Deborah retired with a slightly red face on account of the uninhibited freedom exercised by the students in their choice of costumes. It seemed to Deborah that the effect most students strove for was revelationary, and it speaks well for Deborah's queenly poise that she indicated by no more than a charming lift of her eyebrow the astonishment she felt as the lack of one bizarre costume after another caught her royal eye.

Students are inimitably themselves the world over, of course, and there is no sect more unconventional than the arty type. Our own students make things look pretty lively at their annual Chelsea Arts Ball, and the horseplay there has left many a negligibly-clad lady simply bereft.

These two students looking like ravishing lovelies were boys with a flair for dressing up.

The guy on the right is telling the two sweet young students that he represe a well-plucked chicken.

5

Ah, Mr. and Mrs. Bighead, we presume

Wrong again—just another pair of whacky students

9

From a spread about the 1954 Chelsea Arts Ball in the soft porn magazine, Spick, *November, 1954. The students are a cross between Punk and New Romantic.*

Jackie progressed to many more boyfriends and sexual encounters, including with the jazz musician Ronnie Scott. "He was one of the first people to ever use that word, 'chick.' 'Hiya, chick.'"

> Around that time, I also met that strange man, Quentin Crisp. We were both modelling at the Royal Academy. We got quite friendly. Except that he was always such a misery in the breaks.

> He used to go round in the evenings with this blue hair, and walk around Piccadilly. And he had a big hat and a walking stick, and everybody used to look at him and he'd go like this, you know, with his hand [camp gesture]. And everybody would say "That's that strange, queer man... Oooh!"

> Looking back, I met an awful lot of gay people in those days.

> Until I got into the arts world, I didn't know what they were.

Jackie posed for Feliks Topolski, Norman Hepple, Fortunino Matania, John Ward, and the illustrator, John Daley. Daley she said,

> ...was in love with me. He told me this all the time. He was jealous of my boyfriend. Even though he'd never met him he'd say horrible things about him.

> Well, I didn't love John at all. He wasn't my type and anyway he was much too old. He had long, bad teeth, all brown, and he was a bit bald. In any case, in our breaks he'd make me great big huge pork chops and fried apple. And his stove was so dirty! – you couldn't believe his kitchen and his stove.

> But sometimes in our breaks he used to get me to write. I used to write down all kinds of poems and anything that came to my mind. In that way, he got the best out of me – whereas my boyfriend didn't.

She also posed for a variety of photographers including the fashion veteran Norman Parkinson and cheesecake merchant Walter Bird.

Then I found an agent in Soho and he got me a proper job as a stripper. After that I was never out of work. It was still the fifties. There was so much work that you just couldn't believe it.

And you never had to take your knickers off or anything like that. You had this G-string thing on, and tassels.

On the Soho circuit, however, she fell in with petty criminals and then mainstream gangsters.

That sort of thing was going on all the time. I mean, there was thieves and robbers – you name it. It was just amazing.

The funniest thing is, you just accepted it.

It was Soho.

Jackie also worked clubs. Like Selim Cattan's The Georgian.

Oh my God! [laughs] Selim Cattan. He was such a character. We all loved him – and we didn't love him. We were all a bit nervous of him. He was the dirtiest old man. He owned the club and he made it really good. Every girl in it was as gorgeous as he could get, or else he wouldn't have them. And he made all of them go to bed with him in this big round bed, in his stinky flat round the corner. I didn't do it actually. I was supposed to go there the night of my birthday, but I wriggled out of it. The stories I was told about his stinky bed... [laughs]. He used to take these girls back when they were drunk and say, "If you don't do it you're fired." But we also used to have lots of fun with him – pull his leg, joke.

Working as a showgirl in The Stork club Jackie had an unpleasant encounter with the Kray brothers.

One evening I was sitting in the bar after my act – you weren't allowed to leave straight away – and a man came up and bought me a bottle of champagne.

And I drank it and I got really drunk, but I thought, "Oh, soon I'll be going home."

113

Clockwise from top left. "Ponytail" (a young Barbara Windsor) gets sisterly advice from "Midnight Franklin" (Jayne Mansfield) in the dressing room of a Soho strip club. Having ignored the advice, "Ponytail" is strangled by a lust-crazed mobster. Poster for Too Hot To Handle, *1960, produced by Selim Cattan (re-titled here for the US market).[28]*

Anyway, there was a big kerfuffle in the corner and three men came in and sat opposite me. And most of the girls were sort of drifting off home. I thought, "Maybe another 10 minutes and I can get out of here."

---

28   As well as running The Georgian, Syrian-born Cattan was a theatrical agent. In 1961 Cattan was stripped of his license after "Miss C., Mrs H., and Miss T." complained about his advances. Cattan "strenuously denied" their allegations. But he was soon back in business. In *Norman's London*, 1969 (a guide to London's underworld by Frank Norman), Cattan was described as "forty-one years old, has a crisp moustache, smokes cigars and has a monocle dangling from his neck which he admits is pure affectation." By that time his club was renamed The Georgian Pussy Club.

But then I was called over to these men and one of them said, "Now, if you ask me for champagne that's it. You can have it. And I'll buy you a fur coat. I'll buy you jewels. Anything."

And he made me dance with him. He pushed me onto the dance floor.

Then he said, "You drink whisky when you're with me." So he pushed me back to the table and this great big glass of whisky...

Then the next one said, "Right, come here you," and he swirled me round the dance floor.

It was getting really late by then. It was horrible.

He said, same as the other one, "I'll buy you a fur coat, jewels..." and so on.

Then the last one said, "Come on, my turn now". So off we went, twirling around, and I was so drunk by then. They kept on making me drink this whisky. They were drinking it too.

I thought, "I've got to get out of here."

I went into the ladies and I got my coat and ran for it, ran out the front door.

And I thought, "Oh, horrible".

And I stood in the doorway and suddenly I saw stars...

Boing! I fell down.

When I got up one of these men was pushing me into a car. And do you know who they were? They were the Kray Brothers. They had been dancing with me.

And now one of them was driving round and round and round Piccadilly. I was begging him to not kill me. I was so frightened.

I never went back to The Stork.

George and Liz Baron at the Stork Club, *early fifties.*

SIR MORTIMER WHEELER & FRANCIS SAVIOUR MELITO

Being a jobbing stripper in 50s clubland had a sinister side.

Jackie Cliff:

> You got used to it after a while. It was so hard. Really, a lot of these women [strippers] were nuts. They were. But we did have a lot of fun. They had a double life I suppose, and they were always drinking.

> The owners of some of these clubs, they used to make the girls take vitamins. Because they drank so much and didn't eat much. So they used to say "Come on, eat your vitamins up."

> I also used to take purple hearts [amphetamines]. You could just get them in the chemist. They made me really ill. I don't know why I took them really. I used to take them by the handful, and when they wore off take another whole stack of them. But then everybody did it.

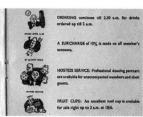

Doing a stint as a showgirl at the renowned Murray's Cabaret Club Jackie met Christine Keeler:

> She was horrible. Well, I say she was horrible: she was bitchy. Put it that way.

> The person that owned that club was Mr Murray. He was so nice. If the girls didn't make any money, he used to give it to them out of his pocket. A very kind gentleman. We all loved Mr Murray.

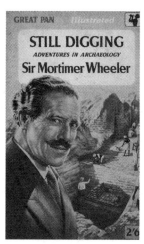

Paperback cover of TV archaeologist and friend of the Queen Mother, Sir Mortimer Wheeler's autobiography. This Pan edition was published around the time that Jackie Cliff, pictured (left) became his mistress.

Then, one day, fate came calling:

> I was doing a striptease one afternoon. I was in a really good mood and walking along – it was in Soho. And there he was, coming towards me.
>
> Mortimer Wheeler.
>
> Of course, he was quite famous in those days, and everybody knew him as Sir Mortimer. [Pop archaeologist and TV celebrity, author of several best sellers, and confidante of the Queen Mother.]
>
> I said, "Hello Sir Mortimer."
>
> And he said, "Hello darling."
>
> Like only he would.

Jackie became Sir Mortimer's mistress. They met regularly at his flat:

> And I would knock on the door – it was Number 27 something [27 Whitcomb Street – there is a blue plaque commemorating the great man], near Soho, Piccadilly.

The plaque on the house where Jackie and Sir Mortimer would meet. The great man frozen in an act of penmanship.

> And he would open the door with nothing on but that long gown that professors wear, black, and a mortarboard with a tassel.
>
> Sometimes he'd have a drink balanced on each corner of his mortarboard - champagne or wine or something, and of course, that made me laugh.
>
> We'd have a drink. Then we'd rush upstairs.

Wheeler befriended Jackie's family and the daughter she'd had by then. He took care of them for around twelve years, presenting a brace of pheasants to Jackie's bemused parents and stealing a handbag from the Queen Mother's home as a present for Jackie.

> He said, 'I've got this for you. I couldn't get a feather from the old girl but I've got you a nice handbag instead.'

But meanwhile, Jackie was determined to save enough money to buy her own flat.

> I was working then, in a place called the Venus Rooms. We used to call it the Penis Rooms.
>
> I was determined to get a lot of money so I could buy myself a flat. In those days, a single woman couldn't get a mortgage. Not unless you had a very, very good job, and I didn't.
>
> So I thought, right, I'm going to do the stripping till I get enough for a flat.

Then Jackie fell for a notorious gangster, Frank Melito, part of a Maltese gang running prostitution rackets in Mayfair.

> And it was the beginning of this awful, really... life.
>
> Fun one minute and terrible the next.
>
> It was like living on the edge of what I can't explain to you really.
>
> I went to Malta and visited his parents lots of times. He had a lovely mum and a lovely dad, and over his bed he had Jesus all

up in fairy lights. And he was a wicked man... Can you imagine – Jesus on the cross with fairy lights?

And he'd go "Aahh..."

Soon she discovered Melito was two-timing her:[29]

I decided I was going to leave him.

I was fed up with him anyway. I knew too much about him by then. Because there were loads of stories...[30]

But he said to me, "I want some money. Give me de money."

---

29   At the same time, Jackie was two-timing Melito with Sir Mortimer!
30   Francis Saviour Melito was born in 1932. He was part of a Maltese gang running the largest prostitution ring in Mayfair. This gang – not to be confused with their precursors, also Maltese, the Messina Brothers – were notoriously violent: "They used to really beat the girls up, threaten to break their limbs, black their eyes." The Met Police left the gang alone – officers were being paid off. Frank Melito was only exposed after an undercover investigation by *The News of the World*. The paper sent a female reporter, Tina Dalgleish, to track Melito to his heavily guarded home. Dalgleish risked her life to identify him. This was part of a huge and costly sting operation. After running the story, the newspaper gave its files to Scotland Yard – which was then forced, reluctantly, to act. [See description in SJ Taylor, *Shock! Horror! The Tabloids in Action*, 1991] Frank Melito's long criminal career included involvement in the 1956 murder of Tommy "Scarface" Smithson. Here, it was alleged that "Maltese club and cafe owners," headed by Bernie Silver (aka "The Godfather of Soho"), had tired of paying protection money to Smithson, an associate of the Kray brothers. He was shot dead by a Maltese pimp in a Maida Vale brothel. The assassin boasted to *The Sunday People*, "Blood started coming out. Thick blood like liver from his mouth. This man I thought, has had it. Mission accomplished. I was really enjoying myself but I was a bit disappointed that the gun had jammed. I was expecting to see a second bullet go rapidly inside him and see something better. Jamming the gun spoiled the whole rhythm... You could see it in his face. He knew he had had it. And it gave me great satisfaction because many a time I've seen him having a go." [Martin Tomkinson, *The Pornbrokers*, 1982, p23] Melito was acquitted of involvement in the murder, but implicated in Silver's criminal and sex operations. He got four years in jail for conspiring "to live off the earnings of prostitution in an establishment in Half Moon Street, Mayfair." That was only a specimen charge. Melito died of natural causes in Chelsea in 1996.

He meant all my savings.

I said I hadn't got any money. But of course I had.

I'd been saving, and I used to save so much, I hardly got a taxi sometimes.

Then he had a big row with me and he opened the airing cupboard, and took out a gun, a pistol, and he was going to shoot me.

He had such a flaming temper.

Then he got a Hoover out of the airing cupboard and he bashed my head with it and I fell down, and he broke all my nose and my teeth and everything.

Then he got my stiletto heeled shoe and bashed my head in with it.

Anyway, I wouldn't give him my money, and I didn't.

After that, Jackie ran. She ran from her work and from London.

What with one thing and another, I had to get out of all of that.

I couldn't bear it any more.

You see, although I was only really doing the striptease, I was living on the brink of – well, if you said anything wrong about these people...

And I'd found out that Frank had loads of girls working for him.

It's like in these films: you think you don't know, but you do really...

On top of that, now I had my little girl to think about.

A NERVOUS COMPLAINT

The Londoner, at 16 Irving Street,[31] was less than 200 yards from George Baron's previous club, the Festival, but many notches classier. The first floor – above an Indian restaurant – was the main club space. There were apartment rooms over that, and a self-contained apartment on the top floor. George and Paul sometimes stayed above the club and also let rooms to gay friends.

From left. The Londoner club in September, 1954. The sign (circled) at the top was replaced by a discreet brass plaque by the door. George Baron, Londoner club manager, a brilliant dancer – and a psychopath.

---

31 The previous live-in leaseholder had been George Taratooty, an estate agent: apartments for "diplomats and other prominent persons".

15 Paramount for Food. restaurant
15 Paramount Automatics Ltd. merchants
15 Paramount (Laboratories) Ltd. chewing gum mfrs
16 Restaurant Asiatique
16 Pavett Ernest, turf commssn. agt
16 Barker, Williams & Co. chartered accntnts
17 Irving Galleries
17 Irving Theatre Club
17 Invernizzi Bros. cheese imptrs
17 Yonan J. F. & A. Tawfik, export mers
18 Berman M. Ltd. theatrical costumiers
19 & 20 Brown (Ernest) & Phillips Ltd. picture dlrs
20 Harlequin Press Co. Ltd. publshrs
21 Georges (Chemists) Ltd
..... here is Leicester square ......

Clockwise from left. The building in 2012. From a commercial directory showing the area adjacent to 16 Irving Street in 1953. From the electoral register, 1957.

CITIES OF LONDON AND WESTMINSTE
IRVING STREET, W.C.2
—cont.

495	L—Colbran, Bertram C.	6
496	L—Smith, Constance R.	6
497	L—Etchells, Frederick	14
498	L—Fairtlough, Andrew C.	14
499	Harrison, Helen	14
500	Harrison, Ridgway E.—J	14
501	L—Morris, Desmond R.	14
502	L—Appleton, Maurice	15
503	Levinsson, Martha	15
504	Levinsson, Sally	15
505	Baron, George J.	16
506	Clay, Paul F.	16
507	Cresswell, Daniel	16
508	Harknett, Dennis G.	16
509	Wallis, Leslie	16
510	L—Williams, Henry C.	16
511	L—Chaudhari, Dhurjati P.	17
512	Adams, Harry	19

Taratooty moved to Golders Green. On the evening of Wednesday, May 13, 1963, he was dining at a friend's house. Watching television he saw there'd been an accident, "near to where I lived." A small private plane had crashed into a block of flats. "I hurried home to find the plane actually embedded in my flat." Nobody in the block was hurt. The pilot and passenger were killed instantly. Two Australian dentists.

The crashed plane.

The Londoner's address suited a showbiz clientele. Irving Street, named after the Victorian actor, Sir Henry Irving, led off Leicester Square, the hub of theatreland.

George and Paul had big ideas for the club. They first tried a dining venue. That proved complicated so they switched to snacks. Dark blue flock wallpaper was put up. A grand piano installed. The pianist was Russ Conway.

Liz Baron:

> Russ Conway – I knew him then as Terry Stanford, which was his real name. And he was so gorgeous. I loved him. He used to play there. In fact, I've sung with him when he was playing, and he was composing – he got quite cross with me because he was composing a new song and it went like [hums a tune]. And I sang it to him one day, and he said, "How did you know that?" I said, "I just listened to you." But he wasn't very pleased. I think he thought I was going to snatch it.

Next door, at number 17, was the Irving Theatre, run by Indian restaurateur, Dhurjati Chaudhari. He lived above the venue with his Irish girlfriend, Kathleen Bryne.

This was where Daniel Carroll – who'd previously worked in the kitchen of the Londoner – transformed into the drag artist Danny La Rue. La Rue described the theatre in his autobiography, *From Drags to Riches*, 1987:

> The Irving Theatre was tiny... On a good day, the theatre held no more than seventy-five people... It was one of the first of the club theatres that sprang to life in London during the fifties, and Chowderry [sic] let it out at every opportunity to managements and individuals who came up with the right kind of money, to stage revues and shoestring productions. At one time, Jill Gascoine appeared in a show there, and the actor, Victor Spinetti, became a regular. The theatre also had a short career as a strip club. It was all pretty daring for 1954.

The year the Londoner opened, the Irving Theatre put on "an evening of intimate Revue, called Men Only, with a talented all-male company." This show was put together by the female impersonator and promoter, Ted Gatty. Piano accompaniment was by a duo, The Gay Bachelors. Victor Spinetti has claimed that the theatre "...was packed with quite a lot of famous people... Philip Larkin was there, and Kingsley Amis, and Alec Waugh. They were all regulars..."

———————

The Londoner was open daytimes as well as evenings.

Liz Baron:

> You'd walk into the place when rehearsing. Sometimes too, I'd just pop into the Londoner for a coffee or something at lunchtime and that's what people did. It was the sort of theatre club where people came after rehearsals or between rehearsals or whatever, and everybody always said, "Hello Darling!" you know – but you didn't always know their names.

Liz recalled meeting Diana Dors there.

> That was when she was with her husband. And GB knew Judy Garland very well, and she came over. But it was all a load of... just on the top – do you know what I mean? Superficial. GB too, he was very superficial.
>
> There was also a younger man living there who used to run the club with George. That was Simon [Austin].
>
> Simon kind of took over from me – if you know what I mean. A very neurotic young man. But you see, I hesitate to say this because obviously all gays are not the same, but there is a type, very volatile and very hypersensitive...
>
> And GB was one of them, and so was Simon.

Simon had had a predecessor. This was Dennis Harknett.

Dennis George Harknett, the son of a chauffeur, was an aspiring actor. Previously a professional soldier, he was discharged from the army because of "a nervous complaint" [possibly code for homosexuality]. He was married to Joyce Phyllis Cole. They had two baby daughters and lived in Kentish Town.

Meanwhile, Harknett was George Baron's lover. The affair was not going smoothly. On the evening of Friday, 2nd July 1954, Harknett came back to the Londoner from the cinema. He and Baron had a tiff. Harknett went upstairs and turned on a gas ring. He was found dead.

"Suicide while the balance of his mind was disturbed."[32]

An interview source for the Harknett incident, a bookmaker who lodged above the club, suggested there was something fishy about this death – about George Baron's role – that Paul Clay, who testified at the inquest, concealed. This source, however, refused to elaborate or go on record.

When and Where Died.	Name and Surname.	Sex.	Age.	Rank or Profession.	Cause of Death.	Signature, Description, and Residence of Informant.	When Registered.
Twenty-fourth June 1954 Charing Cross Hospital	Dennis George Harknett	male	24 years	8/16 Irving Street Westminster Club Secretary	Asphyxia due to carbon monoxide (coal gas) poisoning Self administered Did kill himself while his balance of his mind was disturbed. P.M.	Certificate received from H.H. Stafford Coroner for County of London. Inquest held 29 June 1954 6A	Twenty fifth June 1954

32   Like much else about the Townsend story this memory was buried. But festered. When I located one of Harknett's daughters, she was still bitter about the suicide of a father she'd never known.

MR FASHION

Bermans *in September 1954.*

Only two doors from the Londoner, and next door to the Irving theatre, was the HQ of Bermans theatrical costumier. This was where Jean Townsend worked.

I failed to trace any of Jean Townsend's workmates at Bermans. But her immediate boss there, Michael Whittaker, had left a trail.

John Michael de Bagulegh Whittaker, aka Michael Whittaker, aka "Mr Fashion", was a freelance fashion entrepreneur as well as a designer of theatrical sets and movie costumes, and much else besides. Jean Townsend acted as his personal assistant and co-designer. She was also his friend and confidante.

You won't find out much about Whittaker online. At the time of Jean's murder he was renowned and feted. But the gatekeepers of the internet, in creating a version of history that flatters their Californian *Weltanschauung*, have erased Whittaker. That's because he doesn't fit the enthusiasms and fetishes informing google algorithms, or the fantasies and memorabilia collections of Wiki fan-contributor/experts.[33]

So search engines mostly bring up Whittaker's creation of Honor Blackman's kinky black leather catsuit for the "cult" TV show, *The Avengers* – a suitably commodified pop culture artefact. As I write, there's no online biog, not even a photo of Whittaker.

That said, internet research can throw up wild cards – but you have to be nifty to catch them.

For example, one day, idly googling "Michael Whittaker," I noticed someone on Ebay offering erotic/pornographic sketches "by the famous Avengers catsuit designer."[34]

Naturally, I bought them. They were fairly hardcore. Men, generally in military uniform, involved in flagellation, submission or buggery.

---

33 Wikipedia meanwhile, has 2,000 words on the pointless fashion darling Isabella Blow, and 1,500 on the 1950s TV glove-puppet Andy Pandy – because they correspond to prevailing pop culture nostalgias. A more contemporary puppet, Paris Hilton, gets over 7,000 words – solemnly annotated with 299 references. (Albert Einstein rates 10,000 words).
34 The seller was cagey about how he got them. I gathered however that he was a former associate of Whittaker and lived not far from the cottage where Whittaker held some of his orgies.

Whittaker at the height of his fame
photographed by Angus McBean.[35]

Digging beyond Google, digitised historical and newspaper databases turned up snippets about Whittaker: reviews, ads, short interviews. Nothing substantial.

The Times announced:

> A Memorial Service for John Michael Antony de Baguleigh Whittaker, known as Michael Whittaker, will be held at 11am on Thursday, October 12, 1995, at the Brompton Oratory, Brompton Road, London, SW7.

---

35   From numerous signed and warmly inscribed photographs of Whittaker and his family by the celebrated photographer, Angus McBean, there must have been a friendship between them. Given their shared homosexuality and immersion in theatreland that would be unsurprising. But in another sign of Whittaker's erasure from history, Adrien Woodhouse,

But no obituary.

More surprising was the invisibility of Whittaker and his work in academic databases. These are generally good for obscure cultural figures. But all passed on Whittaker. Not one hit in the Wilson Web sites or Jstor. Not one mention in any database of PhD research.[36]

You might wonder about this if you check the movie database, IMDb. Here again, there's no substance about Whittaker, but there are four citations for him as a movie actor,[37] and five credits for set and costume design – all in mainstream productions.

In 1950 Whittaker got an Oscar nomination for his costume design on *The Black Rose*, directed by Henry Hathaway, and starring Orson Welles and Tyrone Power.[38][For this movie he designed 300 costumes in three weeks.[39]]

However, it appears that Whittaker was a more prolific movie designer than recorded by IMDb. For example, he worked uncredited on costumes for Henry Hathaway's *Prince Valiant*, 1954, and the costume

---

author of McBean's biography, *Angus McBean*, 1982, emailed me, "I'm afraid that there was no mention of MW in Angus's unpublished autobiography and I do not recall Angus, whom I knew well for ten years before his death, ever mentioning MW to me."

36 Most of the material about Whittaker in this book comes from interviews or material in the Whittaker suitcase – see below.

37 This record is incomplete. IMDb doesn't for example mention Whittaker's appearance in Hitchcock's 1929 silent movie, *The Manxman*.

38 As a runner-up, he was given the Hollywood Order of Merit. Whittaker lost out to Edith Head, then at Paramount, for her work on *Samson and Delilah*, directed by Cecil B DeMille, starring Victor Mature and Hedy Lamarr.

39 Including a mink-lined coat for Orson Welles's portrayal of a Mongolian general, to "indicate luxury and opulence." This was created from "brown Russian leather, [and was] 60 inches from shoulder to toe, and lined with 300 mink skins…" The garment was so heavy "that it takes two assistants to lift it onto Orson Welles's shoulder – but he finds no joy in wearing it in the Moroccan location where the temperature stands at around 120 degrees!"

drama, *Star of India*, 1954. In a throwaway comment Whittaker revealed he'd also "designed more than twenty-six productions," for British theatrical impresario Stephen Mitchell.

This proficiency stemmed from Whittaker's background in practical fashion:

> I think the fact that I am able to cut out as well as design costumes is one of my greatest assets. It is all very well to draw a marvellously effective design on paper, but quite another matter to carry out the design – unless you have a clear idea in your own mind as to *how* it can be realised.

Meanwhile, Whittaker was also a professional theatre actor. In the 1940s he played major roles in over a dozen theatre productions, several in the West End. A passable singer, he was praised by the *Manchester Guardian* in 1941 for his part in Eduard Künneke's operetta, *The Cousin from Nowhere*.

Sometimes, Whittaker combined theatrical acting and design. During WW2 for example, he played opposite Ann Todd at the Prince of Wales' Theatre in *The Trial of Madeleine Smith*, and was also credited for the décor and costumes. In the same period Whittaker collaborated with the producer George Black, in mounting and dressing popular plays and wartime revues at the Hippodrome Theatre.

Post-war, in the 1950s, Whittaker was very busy indeed. He created stage sets and costumes for twelve more theatre productions and branched into opera and ballet – including *Pygmalion*, *Tosca*, and *Figaro*. Collaborations with the operatic polymath Dennis Arundell resulted in Whittaker designing several Sadler's Wells productions. Reviews consistently praised his décor and costumes. Meanwhile, Whittaker "dressed" a variety of revues and floorshows.

Top. Whittaker designed the brochure for this 1952 fashion show, devised and compeered by him, again in collaboration with Bermans. Bottom. Whittaker designed outfits made at Bermans for this 1951 Embassy Club Revue, starring the French cabaret artist, Lady Patachou. Patachou's gimmick was to snip the ties of male patrons reluctant to join in the singing at her Montmartre club, Le Lapin Agile. She'd then display the ties on the wall. Jean Townsend would have probably participated in both these projects.

He also found time to become a major producer and compeer of fashion shows.

His style here was speedy and theatrical, in contrast to stilted fashion parades then common. He boasted of showing "228 garments on 24 model girls in less than 80 minutes." He crafted scenes and moods with music, lighting and dramatics. His commentaries were irreverent and risqué.

In the mid-fifties Whittaker founded his own model agency, Michael Whittaker Enterprises. By 1959, it was the biggest model agency in the UK.

In that year, *Theatre World* ran a feature on him.

> Michael has been completely immersed in couturier technique and television for the last five years. He produces frequent Television Fashion Shows, and he is also renowned for his fantastic "live" Mode-shows.

The article described how Whittaker rigorously trained his models: "They spend long hours rehearsing, and he puts them through a special mime-drill."[40]

Later in his career Whittaker became prominent in the influential London Group of fashion promoters. He toured the world (including behind the Iron Curtain) showcasing British design.

Frequently consulted for opinions on style, Whittaker became a familiar newspaper columnist and TV pundit. The media dubbed him "Mr Fashion."

———

---

[40]   HC Corathiel, "Michael Whittaker," *Theatre World*, September, 1959

His Clothes Put Style Into Women's Show →

COMPERING the women's fashion show of "Moygashel" fabrics at the Dorchester Hotel, London, W., on Monday, Michael Whittaker, designer of clothes and decor for film producers, gave a personal men's slant to the proceedings. He wore a dark grey single-breasted suit of fine linen material, cut on Edwardian lines with cuffed sleeves and jetted outside ticket pocket.

With it went a cream linen waistcoat, patterned with a grey pane check and cut in a bold double-breasted style. An individual touch was the set of Georgian mirror buttons—"the latest thing," Mr. Whittaker told "Men's Wear."

The suit and vest were made by Steegan, Ltd., subsidiary of Stevenson and Son, Ltd., the manufacturers of "Moygashel" fabrics.

Featured in the parade was a white evening jacket worn with black trousers.

Left. 1958 modelling competition organised and judged by Michael Whittaker. Note the fat cat with cigar ogling the parade. In the same year, Whittaker rejected an actress, Ann Taylor, who'd applied to his model agency. She said, "I'm afraid I didn't hit it off with Mr. Whittaker. The first thing he ever said to me was, 'Sweety, you're wearing last year's eyebrows.'" Right. Whittaker models his own creation – a linen "Edwardian" suit with cuffed sleeves, "the latest thing" in 1952.

Jean Townsend had been Whittaker's personal assistant from the early fifties.

She liaised for him at Bermans and worked on Whittaker fashion shows in the UK and abroad.

Whittaker counted Jean as a friend and colleague and rated her design skills. Though uncredited, it's probable she assisted with costumes for his Oscar nominated *Black Rose* work, on the Disney production, *The Story of Robin Hood and His Merrie Men*, (1952), and on Hammer Films' *The Men of Sherwood Forest* (1954). [Jean also assisted another Bermans costume designer, Julia Squire, on *Moulin Rouge*, 1952.]

It's noticeable that Whittaker's frenzied pace of costume design slowed after Jean's murder. From about 1955 he focused more on fashion compeering and his model agency. He also drifted away from his role at Bermans after being finally confirmed as a director in March 1955. That might all be coincidental, or maybe he missed Jean's design input.

Michael Whittaker was what people called a "card."

He was also, to use another term then current, a "pervert."

Ostentatiously gay (though he may have been bisexual[41]), he had a fascination for what shrinks call "stuff fetishism."

---

41 Whittaker claimed he'd been married. And that after a divorce, he married the same woman again, and then divorced her again. Whittaker's confidante, Ann Graham:

> They missed each other madly. They were like Burton and Taylor. They were murderous together and as miserable as sin apart. They couldn't live together or bear to be apart. Michael was bi. But if he had a new friend of any sex he'd run him or her past [his "wife"] Sigi. And any new men friends she'd got always had to meet Michael. And then there was a hugely diverting conversation between the two of them about whether he should – or she should – continue with this person.

Sigi was Sigrid Landstad. She had a brief professional acting career, 1940-1945. She often came to Whittaker's shows and was generally introduced as "Mrs Whittaker."

However, I could find no record of Whittaker's marriages or divorces.

From left. Sigrid Landstad performing in The Heart of a Tart *and* Alone by Myself. *Both produced by Michael Whittaker. Dates unknown.*

Asked about his famous leather catsuit for *The Avengers* he said:

> Cathy [*The Avengers*' heroine] is fascinating. She is glamorous. But she is practical too and her wardrobe has to reflect this. That is why I have used such a lot of leather in Cathy's clothes. And culottes – those divided skirts – are just right for a woman who one minute has to look poised and serene and the next could be jumping into a shooting fray with a band of thugs. I designed these in June [1961?] a month before the Paris collections came out, and when they did, I found that they were right in line with the new fashions.

Whittaker didn't mention that the costume was ostentatiously fetishistic.

The catsuit had an antecedent. Whittaker's closest and lifelong friend was the B-movie actress, Patricia (Pat) Laffan.[42] Laffan still has a cult following of fans. Her biggest role was the 1954 *Devil Girl from Mars*, where she stars as a predatory Martian sex siren who descends on the Scottish Highlands looking for men to breed with. The film is notable for preposterous special effects and Laffan's prototype *Avengers* outfit. This dominatrix look was designed by Ronald Cobb, an illustrator who created outlandish costumes for the London nightclub, Eve. But the "leather" element was classic Whittaker.

42　I made repeated attempts to interview Pat Laffan who was born in 1912. Impressively strident over the phone she seemed to find the topic of Michael Whittaker uncomfortable. After several excuses – getting more and more elaborate and unlikely, including one about a leaking bath and a rogue plumber – I gave up.

Pat Laffan in Devil Girl From Mars, *1954.*

Michael Whittaker and Pat Laffan. She has inscribed the photo, "darling! What are you saying!!!? Love Pat."

Such kinky chic chimes with several porno illustrations formerly in Whittaker's sketchbooks [see, for example, Page 30, above]. And with the porno chic that was *de rigeur* at Whittaker's regular sadomasochistic sex orgies.

Whittaker hosted these at his town house in Magnolia Road, Chiswick, and at his country cottage on Dartmoor. They assembled bohemians and celebrities. And soldiers from the Horse Guards.

Whittaker was fascinated by military uniforms and military men. Especially Guardsmen. He liked to dress up in Guards kit, fibbed he'd served in the Guards, and dated soldiers from the regiment. [Members of this elite regiment, which protects the reigning monarch and is famed for its camp uniforms, have always been in demand in gay circles. In the fifties, "guardsman" was gay slang for "rent boy."]

———

At the end of August 1954, a fortnight before Jean Townsend was killed, the *Evening Times* ran a full-page feature: "This Man Stands on the Helm of Fashion." It was illustrated by a natty looking Whittaker giving, "the finishing touch to one of his sketches." The article lauded Whittaker's "entirely successful career" in acting and theatrical design:

Michael Whittaker started early, dolling figures in a toy farmyard with odd scraps from his mother's old dresses. It became instilled into him that clothes have a great effect on people's lives.

Continuing:

> When I met him in a large fitting room abutting Leicester Square, where he acts as supervisor for designers employed by [Bermans] he was beginning to work up a well-mannered sweat about the costumes for next week's big TV show, *Troilus and Cressida*. 'There,' he flung his arm forward, 'are the costumes we have done for the Halloween ball for the British

embassy in Rio De Janeiro. See – witches' robes with red dragons on them. And here,' he fingered a gown, 'are some of Margaret Lockwood's clothes that she used in Trouble in the Glen. I do a lot of private clothes for her...'

Whittaker reeled off other private clients: Ann Todd, Vivien Leigh, Betty Stockfeld, and Joan Greenwood.

The article lauded Whittaker's radio and TV work. It mentioned he'd "conducted the Scottish and continental tour" of the official Court Designer, Norman Hartnell's, Coronation collection in 1953. [Whittaker and Hartnell were close friends. It was Hartnell who introduced Whittaker to fashion show compeering.]

Whittaker:

Mr. Hartnell says I understand his clothes. It's my job to understand all designers' clothes, what they want them to mean, the thought they have behind them.

The "Fashion Man" ended cattily, contrasting British and French designers: "We still design for private customers. The French design purely for the American market."

A HOLE IN THE ALIBI?

Some have wondered if the odd circumstances around Jean Townsend's death suggest an SM routine that went wrong. Particularly the fact that her underclothing had been so meticulously (ceremoniously?) removed. Did she contribute to that ghoulish striptease? Did someone partial to this kind of fetish, someone known to or close to her, take part in her murder?

Which leads us to enquire about Michael Whittaker's movements around the time Jean Townsend was killed on the night of 14th September, 1954.

Did he have an alibi?

He had a good one. But there was a possible flaw in it.

From late August, 1954, Whittaker spent a lot of time in Scotland. He was designing and producing a fashion show to promote Scottish fabrics at the Kelvin Hall, Glasgow. This show ran during the first fortnight in September.

The private showing was on 2nd September. It was in the presence of the Queen Mother, and suitably tasteful.

Norman Hartnell displayed evening gowns "of tartan taffeta," and "pheasant feather embroidery." Poupée Hart, one of Whittaker's favourite models, displayed an "Evening Dress and Jacket in Silk Organza" by Frederick Starke. The band leader Victor Silvester's wife,

Patti Morgan (a TV compeer for his *BBC Dancing Club*), paraded in an organza cocktail dress, topped with a hat by Norman Edwin.

While this private show featured nineteen garments, the public shows counted 57. Throughout, Whittaker was on his cheekiest form. In one, he quipped that a model was about to appear in her "fancy pants." The Soviet ambassador, Yakov Malik, thought he was about to see a beautiful woman in her "panties." Sniggers all round.

After compeering the show for the first three days, Whittaker flew back to London. The TV personality, Joan Griffiths, took over his role. According to the programme, Whittaker was due to return to Glasgow to compeer the two final shows, one on the 12th, and the finale on the 18th.

There is ambiguity about these dates. The 12th September was a Sunday, and in Presbyterian Glasgow, there was no show. That might have been a misprint for the 13th. It's unclear whether Whittaker stayed in Glasgow after that, between the 13th and the 17th September. It's likely he returned to London. Glasgow in those days was not inviting for someone as mercurial and debonair. Also, Whittaker at that time had pressing business in London.[43]

During that interval, Jean Townsend was murdered – on the night of the 14th. That would have been the most likely date for Whittaker's return flight.

In 1954, all commercial flights between Glasgow and London left and arrived at Northolt Aerodrome. This was adjacent to South Ruislip,

---

43   A letter addressed to Whittaker at Bermans by the Festival promoter, Elson Gamble of House of Fraser (30 April, 1954), hints at his hectic schedule around then. Whittaker, it seems, had problems fitting a pre-arranged London schedule (which included the Selfridges show that season) around his Glasgow dates. Gamble was also anxious that Whittaker feature in the national televising of the Glasgow show, broadcast on September 6, at 8.40pm. But it seems that Whittaker missed that date as, once again, he was in London.

about five minutes' drive from the murder scene. The London-Glasgow schedule operated twice daily and included an evening service.[44]

South Ruislip was respectably dreary. But nearby Northolt Aerodrome was chic and metropolitan. In the early 1950s [up to October, 1954, when Heathrow was fully opened] Northolt was the busiest airport in Europe. It was the favoured hub for British and foreign royalty, and a prime location for the paparazzi to snap Audrey Hepburn, Judy Garland, or Frank Sinatra.

My mother (right) worked as a BEA stewardess at Northolt in the 1950s. Here, she poses with Danny Kaye, who has just landed.

In those days there was no public transport from the airport to central London. You would get a taxi, or be picked up by a friend…

---

44   Though at what time the return trip touched down I've been unable to discover.

Details of Whittaker's movements on the fatal night, and more general details about his life and appetite for "dangerous" sexual play, as well as his relationship with Jean Townsend, may be in the locked police file.

Or maybe not.

Top. September 1954, Programme *cover designed by Whittaker. Bottom. Portrait of Whittaker by Angus McBean.*

TASTEFULLY DONE OUT

After reading the gangster Dennis Stafford's memoir about the Londoner club I found his phone number. We talked for an hour.

He said that at first he was a "little bit reluctant" to finance the Londoner. "In England in those days it wasn't accepted. And I wasn't gay or anything. But anyway, I put the money up."

Stafford also remembered the Festival club: "That was a bit of a... that was like a toilet actually! What we called Cottage Greens. (Laughs) It was a place for closet queens."

The Festival's location next to a notorious male urinal was handy. Festival members would occasionally smash its glass canopy with ashtrays hurled down from the club windows, "so they could see inside – they thought this was very funny."

The Londoner had a more dignified face:

> We used to have a royal commissionaire on the door, with a white hat. So it was strictly members only.
>
> The interior of the club – you went upstairs and there was a small entrance, very, very unassuming. Then you turned right, then came to a door, on the level of the first floor. And then you opened a door that went onto a balcony, and then you went downstairs into the club. It was very theatrical.
>
> Then, as you went down – down the flight of stairs, you had this old floor, with beautiful wooden windows open above it

that you could see from the street. There was a window seat there with a wonderful view.

And it was all well tarted out, and the furniture was replica Louis XV style, and the glass as well – all crystal – it was really tastefully done out.

Stafford confirmed his closeness to George and Paul, recalling they'd once all gone on holiday together. This to check out a villa Stafford had won in a poker game at the Astor club.

I said to Paul I think I'll go and have a drive [to Aleppo]. And I'd just bought a Ford Zephyr convertible (laughs), so Paul said, "Oh, me and George, we'll go." He said, "can I bring a friend of mine, Paul Andre? He's a hairdresser." So I said, 'alright.' So we all went in the car. And when we got there they went out and done their own thing [picking up sailors], and I looked for women.

Stafford expanded on the Londoner clientele.

Sarah Churchill. She was an old love pot. Liked to screw about. Terrible drunk. I took her home a few times. Only because she was drunk. She wasn't my type, you know. But her legs would spread after a few drinks for anyone, sort of thing. Shame to say that, but that was the way...[45]

---

[45] The journalist Frederic Mullally confided of Sarah Churchill: "I never saw her less than drunk." And the writer Gwyn Robyns told me how once, when Churchill came visiting, Gwyn's starchy husband was so offended by the actress's drunkenness that he arranged for a cab to take the her home. An hour later he went out, passing a nearby pub. The prime minister's daughter was in the public bar, astride a stranger's knee, surrounded by enthusiastic punters. So brazen were her antics – nights in police cells and trips to magistrate courts – that Sir Winston arranged covert surveillance of his errant child. In her autobiography, *Keep on Dancing* (1981), she described being watched from unmarked police cars, as she went on regular "midnight prowls mostly up and down along the river." When after one adventure she ended up in Holloway prison, "I was asked whether I would like a private cell in tones which might have been employed if they were showing me to

[Lady] Nora Docker. She was a pain in the arse. She was alright, but when she came in she wanted full attention... Nora... yes. We called her the old bicycle. She loved to be round gangsters, you know, the East End gangsters and all that. She used to like to drink in the clubs with them. She was an outrageous woman and she loved sex. As long as it was a known face sort of thing. Daniel Farson [writer and broadcaster] – he was a good friend of hers, and he used to find her rough trade [laughs].

Stafford added that Jack Profumo, a regular, "brought his wife," the actress, Valerie Hobson, "and she was fascinated because Johnnie Ray was there at the time." She propositioned the pop star. But no luck, as Ray was gay.

And: "I tell you someone else who used to pop in – the Duchess of Argyll. That was a right pervert."[46]

Stafford recalled other prominent gay Londoner regulars: Lord Boothby, the Tory politician and at one time the lover of the gangster Ronnie Kray; Peter Wildeblood, the novelist and early gay rights campaigner; and – later on – the Beatles manager, Brian Epstein...

a room at the Ritz... It proved to be a perfectly adequate place, with a high hospital bed, and I was given a red flannel nightgown."

46   The Duchess of Argyll featured in the Profumo scandal when two photos of her surfaced: performing fellatio, and watching a man masturbating. In both pictures the man's head was invisible. There was press speculation about the identity of this "headless man." Nowadays it's thought there were two "headless" men – one in each picture. The masturbator being the actor, Douglas Fairbanks Jnr, and the "fellatee" being Duncan Sandys, a Tory cabinet minister, and son-in-law of Winston Churchill. These photos featured in the Duchess's 1963 divorce proceedings. In his summary of the divorce case, the Judge, Lord Wheatley, complained that the Duchess was: "a highly sexed woman who had ceased to be satisfied with normal relations and had started to indulge in disgusting sexual activities."

Several Londoner members and associates had royal connections. For example, the then trendy Pietro Annigoni, known for his paintings of the Queen, the Queen Mother, Prince Philip and Princess Margaret.

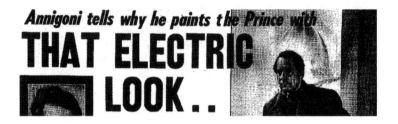

Annigoni tells why he paints the Prince with
THAT ELECTRIC LOOK ..

Stafford recalled Annigoni as,

> a big blustering guy. He used to wear that thing, a badge, a citation from the government of Italy. I often puzzled at that. In this country we don't do such things, we have Lords and Honours, but not – this sort of badge on his lapel. Yes, Annigoni was a boisterous man! Yes. Yes. Noisy. You know the type? He wasn't gay though, not to my knowledge.

Another frequenter was the society photographer known as "Baron." Baron was close to both the osteopath Stephen (Profumo Affair) Ward and Prince Philip, and frequently photographed the Royal Family.[47]

---

47   Baron Stirling Henry Nahum was born in 1906. "Baron" was his first name, not a title. The son of an Italian Jewish shipping tycoon, Baron was raised in Manchester. "No problems of poverty complicated our lives." His twin brother, Jack, became a QC. Originally, Baron specialised in portraits of theatrical and showbiz personalities. Following a chance meeting with Earl Mountbatten in Malta, Baron became a regular and semi-official photographer of the royal family. He was also a key member of the nightclubbing coterie around Prince Philip and his first cousin, the notoriously promiscuous David Michael Mountbatten, 3rd Marquess of Milford Haven.
It was Baron who, in 1946, invented The Thursday Club, a weekly lunch, rather than a club proper, convening in the private upstairs room of Wheeler's Oyster Bar, in Soho.

Of course, most Londoner habitués were not so famous or well-connected.

Representing this lower rank of arty and theatrical Londoner club chancers was a character close to Paul Clay, and a friend and "business partner" of Dennis Stafford, Douglas Sergeant. A failed actor and playwright,[48] Sergeant was also known as Ian Douglas, Quintin Siegfried, and Baron Rio de Branca – the supposed son-in-law of the

---

[Anthony Summers and Stephen Dorril in Honeytrap, 1987, comment it] was a strictly male affair. Lunch, a euphemism for a booze-up that often lasted into the evening hours, was the occasion for the telling of long, funny, and often bawdy, stories… Each month, the members elected one member 'Cunt of the Month', honouring the man who had made the biggest fool of himself in recent weeks.

Artists, photographers, and socialites met there with top ranking actors, politicians, lawyers, and newspaper editors. Frederic Mullally, an occasional guest, reckoned these were the "most influential people" in Britain at that time. Stephen Ward attended. Prince Philip was a founding member. While lunch-time gatherings barred women, evening run-on parties afterwards featured plenty. These parties were held in Stephen Ward's flat in Cavendish Square, or in Baron's Piccadilly flat. Visitors here might be waited on by "girls dressed only in leather Masonic aprons," "flicked up and down like a sporran." Inevitably – given the distinguished British clientele – these parties ventured into "Satanic" rituals with SM trimmings and stock gadgets: whips, chains, gags, etc. In a memoir, Stephen Ward recalled sedate drawing rooms in which huge effigies of devilish phalluses were worshipped. Sarah Churchill's photographer husband, Antony Beauchamp, who acted as record keeper for the Thursday Club, is said to have taken compromising snaps of some of these gatherings. There are claims that some of these featured Prince Philip in flagrante.

48   From a well-to-do family the public school educated Sergeant claimed to have joined the French foreign legion as a teenager, then trained as an actor and worked as a stage manager. He also boasted he was a prolific song writer. It's true he wrote two musicals which were staged, *Lisette* (1950) and

President of Brazil. This chameleon identity came in handy dodging numerous creditors and fraud victims.

Sergeant featured in various court cases for libel and bankruptcy. Particularly in connection with his attempt to launch a men's monthly, *Adam*. This left a wreckage of distressed creditors and unpaid employees. Some of these employees "decided to sell up the office furniture and share the proceeds, having been left practically destitute."[49] Sergeant promptly went missing and was found wandering in the Great West Road, pleading loss of memory.

Sergeant's nickname in the Londoner was "Johnnie Ray's mother" on account of his hearing aid.[50] Dennis Stafford sheltered with Sergeant in Trinidad whilst on the run from the police. Mysteriously, in Stafford's autobiography, he calls Sergeant "the heir to the Sandeman Port business [in Trinidad]." Declining to elaborate on this to me, Stafford described Sergeant as a

> Very colourful character. He came from a very wealthy family. But he was weird. He was a bit of a masochist; he liked to be hurt, you know? And apparently he used to tie chains round

---

Lucky Boy (1953). Both efforts bombed. Of *Lucky Boy*, *The Stage* wrote it used "practically every cliché of situation, character and dialogue," and that its "humour [was] of the kind that makes people mistake the name Bagshot for Bagwash and the rearrangement of a bridge date for talking about a date pudding." On its opening night a scene had to be cut as the choreographer suddenly quit the show and five advertised actors failed to arrive. On the second night, with the missing scene reinstated, the audience "was content with an outburst of booing in the second act – but made up for it by laughing in the wrong places."

49   "What has Happened to Adam," *World's Press News*, April 13, 1933
50   Ray was an unlikely pop star and sex symbol. Among other things he was near deaf in one ear and wore a hearing aid in concerts. This didn't stop his performances creating unprecedented hysteria – more so than Sinatra and anticipating Elvis and the Beatles. When Ray first came to the UK in 1954 the *Sunday Pictorial* installed a psychiatrist in the London Palladium to analyse his "hypnotic" effect. The doctor reported: "Ray is a child playing with the key which can unlock, control or divert the HIDDEN impulses in human beings."

his balls, his testicles, and heavy clips on his nipples for sex and they'd pull up and he had nipples about that long. Strange it was. A bit weird. His whole sex life was. He was alright, I mean I socialised with him a few times.

Quintin Siegfried

Mr. QUINTIN SIEGFRIED desires to thank Messrs. METRO-GOLDWYN-MAYER, FOX FILM CO., BRITISH INTER-NATIONAL PICTURES, UNITED ARTISTS CORPORATION, and PARAMOUNT for their kind co-operation, which has enabled him to produce this booklet.

CONTENTS

Sergeant claimed to be a professional numerologist. Above is a pamphlet he produced on the topic, illustrated with movie and stage stars. At the same time, he was the director of Quintin Siegfried Limited, Cornish Industries Limited, *as well as* Joan the Wad Limited. *These companies marketed lucky charms, particularly* Joan the Wad: *a metal mascot dipped in the well of a Cornish saint, which assisted wins in the Irish sweepstake – as 1,400 lucky prize winners could attest. "Joan the Wad is the lucky Cornish Pisky who sees all, hears all, does all. That is why there is more health, less unemployment, and more contented people in Cornwall that elsewhere, but all these benefits can be obtained if you live elsewhere by adopting Joan the Wad."*

Ray's fans were unusually libidinous. In an interview with a Palladium stage hand I was told, "It was the first time we found knickers under the seats." And Jack Lewis, a veteran showbiz commentator, reminisced,

> It was pandemonium in the concerts. They used to stand on the seats, they did a tremendous amount of damage. Broken seats and broken railings. The place was littered with things.
>
> Q: Did girls wet themselves?
>
> VL: Oh, Good Lord, yes. That was the whole bit, wasn't it? And the whole idea was they got sexual orgasms out of sitting there watching somebody. And we used to talk about it in those days as saying it was a kind of group therapy.
>
> We would wonder: what was it? Hypnosis? Maybe a group hypnosis. I mean, that he could go on stage and make all these girls do what they were doing. And without anybody touching them. Which to me is an amazing thing. But I suppose if your mind's that much excited, your body can get that excited. Oh good Lord, yes. [Fred Vermorel, Unpublished interview, 1987]

Stafford's connection with the Londoner, and George and Paul, had been intermittent, due to several long prison sentences.

He'd last seen the pair, "in the seventies."

> When I came home [from jail] I saw them again, they were living in Maida Vale. And this girl I was taking to South Africa – I ended up marrying her – she was a beauty queen – Lorraine Brown – I took her round to meet them.

In that phone conversation, Stafford also told me about a gay man, Leslie (Les) Wallis.

I already knew a bit about Les. That he'd lived with George and Liz Baron at Brydges Place and then above the Londoner. That he was notoriously promiscuous even in Londoner circles. That he dabbled in acting and probably earned a living as a male prostitute.

Dennis Stafford:

Les Wallis

> I can tell you a story, but I don't know how far you're going to get with it.
>
> There was a guy called Les Wallis, Aunty Les. Rather fattish old quean. Always came into the Londoner about seven o'clock, regularly, and had his pink gin. Then he'd cruise around afterwards.

It was regular, you could time yourself with him. Anyway, at one time he – this was when Armstrong-Jones was marrying Princess Margaret – he started mouthing off about Armstrong-Jones being his toyboy.

Saying he'd had Armstrong-Jones in bed with him and so on. And he's mouthing off a lot. Telling everybody. He was talking about a time when Armstrong-Jones was with Jackie Chan.[51]

One day when I was going out [of The Londoner] I saw two guys coming up the stairs – they looked like police – you know, well dressed police. They said to me,

"Can you tell us the entrance to the club?"

I said, "Yes, it's up there."

Anyway, they were there to see Les.

They talked to him and after that Les is mouthing off, "They came and threatened me! It was Special Branch, and they threatened me..."

But Les took no notice. He kept on mouthing off about him and Armstrong-Jones.

So they came and warned him again.

Now remember, this man Les was there every night at seven o'clock.

So they warned him again, and after that nobody ever saw him.

He disappeared completely. He completely disappeared off the scene.

And to this day... He was warned twice and there he was still mouthing off – a few pink gins and away he used to go...

And he vanished.

---

51   1955-59. My letter to Jackie Chan about the Londoner went unanswered.

THE PYRAMID CLUB

In 1954, several news stories billed Jean Townsend's killing as "The Pyramid Club Murder."

This wasn't a reference to a nightclub. Pyramid clubs were a fifties' craze: impromptu social events devoted to getting rich quick, and having fun.

They started in the US around 1949. In March that year, *Life Magazine* announced, "PYRAMID CLUB SWEEPS NATION." It said, "several million Americans" were trying to get "a few fast bucks via the wackiest route since the chain-letter mania of 1935." It called this "mass hysteria" which began:

> like so many other strange and wonderful notions – somewhere under the balmy skies of California. By last week it had spread right across the nation and into staid New England, moving as fast as a tornado and causing almost as much upset along the way.

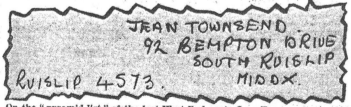

On the "pyramid list" of the last West End party Jean Townsend attended is her name, address and telephone number.

It worked like this. You went to a pyramid party and gave the host a dollar. The host then gave you a number. This started you off at the bottom of the pyramid. To move up you had to go to another party. But this time bring two friends. All three then gave the new host a dollar each. You'd then be eligible to move up a notch in the pyramid. Then your two new members invited another two new members. And so on. As the pyramid swelled you moved up and up. By around the 12th day you should have got to number one. At this point you gave the party yourself. As the host you collected a dollar from everyone who came. The bigger the pyramid the more money you got. Some people were reputed to win $2,000 or more.

The US authorities didn't like pyramid parties and tried to stop them. It was said they broke lottery laws. But pyramiders were defiant. There were mass protest meetings where people wore pyramid shaped hats and demanded their rights. They lobbied and mobbed judges. A prosecutor said, "I don't think these people need the protection of the police or courts. More likely they need a psychiatrist."

In the early fifties the craze crossed to Britain. It had a glamorous and risky feel. Pyramid parties were cool and "American," they featured getting drunk and joshing strangers, and jiving to jazz music. The rumour was the trend had been imported by "Two lonely American visitors, not known by name but friends of stage stars." It then spread through London nightclubs and "the dressing rooms of West End theatres."

The *Daily Express* described,

> Bowler-hatted barristers, clerks, army officers, students, typists... all at a pyramid party in a flat off Cheyne Walk, Chelsea... Most of the guests had come from other parties in Kensington, and were on their way to still more parties in Westminster. At 9.45 the radiogram was playing "La Ronde." By 10 o'clock it was going on to Dixieland music. It ended at 11. The guests were drifting out. But the telephone was still ringing: "I hear you're giving a party..."

The socialite cartoonist Mark Boxer was an enthusiast. He said the parties were:

> rather fun. All sorts of most eccentric people arrive at the house. My place suddenly became full of coloured men, chorus girls and business men whom I had never met.

Tony Overman, a restaurant manager, married to the actress, Sylvia Overman, a "negress star," vouched that:

> The whole thing is innocent, if somewhat hectic. I believe the church and the police have been condemning the craze, but there is nothing illegal or immoral about it.

Another pyramider, Leon Maybanke, a scriptwriter, enthused, "The parties [are] terribly crowded, awfully exhausting, but madly gay." They were, "just a way of meeting people." He claimed that with the money he'd won he was opening "a coffee snack bar."

But the *New Statesman* denounced pyramid parties as "the exploitation of the credulous by the fraudulent." It said they were "undesirable, since the 'pyramid' stooges are brought into excited and promiscuous contact at parties attended by the criminal fringe."

When Jean Townsend was found dead, police found a list of names for a pyramid club in her handbag. Her name was at the top.

She'd gone to the Londoner Club on the night of her murder to celebrate her win with close friends. Her actual pyramid party was due to take place the following evening, at the Gerrard Street home of the Londoner manager, George Baron.

Jean's link with the cosmopolitan pyramid party scene became another element in casting her as a "bad girl" with sordid nightlife connections.

"OVER PYRAMID PARTY LIES SHADOW OF JEAN."

The *News of the World* carried a front page picture of Jean Townsend, "wearing the scarf with which she was strangled." Inside was a feature about pyramid parties and the "spivs" who organised them for "a rake off."

As to the moral aspects of the craze, the dangers are clear. Large numbers of young people are induced to go to houses and meet people about whom they know nothing. This promiscuous association has evils that are obvious.

The *Daily Express* captioned images of one pyramid party with ominous ellipses:

...a girl dances in her stockinged feet... a man tries a trick with a handkerchief on his chin... a bottle or a glass rests in nearly every hand... On the walls of the flat... [is] a pyramid chart. It tells you where the parties of the future lie... the parties at which you never know the host... or your fellow guests.

After Jean Townsend's murder, pyramid parties in the UK abruptly stopped.

AMERICAN ACCENTS

"American accents" featured a lot in the Townsend case.

There were the accents of the two men Brenda Thomson heard arguing just after that scream around midnight...

The driver of the flashy American car who pestered Jackie Cliff in Victoria Road...

And the manageress of a local dry cleaners, Dorothy Church, reported that a customer "with an American accent" had handed in "a blood-stained red checked shirt and a pair of grey gabardine trousers." This man had "fresh scratches over his left eye and on his cheek." She asked him if he'd been "in a scrap." He said, "Sort of." When she reported this, the items had already been sent away for cleaning. The police raced "to take possession of the shirt and trousers." They interrogated the American. He had an alibi.

Previous page. Front gate of the South Ruislip USAF base. *Above. The bowling alley.*

During the war, hundreds of American servicemen were stationed around Ruislip. Many were connected with Northolt Aerodrome – at that time a mostly military facility.

Then, in 1949, the USAF built a huge complex in South Ruislip at the lower end of Victoria Road, opposite what in 1952 became Queensmead secondary school.

This Base became the European intelligence HQ of the American military in the Cold War. Its importance was recognised by the fact that CND marches from Aldermaston to Trafalgar Square sometimes climaxed in the suburban streets around the Base, where protesters staged "sit downs."

Right. H Bomb test explosion, April, 1954. Middle and bottom left. American seduction. "There was always a sprinkling of American servicemen who staked out their own corner of the hall where they jived fervently to The Jersey Bounce and Pennsylvania Six Five Thousand. Their look of dedication never altered even when sweat plated their faces, and they chewed gum incessantly as though it contained a secret ingredient, a drug perhaps, which was the source of their boundless energy.

'The most dedicated dancers brought their own partners; tense, rubbery girls who trucked and spun through intricate routines without missing a beat or conceding that any other couple shared the floor. They were exclusive. No one else dared ask them to dance. Between sets they sat together, comparing bracelets and puffing sulkily filter-tipped cigarettes. They always appeared to be in a bad temper. When they were not dancing they were bored. Their make-up was thick and even, with rims blue around the eyes and mulberry mouths which ignored the outline of the lips beneath. Collectively they were known as –'Yank bait'…

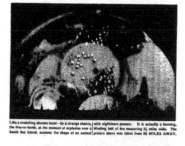

IT THREATENS THE WORLD

Like a crouching obscene beast—by a strange chance, with nightmare powers. It is actually a burning, the Horror-bomb, at the moment of explosion over a blinding ball of fire measuring 3½ miles wide. The South Sea Island, assumes the shape of an animal picture above was taken from 50 MILES AWAY.

20¢ AUGUST 1956
SCIENCE and MECHANICS
The Magazine That Shows You How

Raymond Loewy's Car of the Future

Electronic Garage Door Opener

"The Lieutenant held Sadie at arm's length, guiding her with the tips of his fingers while she jerked and twisted in the centre of an admiring crowd. Her skirt rode up over her thighs. Her breasts jogged busily beneath her sweater. Her face had set like custard in a look of disdain as if she preferred not to know what her body was doing. The tune throbbed through its two false endings then soared into its blithe finale. The Lieutenant led Sadie back." — *Philip Oakes*, At the Jazz Band Ball. A memory of the 1950s, *1983*.

For locals, the USAF Base was a forbidden zone, guarded by US military police, in white helmets, belts and sashes, some armed with machine guns, who checked people in and out the gates.

Inside, was miniature America. A plush cinema, a theatre, a night club. The décor and furnishings were extolled as "palatial" – "just like going to America!" Stars like Bob Hope and Sammy Davis Jnr. performed there. There was also a gymnasium and a ten-pin bowling alley. A tunnel under the nearby railway led to a baseball ground. The Base had its own bank and its own currency (US military dollars) and a high-tech hospital.

Some US servicemen brought their families over and settled around Ruislip. Some imported American cars. Fantailed, abundantly chromiumed and sensuously upholstered monstrosities that looked scandalous, parked in our suburban streets.

Also scandalous was how well paid, well dressed, and handsome, these Americans were. They were generally taller than British men. They seemed to glow.

Reg Hargrave recalled,

> The Yanks looked a different race. They had smart uniforms – whereas the British Tommies, you know, their uniforms didn't really match up – the Americans had decent caps instead of those funny little hats our soldiers used to perch on their heads. Even the American squaddies looked like officers.

The South Ruislip-raised TV producer, Gay Search,[52] recalled that,

> The Americans seemed very big and very milk fed. Very kind of healthy. And sort of a bit exotic.

Most striking – almost shocking, to locals – was the lushly provisioned PX supermarket. Here were ranks of streamlined fridges taller than a

---

52 I initially contacted Gay Search to see if there might be a connection between the secrecy surrounding the Townsend case and the Kroger spy case (see below, The Krogers of Cranley Drive).

man, space age gadgets like Osterizer blenders, and pyramids of tinned ham and tropical fruits.

Gay Search:

> To walk into that place which was full of food and exotic stuff. Sweetcorn! Hard to think now but it was something you never saw. And Hershey bars.

I had a child's perspective on the Base, which was ten minutes' walk from my house. I used to sneak in disguised as a junior Yank, courtesy of my émigré grandmother.

Isabelle had emigrated to New York just after the war. She sent gifts like genuine jeans and American-style chequered shirts and jackets from Saks Fifth Avenue. To perfect my outfit I adopted a crew cut and an Audie Murphy drawl.

Once inside, I'd head to the PX for chewing gum – and, especially, American comics.

American comics were about winners. They had grown-up story-lines and slick illustrations. They were heart-warming and uplifting. They were printed on quality paper with shiny full-colour covers. They smelled like new toys.

Whereas British comics, like the *Beano* and *Dandy*, were dowdy and shrill and crudely drawn, their paper fragile and meagre, and they smelled of cheap ink and newsprint. The stories featured rowdy losers like Beryl the Peril, or ragged yobs like the Bash Street Kids.[53]

---

53   Differences highlighted in the British and American versions of Dennis the Menace. British-style Dennis was a knock-kneed scowling bully who battled sadistic teachers and a furious father. His dog was a scruffy mongrel called Gnasher. Whereas American-style Dennis lived in a large

———————

The American way of life was seductive.

But fraught with peril.

The Sunday before Jean Townsend's murder, the Rev. George Bennett had read a sermon in the 13th Century church in Ruislip High Street, titled, "Cosh boys, Teddy boys and the Hydrogen bomb." The connections would have been obvious to the congregation: Americanization was stalking our suburb in the guise of errant youth.

That same September, 1954, the detective magazine, *True*, ran an editorial, "Crime and the Dollar:"

> Young men and women demand the luxuries of life before they have prepared themselves to give anything to the community in return. In short, they want it all for nothing.

True trumpeted a crime wave spreading from the US to the UK. "Can it Happen Here?" "America's 'Teddy Boy' Menace."

True told of a spiral of disorder. At first, the "antics" of British Teddy Boys caused amusement. Then came violence on "foreign" students out

———————

house in a leafy suburb, and his parents cherished him. He had golden curls, was chubby and freckled, and charming and mischievous. And his dog was a benign shaggy sheepdog called Ruff.

Oddly, however, American comics were considered dangerous – more insidious, than the home-grown variety. In the mid-50s a moral panic about American comics erupted. In 1954, Lady Elizabeth Pakenham warned in the *Daily Express*,

> These magazines come from America… Do not let us [extend] the power and the profits of this germ-laden matter. Allow it no fresh breeding grounds over here!

The same year, George Pumphrey's pamphlet, *Comics and Your Children*, ignited a discussion that reached Winston Churchill's cabinet table. Offensive American comics (preserved in a manila envelope in The National Archive) were passed round in Cabinet. Examples included *Captain Marvel, Jesse James, Frankenstein, Black Magic Comics*, and *Famous Yank Comic*.

with English women. This was followed by "scuffles in milk bars..." [and then]

> riots began to occur in dance halls... Clothing stores were broken into and robbed. Old women were beaten up and their handbags snatched. Pedestrians were waylaid at night, the police and all those in authority were insulted and openly defied. And in each and every case, the thugs, the cocky young lawbreakers were dressed in the stove pipe trousers and long jackets of the Teddy Boys.[54]

An accompanying Cabinet memo:

> Many of [the comics] have a strong element of sadistic cruelty and an undue emphasis on violence. A number have an erotic streak and abound in representations of scantily dressed women. Some of the scenes portrayed are horrifying – macabre supernatural scenes with zombies and ghouls, the frenzy of drug addicts, the grimmer aspects of modern war, and scenes of torture and murder... The emphasis on violence and cruelty is heavy and unwholesome. The idea that violence has to be countered with violence is commonplace. The prevailing sense of values is shoddy and distorted.

This resulted in the Children and Young Persons (Harmful Publications) Bill, 1955.

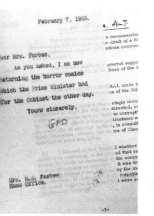

Left. Cabinet Office Letter Right. From one of the comics examined in Cabinet. 7 Items extracted from PREM 11/858.

---

54   *True Detective*, Vol 4, No 10, April 1955.

A panic enacted all over Britain. Even in my own Downbarns Road, South Ruislip. Where next door to the Vermorels, lived the Spencers.

The father, Norman Spencer, was a cheerful Yorkshire builder. He was making a mint out of the post-war housing boom. Norman would buy a new motor every year. Always a Jag, a Rolls, or a Bentley. Parked outrageously outside his red-brick council house.

The Spencers were first in with every mod con: washing machine, fridge-freezer, hair dryer, teabags...

The Spencers also had the first TV in our street. In 1953, neighbours squeezed into their front room to watch the Coronation. Mrs Spencer served tea and tarts. People admired her mahogany radiogram.

The two Spencer sons had pocket money and attitude to burn. I first heard rock and roll when it thundered through our party wall. When they got bored with their 78rpm discs the Spencer boys spun them like Frisbees to smash against walls. My mum declared they were just like Americans who didn't know "the value of money."

They were the first Teds in our street. The older boy changed his name from Tony (Italian: poncey), to "Sid" (British: hard). Sid then bought a motorbike and became a ton-up boy. Many of his biker mates were killed or maimed up and down the A1 and North Circular. Sid survived a crash with his neck set in plaster.

Norman Spencer, meanwhile, was besotted with his peroxided wife, Elsie. He bought her jewellery and furs. Proper mink and stuff. They drove to West End shows in his luxury cars. But Elsie dumped Norman and ran away to America with an American quarter-master sergeant from the Base. No one was surprised. A sign of the times. In any case, Elsie was "that kind of woman."

Tony (Sid) Spencer (left) in pre–Teddy boy days with me on holiday in Clacton. When Sid upgraded his flick knife to a stiletto rather than side opening version, he donated me the old one.

Pyramid parties, easy money and silly money, hedonism and lawlessness, violence, Americans, late night trains, West End clubs…

And Jean Townsend sprawled in the weeds of a wasteland. Immaculate and fashionable. Stripped: "Her knickers, suspender belt, panties, stockings and right shoe were by her feet."

Coroner: "Completely off her body?"

"Yes."

THE WHITTAKER
SUITCASE

Jean's boss, Michael Whittaker, seemed to have a perfect alibi for the night of Jean's murder.

But there was that gap in his overseeing the September 1954 Glasgow fashion show which coincided with Jean's murder. A gap which could place him at Northolt Aerodrome – a five-minute drive from where the murder took place in Victoria Road, on the night Jean was killed.

Moreover, Whittaker would have been privy to Jean's habits and vulnerabilities. He possibly knew she'd topped the pyramid club and was celebrating that night at the Londoner, and he would have known she often caught the last train home.

Time to take a closer look at "Mr Fashion."

———————

Fathoming Whittaker was made difficult by trails of misinformation Whittaker himself left, teasing decoys for nosey parkers such as myself.

And most of his associates were dead or untraceable. But eventually, I traced John Michael Guest, an ex-director of Whittaker's model agency. He'd only known Whittaker from the sixties. He was unaware of Jean Townsend or the Londoner.

But he put me on to Ann Graham.

Ann Graham's relationship to Whittaker had been complicated. She was the girlfriend of Whittaker's last boyfriend. She was keen to talk about the man she'd known as Mike. They'd been close for over 20 years.

A retired actress and dancer, Ann lived in a fisherman's cottage, in a picturesque enclave of Margate.

Ann Graham

Height 5'3½/1.61
Bust 32/81 Waist 22/56 Hips 34/86
Dress 8-10/36-38 Shoes 3-3½/36-36½
Gloves 6½/6½ Hair: Fair Eyes: Blue

JB agency

Television/Films
Photographic

7 Stonehills Mansions
8 Streatham High Road
London SW16 1DD

01-877 5161/2
01-769 0123

SHOW SERVICE

CAREMOLI

Coursa Porta Nuova 46
654456 - 695002
MILANO

Ann had met Whittaker's boyfriend, Michael Trilling [Surname changed], in the 1970s. They were both actors and both "resting." As traditional for aspiring actors, they were temping at Selfridges.

Ann Graham:

> One day in a coffee break I had my foot out and he accidently tripped over it. He fell flat on the floor. So I had to buy him a coffee. It turned out the most expensive cup of coffee in my life. We were together for years, and he was a complete case.

When Ann met him, Michael Trilling was living with Michael Whittaker at his house in tree-lined Magnolia Road adjacent to the Thames.

The three soon made a ménage a trois.

> Often, we'd come home after a night out at a show and have fish and chips and champagne sitting in the front room.

Whittaker delighted in introducing Ann to high culture and high society. She was entranced by his savoir faire. He took her to Ascot – to the Royal Enclosure, where he went every year.

When asked how he managed this entree, he claimed a "special connection" with Princess Margaret.

Ann relished Whittaker's catty witticisms behind people's backs, his relentlessly camp frivolity, his cultural sophistication, his 40 plus cigarettes a day, his dandyism.

> He always wore three-piece suits – always with a waistcoat, and matching shirts and ties, and shoes polished like mirrors, and he'd have a hat... you couldn't NOT see Michael, he was relic of a time gone past.

Whittaker cherished his dog, Hell. He would take Hell everywhere: to meetings, fittings, fashion shows. Hell was a badly-behaved animal, prone to running loose and snapping at models' heels. One of Ann's tasks was to feed and walk the beast.

Whittaker was a hoarder. He collected thousands of vinyl records to use in fashion shows. He bought engravings and paintings and exotic costumes, and had cupboards stuffed with bric-a-brac.

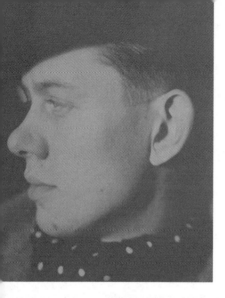

*Anticlockwise
from top left.
Whittaker
as a suave
young blade.
Compeering a
show in the mid-
1960s. With Hell.*

His Chiswick home was especially crammed with anything connected to the Horse Guards: tea caddies, mugs, memorabilia, prints, postcards, photos, cuttings, cartoons...

He'd even turned a plumed Guards' helmet into a table lamp, claiming it was a relic from his own time in the regiment. On a wall hung "his old sword."

Ann was close to Whittaker for twenty years. She saw him through a crisis when the taxman came for a huge unpaid bill. Whittaker was forced to sell his Dartmoor cottage and many art works.

"But he still had to have the best wines. He found them in Morrisons."

Whittaker worked into his seventies. Looking at videos of later shows, you can see why he went out of favour. They're more likely to feature Sinatra than the Stones.

Even so, he shocked his godson, Alistair Cameron.

Alistair nowadays runs a fashion emporium, Ambers of Amersham. He started this with his mother, Carla Cameron, who'd managed Whittaker's model agency in its heyday. Ambers holds annual fashion shows. Once, Whittaker, then in his seventies, was asked to give an impromptu commentary. It was so blue there were red faces all round. It was too much for Amersham. He was never asked back.

In 1995, Whittaker went into hospital for a minor operation. He caught a hospital bug.

Ann: "He started to look quite yellow. He began fading. Then one day he just went."

Ann and her – and Whittaker's – boyfriend, were left to clear up the estate. There were no relatives. Objects of obvious value were sold. Ann retrieved Whittaker's family heirlooms, including a grandfather clock, and some minor art works. Whittaker's historical costume collection and his racks of bespoke suits were donated to a nearby art school. The LP stash went to Oxfam.

The boyfriend wanted a clean sweep. He went through the house, throwing anything that remained into a skip. But, says Ann, "I thought, 'this was an important man.' So I went round the house and grabbed everything that seemed to be about him."

Ann scooped up cuttings, playbills, photos, letters, telegrams, legal documents...

All this she stuffed in a suitcase and several art folders labelled "WHITTAKER'S LIFE." It was stored it in her attic until I arrived, when she gave it all to me.

Michael Whittaker had been born 13th April 1918. His father was Major William Edward De Baguleigh Whittaker, MBE.

The Major was a daredevil adventurer, soldier, professional racing motorist, and a journalist and author. He wrote an eccentric genealogy, *The Glynnes of Hawarden*, for the Flintshire Historical Society, and translated erotic poems by the Persian poet, Omar Khayyam.

Though partially disabled, he joined up for WW1 and got a chest-full of medals fighting in France, Flanders, and Gallipoli. Invalided out he then joined the Home Forces and got an MBE for the air defence of London.

Anticlockwise from top left. Whittaker's father. Whittaker in 1925. The inscription on the back reads, "John Michael de Bagulegh Whittaker, age 7 years." Whittaker as a teenager, casting a debonair shadow.

175

After the war, the Major became a correspondent for the *Daily Express* and *The Times*. He died in 1933, at 48.

His *Times* obituary was gushy. No doubt written by a chum. It said he was a scholar and a soldier, "an accomplished horseman with beautiful hands, a good shot... and a devotee of aviation in its early days." Also that, "He was most in his element in a powerful motor car, which he drove like the artist he was, never taking the least risk... yet putting up most remarkable performances for speed and skill."

The obituary ended saying that Major Whittaker had been "a fine talker" and "a delightful companion."

———

Not so delightful at home. In 1912 he had married Elsa Pauline Burn. He was 27, she 24. They had their son, Michael Whittaker, in 1918. They divorced in 1920.

The divorce papers list Elsa's complaints. The Major had "caught hold of [her] and pinched her arms and wrists bruising them..." He struck her "on the head with his fist and threw her on to a couch." He "took up a lighted stove to throw at her." He threatened to kill her and also to shoot her. He "committed adultery with some woman" at the marital home, and elsewhere.[55]

Elsa got custody of Michael. Plus maintenance. But the maintenance never came. Major Whittaker was broke.

That didn't stop him marrying again in 1924. This was to Dorothy Francis Blood. With her, he had two more children. Letters in War Office files, sent by Dorothy, show he left this family too, "entirely without means."

---

55   TNA: J 77/1687/2504

But Elsa was luckier than the Major's second wife. Elsa came from money and was well connected. She used her contacts to top up her income with work as a fashion model.

An unkind person quipped that, "like all English women, she was pear shaped." Notwithstanding, Elsa featured in upper crust fashion catalogues and fashion ads in theatre programmes.

Anticlockwise from top left. Modelling in The Lady, *June, 1933.* Barkers Outsize Fashions, *nd. Whittaker's mother (centre) in an ad for Seagers BRONX gin, 1936.*

Elsa was also lucky in her younger sister, Mabel.

Mabel Cecilia Burn was born in 1889. She was the family beauty, and became the actress and opera singer, Mabel Twemlow.[56]

Mabel established herself as a singer at 20 (1909) when she appeared as Schwertleite, a Norse goddess in Wagner's *Die Walküre* at Covent Garden Opera House. She also sang at Drury Lane Theatre in Wagner's *The Master Singers*.

But her forte was comedy. In 1917 she played in a sketch at the Hippodrome, *Beautiful Mrs Blain*. The year after, she was the lead in a rom-com opera, *Valentine*, by Napoleon Lambelet – libretto by Arthur Davenport. This had a risqué lesbian subtext. Mabel was Diana, Queen of the Amazons. "There's a country that we hail from ... Flada-rada-rad tzing bom! ... That we've banished ev'ry male from."

Mabel was also a professional dancer. She performed with the troupe, Cochran's Young Ladies, in *Mayfair & Montmartre* (1921), and *Babes in the Wood* (1921-22).

The troupe's founder, Charles Cochran, known as the English Diaghilev, had a crush on Mabel. One telegram he sent her went: "I saw you a few days ago and thought you looked superb. Something must be done about it. Your friend and admirer, Charles B Cochran."[57]

---

56 Twemlow was Mabel's mother's maiden name. Mabel and Elsa's parents divorced in 1885, following their mother's repeated adultery with a Thomas Fielden. The Twemlows were minor landed gentry from Hatherton in Cheshire. Whittaker kept a file about his descent from the Twemlow line. It included a print of Hatherton Lodge and the Twemlow family crest.
57 The telegram address was: "Cockranus, Piccy, London." Cochran had a appalling death. One day, he jumped into an hotel bath to relieve his arthritis. The water was scalding hot and killed him.

Left. Mabel pursues "Adonis," supposedly unaware that "he" is a girl. Right. From a review in the Illustrated Sporting and Dramatic News, *Feb 16, 1918. Mabel Twemlow, as Diana, Queen of the Amazons, in* Valentine, *1918.*

Mabel also acted in movies. She was Lady Blarney in Oliver Goldsmith's *The Vicar of Wakefield* – a silent movie of 1916. After that she acted in six talkies – up to 1947, when she retired.

Mabel never married or had children. She used her earnings to support her beloved sister, Elsa, and her beloved nephew, Michael Whittaker.

She was a second mother to Whittaker, especially after Elsa's death in 1951. For many years they shared a house in Holland Park.

Whittaker, in turn, treasured Mabel. He amassed her playbills, cuttings, and promo photos.

When she died in 1964, she left him everything – all her money and all "my furs and jewellery," and "The Grandfather Clock with Victory Ship and the Coral Wedgewood Tea and Breakfast Service."

Whittaker also inherited his aunt's old makeup box. It was labelled, "Miss Twemlow."

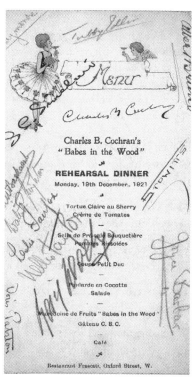

Top. The Whirligig, *by Edgar Wallace and Wal Pink,* Palace Theatre, *1919. The set is the "Temple of Chance." Mabel Twemlow presides (dead centre) over a pyramid of Palace Girls as a Goddess. Edgar Wallace was so pleased with this production that every Saturday he'd entertain the chorus girls at his home "to roast lamb and ice-cream… crowded on assorted chairs around the dining room table, and greeting the popping of champagne corks with ladylike shrieks."[58] Bottom. Mabel's signed menu for Cochran's* Babes in the Wood, *rehearsal dinner.*

---

58   Margaret Lane, *Edgar Wallace. The Biography of a Phenomenon,* 1939

Top. A close-knit threesome. A moustachioed Whittaker with mother (right) and aunt (left), nd. Bottom Mabel poses for her fans in a postcard, nd.

When I came across this box, in Margate, in 2010, it still smelled of Mabel's greasepaint and powder.

Clockwise from top left. Whittaker was the costume designer for Walt Disney's The Story of Robin Hood and His Merrie Men, *1952. This image is Will Scarlet. Costume for Joan Greenwood (for whom Whittaker also designed privately) which featured in a compilation celebrating the British Film industry, staged at the Royal Film Show, 1953. [Billed as "the first Royal Film Show of the Elizabethan reign" the main attraction was the Hollywood musical,* Because You're Mine, *starring Mario Lanza. At the reception, "Hollywood's Yvonne de Carlo was anxious to tell The Queen she was going to make a film with Alec Guinness. The Queen responded, 'How nice.'" Princess Margaret meanwhile confided to Gene Kelly that she'd seen* Singin' in the Rain *six times. Fashion sketch, nd.*

Clockwise from top left.
Two woodcuts by Whittaker,
nd. Right. Landscape
from one of Whittaker's
sketchbooks, nd.

Top. Sketch in gouache for a lighting set-up, nd. Bottom. Chalk sketch for unidentified stage set, nd.

Ann told me lots about Whittaker. She put me on to others who opened up his life. But much remained mysterious. Whittaker would have enjoyed that. Asked how old he was, he'd quip, "I'm older than I seem and younger than I look."

He boasted of French and Scottish ancestry. But he was not very French, and not Scottish at all. The "de Bagulegh" tag [John Michael de Bagulegh Whittaker] which Whittaker's father claimed was allied to the French de la Rochefoucauld aristocratic line, was at best distant, and possibly made up. Whittaker's male line came from the Blackburn area of Lancashire. There was also an Irish – not Scottish – family connection.

Whittaker claimed he'd gone to a British public school. He had the manner. But it wasn't a school I could identify. Unusually, none of the many schoolboy – and school group – photos in Ann's suitcase showed him in school uniform. Perhaps he went to a private school run on liberal lines.

Whittaker later went to Chelsea Art College to study architecture. Then switched to fine art. He collaborated with the designer Sherwood Foster at Chelsea, creating some of the outlandish floats and costumes that each year were made for the Chelsea Arts Ball. He then travelled to South Africa, where he studied drama.

He returned to Europe to study industrial design in Holland and Belgium. He was back in London in 1939, just before war was declared.

———

Maybe it was because of his father's military past that Whittaker bragged that he'd served in the army during the war. Specifically, in the Blues and Royals as a Horse Guard. Ann Graham was convinced on this point. She told me it was a shame I'd turned up so late – so many of his old army comrades were now dead – they could have told me many interesting things…

In fact, Whittaker was exempted from army service – probably because he was so camp.

His war was strictly on celluloid. He became a movie poster boy for British grit.

In 1942 he played three military roles. He was a sub lieutenant in *The Day Will Dawn*, starring Ralph Richardson and Deborah Kerr, directed by Harold French. He was an RAF beam gunner in a B-17 bomber, raiding Nazi Germany, in *Flying Fortress*. He also played a plucky Royal Navy sailor in *In Which We Serve*, directed by Noel Coward, starring John Mills, Celia Johnson, and Richard Attenborough.

In that same busy year Whittaker also played a more substantial part, as Dr Arne [composer of Rule Britannia], in the biopic *The Great Mr. Handel*.

Whittaker in a matinee idol shot for In Which We Serve, *1942. As well as acting the warrior in three WW2 movies, Whittaker had a military role in the 1945 Adelphi Theatre production of* Desert Rats, *by Colin Morris. Opposite page, bottom, Whittaker (standing), plays Lieutenant Lord "Jimmie" Eccleston.*

Above left. Whittaker plays the Hon Ernest Woolley in JM Barrie's The Admirable Crichton, *at Her Majesty's Theatre, London, 1943. Right. He also had a role in* A Party For Christmas *at the Haymarket Theatre, 1941, at the height of the London Blitz.*

Whittaker's military service was fantasy. He never was a guardsman. But Whittaker and Ann Graham's mutual boyfriend, Michael Trilling, did serve in the regiment. He spent 12 years in the Blues and became a warrant officer.

The Whittaker suitcase had many pictures of Trilling in Guards' uniform, broody under thick eyebrows. In other pictures, Trilling was done up in a camp leather chauffeur's outfit, like a cocky young stud out of Joe Orton.

After leaving the Guards, Trilling took up acting under the name "Philippe". He had parts in TV shows like *Hi-De-Hi!*, *The Two Ronnies*, and *Dr Who*. He also worked in commercials. *The Stage* reviewed him in a satirical farce, *Who Killed Who in Timbuktu?*: "[He] displays a fetching grin and considerable pelvic mobility."

Later, as Whittaker's chief assistant and factotum, one of his duties was to organise and assist in Whittaker's orgies. Ann Graham said his role was like, "a Maitre d'O."

Ann Graham:

> My Michael he used to be like – you know these high-class hookers when they have a maid who lets people in and out and takes the money and all of that? Well, Michael [Whittaker] used to have a sort of clique that used to visit him at the house, and they'd all go into his front room and I don't know how it worked actually – but my Michael was like the maid – I don't think any money was involved – but you know, he'd say, "it's your turn now you can go up." Then afterwards, he'd shepherd the last one out.
>
> And Michael had a fetish for leather... And they all wore leather. And they had these wrist thingies on, and leather underpants, and anything else they could think of.

And there was a sort of a rubberised sheet thingie that went over the bed. And they had ampules of some sort to spice things up a bit – or to get you going if you couldn't, or whatever...

It was like that lady who had luncheon vouchers [the brothel keeper, Cynthia Payne] and it was all so – not sexy – it just amused me: you could almost imagine anything going on. I mean, laid back isn't the word. It was practically horizontal.

And of course it didn't matter who belonged to who. Larry [surname suppressed] was an example of that. He told me very firmly he loved his girlfriend very much. But he still fancied me for the night...

She, too, assisted at these events. But, she says, as an occasional spectator:

I went on the wrong afternoon once. And there were all these blokes sitting about, so I said I'll come back later and I ran away...

———————

Who were the participants?

Here, Ann was cagey. But in our second interview, sipping tea from Whittaker's china cups under the grandfather clock Whittaker had inherited from Mabel Twemlow, she told me names.

They fitted with the Londoner crowd: Princess Margaret and Lord Snowdon (as well as Snowdon's half-brother, Peregrine Armstrong-Jones), Sarah Churchill... There was also Norman Hartnell. Even, it seemed, the demure and remote fashion model, Barbara Goalen.

Ann Graham:

It was all very light-hearted, I couldn't even be shocked. It was just the way things were. It was this louche crowd, and everybody flitted about and they all went to clubs and out to dinner and danced and did shows and went to shows and saw other people's shows.

It was like the tide. It just came in and went out. People got dragged in with it this week, and another lot came the next time.

A continual washing in and out of all these people. It was like a washing machine. They were all going round and round. They'd all mix together and then separate and then come back together...

I'd noticed that Whittaker's artwork and sketchbooks sometimes featured burly men in what looked like Nazi uniforms doing what looked like unspeakable things to other burly men. These ambiguous images were adjacent to fashion illustrations and landscape sketches.

Two facing pages from a Whittaker sketch book switch from an evening gown design to an assault by men in quasi military uniform.

Left. Whittaker camping in middle age. Right. From a sketchbook: an unfinished scene.

I also noticed that pages had been razored out of Whittaker's sketchbooks. Presumably after his death. They had been censored – only to turn up on Ebay decades later…[as mentioned above]

From contact sheets showing a Whittaker show, unidentified location and date.

Left. Whittaker the stylist in action, magazine feature, mid-fifties. Right.
Whittaker styles an unidentified woman, c.1953.

Whittaker was a fantasist, a storyteller – and a liar.

And charming and brilliant.

For Jean Townsend, he must have been a fascinating boss. There was no one like him in South Ruislip. I would guess she doted on him.

In Ann Graham's Whittaker suitcase there was only one image of Jean. Whittaker had cropped it out of a larger news photo showing her about to board a plane with a troupe of models to show Norman Hartnell designs in Le Touquet, France.

Several newspapers had featured this image. One of them arrowed Jean with a caption: "The girl apart… Marked down for murder"

The image is revealing. Jean stands aside from the models. She looks self-effacing. Her posture suggests withdrawal. She positions her feet diffidently, in contrast to the best-foot-forward of the other women.

The typed inscription on Whittaker's crop of this picture – which featured only Jean, recorded she was "a colleague as well as a friend."

Whittaker's godson, Alistair Cameron, had listened in on many conversations between Whittaker and his mother.

Whittaker had talked about Jean Townsend frequently and warmly. He enthused over her efficiency and design flair and eye for fashion. But he never mentioned she'd been murdered.

When I told him, Alistair was astonished and bewildered. I could see his mind churning. Previous to that I'd not told him why I was so interested in Uncle Mike.

THEY WERE ALL AT IT REALLY

Stanhope Castle, home to Dennis Stafford.

Dennis Stafford had been more indiscreet over the phone than in his book. Face to face he might tell me even more. I arranged to interview him at his home.

Meanwhile, I'd noticed a news story from 1959 showing that while the Londoner was still going, George and Paul tried to branch out with another club, the Downstairs Room club, at Gerrard Place, Soho. This venture ended suddenly, in circumstances suggesting the couple were more mixed up with gangland than I'd supposed.

SOHO CLUB OWNER TIED AND SLASHED

Club owner Paul Clay, a friend of film stars, was found yesterday lying bound and slashed on the steps leading from his basement club in Soho.

Mr. Clay – grey haired, aged 42 [in fact, 55] – was found by taxi driver Harry Hawkins who drove past the club... at 9 am... "I saw him lying on the steps. His hands were bound behind his back and his coat had been pulled down off his shoulders and halfway down his arms. His face had been very badly slashed and he had obviously been trying to get up the steps for a long time."

Meanwhile, the club's co-owner George Baron, "slender and fair haired, was asleep in his fourth floor flat in Gerrard Street, 200 yards from [where] Mr. Clay was found. Next door was Clay's locked flat."

George Baron had, it seemed, been woken and alerted to the crisis "by 43-year-old Robert Ashkettle who runs the nearby first floor club, the Cross Keys."

Ashkettle reported that Baron "was very shocked."

Lancashire-born Mr. Baron, now a choreographer and film producer, talked to detectives for more than an hour.

There was no money missing from the club. Mr. Clay's gold watch was still on the bar.[59]

Had this been a warning? Facial razor slashings were not unusual in those days. Inflicted to establish territory or punish grasses.

It was also reported that a bottle of acid had been thrown into the club two weeks before. So were George and Paul being targeted by a gang?

But some things didn't add up.

Paul was supposedly razored at around 7am. His face was "crisscrossed with slashes." He needed thirty stitches. Surely, if – as was reported

---

59   *Daily Express*, June 2, 1959. The story also referred in passing to Jean Townsend's murder and its link with The Londoner. It wrongly referred to the Londoner as George's "former club."

– there had been a two – hour interval after the attack before he was discovered, Paul would have bled to death.

It was said the bar had closed at 11pm the previous evening. What, then, was Paul doing there that morning – with his gold watch on the bar, while his partner, George, apparently slumbered 200 yards away in Gerrard Mansions?

It seemed fishy.

I also wondered about Mr Ashkettle.

———

Ashkettle had form. Two years earlier, in February 1956, he'd been convicted for shooting a man at the Checkers Club in Macclesfield Street. The tabloids gloated that Ashkettle had shot "a professional punter" called David Haylock with a "pearl-handled revolver" just as the pianist was playing "Love is a Many Splendored Thing."[60]

———

60   The Met Police case file recorded that the shooting occurred after Ashkettle had propositioned Haylock. This caused an argument. Ashkettle then shot Haylock in the arm, almost casually. Then the two men strolled together to another club and stayed there for around 10 minutes. After that, Ashkettle hailed a taxi and took Haylock to casualty at the nearby Charing Cross Hospital.
The police were called by the hospital. They took Ashkettle to a police station. He said, "I'm saying nothing, and signing nothing. What am I held here for?" He was cautioned. He then admitted, "I shot him," and began to cry, adding, "Go on write it down." [TNA: CRIM 1/2692]

Ashkettle was a career criminal with 17 previous convictions, mostly theft. He'd been imprisoned twice. He'd last been released in May 1954.

He was also part of the gay fraternity around Soho.

The police notes read:

> He states that although he lives with his wife [at 15a Gerrard Street], they have "little in common." He is of an effeminate disposition and associates with men of a similar nature in the West End of London.

Ashkettle was sentenced to three and a half years. He was out by June 1959 – in time to wake up George Baron…

Or maybe to provide the notoriously violent George Baron with an alibi…

But surely, George couldn't have been the assailant? Couldn't have acted so brutally, and potentially murderously, to his long-time lover.

I knew about his violence under drink.

But a potential killer?

When I first mentioned Jean Townsend's murder to Liz Baron, she asked whether I thought George might have done it.

She thought him capable.

But Baron was performing in *Guys and Dolls* that evening – and South Ruislip was a long way from the London Palladium.

However, the story suggested that Paul and George's links to the underworld went deep and dodgy. Could Jean Townsend's connection with George and Paul have embroiled her in some dirty business?

Some business linked to the Londoner?

When I met him in 2011, Dennis Stafford had changed his name to Dennis Scott. He lived quietly in the picturesque town of Weardale.

But he was still managing, one way or another, to be on the wrong side of the law. He claimed this was because of a vendetta by local cops. This was plausible. Here, on their patch, was a convicted murderer and career criminal. But he wasn't in sackcloth and ashes. Rather, his home was a luxurious four-bedroom apartment in the 18th century Stanhope Castle, dominating the centre of Weardale. This apartment had a private gym and a twelve-seater sauna. The view from the enormous double-arched windows in Stafford's lounge was over his own scenic grounds down to the River Wear.

Stafford reckoned his place was worth around £2 million. He'd almost secured planning permission to build chalets nearby, which would bring the value up to around £6 million. [The source of these riches should remain murky – they have nothing to do with this story.] When I mentioned Stafford's lifestyle to Liz Baron she laughed, "And they say crime doesn't pay!"

But Dennis had local enemies. Enemies in the town planning department and local police station. Enemies in the pub over the road. Even in the local supermarket.

The police had allegedly tried to fit him up – accusing him of torching a car in a quarrel involving a shotgun fired through a neighbour's window. Stafford was acquitted.

Then he was accused of shoplifting in Weardale Co-op. The haul was cheese, frying steak, lamb, and pork chops.

In court, Stafford ridiculed the charge:

> If I'm going to shoplift, am I going to stand in front of the store's biggest camera in the pet food aisle? I don't need to shoplift. It's ridiculous.

Adding,

> As for the pork chops, I'm Jewish so I don't eat pork.

Stafford was surprisingly fit for a 77-year-old – he looked at least 10 years younger. He was affable but guarded, crisply dressed and manicured. I noticed his eyebrows had been trimmed with scissors and glossed. While we talked, his large, watchful dog lay between us.

First, we talked about the disappearance of Les Wallis.

Stafford claimed that Les had been voluble about Antony Armstrong-Jones being his "bitch," "fucking him up the arse," "and so on."

Then came the visits by two "Special Branch" men to the Londoner, and their warnings.

The context was the impending marriage of Princess Margaret and Tony Armstrong-Jones.

It's well known that Armstrong-Jones' bohemian lifestyle, and his promiscuity and bisexuality, had alarmed the Palace.

In *Snowdon: The Biography* (2008), Anne de Courcy writes that when the engagement was announced, "A frisson of horror ran through many of the courtiers. Sir Alan Lascelles... [lamented that] 'the boy Jones has led a very diversified and sometimes a wild life and the danger of scandal and slander is never far off.'"[61]

So the potential for embarrassment was great. In that context, the warning to Les Wallis is believable.

Whether or not Les was really Armstrong-Jones' lover is, of course, hearsay.

What is more certain is that Armstrong-Jones was a regular at both the Festival and the Londoner. As was Les Wallis.

---

61   Anne de Courcy, *Snowdon*, p85

A letter I sent Snowdon asking about his association with these clubs brought an email from his PA:

> 5/19/11
>
> Lord Snowdon has asked me to thank you for your letter to him regarding the above clubs in the 1950s. I regret to inform you that Lord Snowdon has no recollection of these two clubs.
>
> Kindest regards
>
> Lynne Wilson

Lord Snowdon lived a full life after the fifties. A lapse of memory would be understandable.

Dennis Stafford:

> Yes, [Armstrong-Jones came to the Londoner] quite often. He was a strange fellow. You could meet him in the daytime and you would never know he was gay... and other times he'd come in like a screaming old quean. Strange innit?
>
> Don't know whether the drink got to him or what, but...
>
> FV: But did Les Wallis really vanish after that second warning?
>
> Oh definitely, because look, he was like an old quean. He had his routine, even had his own special glass. You know. It was his world. Where else was he going to go? To a pub? But, yes, I would lay odds on it.

Stafford added,

> Paul [Clay] was concerned when he disappeared. I remember that. They were very close, in the sense that they were a similar age and they used to – not fight, but be bitchy to each other – but they loved each other. You know the type of relationship.

Later on, Paul even went to Les's flat [in Paddington.] He found it all just abandoned, with Les's things still inside.[62]

———————

I then asked Stafford about the 1958 razor slashing.

> Yes, well I tell you the actual truth to that – I know it for a fact. George attacked Paul.

> FV: Did he really? Because that was a razor attack.

> Stafford: Yes. Let me tell you something about George. George in drink was a very aggressive person, and I know a couple of people he used to associate with that he used to beat up and that. A friend of mine, a guy I knew, who I went to school with, was with George for a short period and George hit him over the head with a glass ashtray and things like that, you know...

> And I lived in... I bought it off Paul actually – he had the lease on a mews house in Queensgate, behind the Albert Hall – I bought the lease off him, and I had it as mine – and I threw a party there, and George came.

> And, you see I'm not gay, you must understand. And though I understand it all, it's just not my scene, you know? If it was I'd indulge – only it doesn't interest me.

———————

62   I found no documentary evidence of the death or emigration of any Leslie Wallis around that time. Nor any death certificate that corresponds to his birth date. That's not to say Les was bumped off. Stafford admitted various other theories were mooted about his disappearance. One being that he'd done a runner from debts. Les's friends, however, were puzzled that his disappearance was so sudden, and that this gregarious man was never seen or heard of again. And why had he abandoned all his possessions? Stafford inclined to a sinister explanation.

But I'm very sympathetic. I like gay people, I like the scene, talent, culture, everything.

But George always had a crush on me. He never tried anything or anything like that. But I was with a girl called Salena Jones at the time, an American [Jazz] singer, and we'd bought this lease and done the place all up.

Anyway, George came round and then he starts his nonsense after a few drinks, and he's with one of his boyfriends, and then he started being aggressive.

I said, "George behave yourself or..."

But he went on with his nonsense and I'd just had enough that day, and I went Bang! I cracked him.

So he says, "Oh, you of all people hitting me!"

I said, "Come on, get in. You're going home."

I threw him in the car and I was going to take him back to his place. He was living in Gerrard Street.

So I was getting out of the car to take him upstairs, and he ran off. And he run through the alleyway up to the Two Decks. I thought, I can't let him go like this you know? Because he had a cut eye...

So I go to the Two Decks and as I go in he attacked me!

And two homies or whatever you want to call them started on me, and I cracked them. I ended up having a fight with them too.

But George, in drink, was a very nasty individual and he was the one that cut Paul up.

FV: But they were supposedly...

Yes, I know, but George... He committed a lot of injuries on Paul over the years you know? Oh yes.

He was very aggressive, and he was the one that committed the slashing.

That's a fact. Because I was away [in jail] at the time, and obviously I asked a friend of mine, Wally, to find out what happened because then I could send someone round to sort things out.

Then it came back to me and I spoke to Wally, and Wally said it was George that done it.

He used to come in drunk and they fell out. But it definitely was George.

And that's not hearsay. It's a fact.

———————

I now asked about the Stephen Ward connection.

Dennis Stafford:

I used to go to the Embassy with him. He used to like the Embassy, and the Eve club in those days, and I used to see him quite often, and [later on] I knew what's-her-name, Keeler. She was a slut, you know? But she was a bit of rummy. So was Amanda Rice-Davies.

Stephen was involved with a guy called 'Dandy Kim' [Caborn-Waterfield]. Dandy Kim was involved with a circle who had... perversions, you know, copper files [coprophilia] and all that crap, and Stephen got involved in that.

And Profumo too, he was involved in all this. In parties in Chelsea, they used to pee on each other and... [indecipherable] you know.

Now, through that, Stephen got connections with all these top people who... Well, they were weirdos – and that's how he earnt his money.

Like they want a bird, they want a boy, whatever – he used to supply it. But he had so much on so many people. If it had come to court and come out, I think... you know.

Yes, I knew Stephen. If I saw him I'd have a drink with him. I went to his place a few times.

———————

The interview moved to Sarah Churchill.

FV: You said you had a bit of a fling with her?

Well, a fling... I had a dabble a couple of times. Not a fling. You'd be in the club, had a couple of drinks: "You going to take me home, darling?"

FV: What, did you go upstairs [to his apartment]?

Yes, and it was one of those things you know. It happened to so many different people. It was very open in those days, you know? They were all at it really.

Because you must understand that the Londoner attracted so many people of, you know – these high class standing people – because it was illegal to have a gay club. Yet such important people used to go there, that a blind eye was, you know, given to it.

And that's why it attracted such a calibre of people. Because there was nowhere else they could relax, you know?

And most of these people were weirdos – for want of another word.

But nobody ever spoke out of turn as far as I know, outside the club. It was a closed community and whoever went in there...

I mean, who knew Rock Hudson was gay all those years ago? And Burt Lancaster, Johnny Mathis, Johnnie Ray...

MURDER MILE

The evening after Jean Townsend's murder, police cars toured South Ruislip with loudspeakers asking for information. Appeals flashed on local cinema screens. "Attractive women police officers were told to dress in civilian clothes and walk casually around the murder area."

The police looked for "a wavy haired young man" and a small red sports car. Neither was traced. They looked for two men in "dark grey black plastic Macintoshes and gabardine suits." These men had been hanging around the crime scene the evening before Jean's murder, trying to chat up women. They were found and interviewed, then cleared.

Fragments of two teeth "found near the murder spot" had detectives looking for a man with two front teeth missing. A candidate was found in a nearby boarding house. Interrogated. Then cleared.

Forensics examined two half-pint milk bottles and "a number of small objects including a cigarette pack" found near Jean's body.

No result.

The local paper ran an editorial about "young females" "done to death on open ground."

This it said,

> went back and back through the centuries till it merges with savage times from which it springs. Such throwbacks to primitive lust are unpredictable and defy all precautions... [a] maniac [had pursued] his lust to the death.

A panic began in South Ruislip. The local Highways Committee announced that street lighting would be extended from dawn to dusk. *The Ruislip Advertiser and Gazette* reported a "curfew" on local girls.

Under the headline, "Vigilantes patrol Ruislip's 'murder mile.'" it was announced that fourteen "fathers of young teenage daughters" "unarmed and carrying torches," had formed themselves into three-man vigilante squads to patrol "murder mile," from 10.45pm to 1 am.

————————

Meanwhile, the press knocked on doors for angles.

Three sisters spoke up. Sixteen-year-old Violet Ingram claimed she was once "followed by a man on a cycle. He got off his bike and chased me down the road." She described him as balding in front with bushy hair at the back. His accent was "either Irish or Scottish." Twenty-one-year-old Margaret Ingram said she'd been approached several times by "strangers." Twenty-three-year-old June Ingram had been asked to get into a car a week before, by "a man with an American accent."

James O'Dell, a 25-year-old American Embassy worker, explained he'd discovered a "Peeping Tom" in his garden, "less than 100 yards from the murder spot."

> I slipped on a pair of trousers over my pyjamas when I heard someone moving about in the front garden. I picked up a tennis racket, chased him up the road, and finally caught him. He was about 5ft 10in tall and rather bald. I told him to stop hanging around my place so late.

————————

209

More disturbing was the story told by twenty-two-year-old Joan Galer.

A few days before Jean Townsend was killed Joan Galer had been to the cinema and taken the last train home. She noticed a man walking parallel with her on the other side of the road. This was about 700 yards from the murder scene.

The man suddenly ran over, grabbed her by the shoulders, and pushed her to the ground. She was wearing a grey silk scarf. He pulled it tight. She screamed. A cyclist appeared. The man ran off. He was between twenty-five and thirty years old and wore a sports coat. He had a "high forehead."[63]

BUTTONS CLUE TO WOMAN'S ASSAILANT
Man with high forehead makes midnight attack

None of these women had previously reported anything to the police. It wasn't something you talked about. As if being attacked was shameful.

Joan Galer subsequently married and moved up North. She'd since died. I found her son, a university lecturer, born after the attempted strangling. He was shocked. His mother had never mentioned the incident. Or Jean Townsend.

As when after a long search, I found the only surviving relative of Jean Townsend, a niece.

---

63 Jean's friend June Sweetzer also reported an assault several months before the murder. She said she'd been "attacked in the fog" by a man who jumped out of an alley. "It was a terrible shock." He pinioned her arms but ran when she screamed. He was short and wore "crepe soled shoes."

She remembered Jean's death. She'd been four at the time.

But the family hushed up the details. She was told Auntie Jean had died in a car accident. Years later, a teenager, she read the truth in a local paper. She was as upset by the deception as by the murder. And, even now, too upset to talk about Jean. Like the Met Police, like the QC David Farrer, like so many others, she seemed to wish the thing would go away, that Jean Townsend be forgotten once and for all...

———————

In 1954, the police found no leads in the Townsend case.

Time went by.

The rest of the fifties. Then the sixties.

In 1970, Jean's father died of a heart attack working in his garage. He was 62. His wife, Lilian, blamed the stress of losing Jean.

Then, in October 1982, the police announced they had unexpected new leads in the Townsend case.

Someone (in some versions, two people) had made anonymous phone calls, "revealing new facts." The police were giving nothing away, but wanted the person(s) to call them back.

Detective Superintendent Tony Lundy was put on the case. He looked over the file. The mystery informants never called back. Lundy returned the file to storage.

A few years later, Lundy got into trouble at the Yard. Accused of major corruption: supergrasses, paybacks. He resigned and departed for the Costa Brava. Contacted there by Reg Hargrave in 2005, he said he remembered nothing at all about the Townsend case. And who had given out his phone number?

DEAD FASHION GIRL

Interviewed in 1983, Jean's mother, Lilian, confessed,

> I never really got over her death. A clairvoyant told me whoever did it was far away across water. But now it's nothing to me. I am not vindictive. I don't know why they should reopen the case.

Lilian Townsend eventually retired to Canvey Island. An odd choice for a snob.

She bought a modest bungalow on the island. She lived out the rest of her life there. She died in September 1992, aged 87. She left her wedding ring and "small gold ring with diamonds" to a neighbour. And requested that, "the funeral cortege shall not leave from my home but shall leave from the Chapel of Rest and that my body shall be cremated."

Jean too, had been cremated back in 1954. Her ashes are buried in Golders Green Crematorium, Plot "J".

Jean Townsend on holiday with her family.

THE STRANGE MATTER OF

Stories mooting an American dimension to the Townsend case have been persistent. That maybe an American serviceman – or several such – killed her. It was even rumoured that suspect Yanks had been whisked out of the country to avoid prosecution.

This was plausible. It's known the American military in those days objected to having servicemen questioned by British police, or judged in British courts. There were cases in the 1940s and 50s when, following assaults and rapes, and even murders, American soldiers had been quickly shipped out of the country.

The British government was complicit. This American quasi-independence – a state within a state – was a price the British paid for their "special relationship."

———

In 2009 I placed a notice in the *Police Pensioner* asking for contact with officers who'd dealt with, or knew about, the Townsend case.

I got a dozen calls or emails. Some led to further contacts and sources.

I was impressed by how many of them remembered – and still cared about the case. It irked and offended them it was unsolved.

They came up with various angles. Three suggested an American was the culprit.

One telephoned me that he'd always had "a gut feeling" an American did it. He'd heard about Americans being hurriedly transferred out of the base after the killing.

But when I asked for details he rang off.

Another ex-policeman told me "off the record" that American servicemen had been transferred back to the US after the murder.

This informant had once lived locally and befriended Jean's mother, Lilian, during the investigation. He used to drop in to see how she was, and update her on the case. He'd kept in touch with Lilian until she died. He thought the Townsends had been let down.

Another American link emerged out of the brief 1982 re-investigation.

A retired Detective Constable emailed that while serving at Acton in West London from 1982 to 1985, he was "involved in the investigation of several local murders." During this time he worked with a Det. Supt Nick Carter.

Email:

> Around 1982/83 Nick was transferred to SO1(1) at New Scotland Yard (NSY). His new posting [enabled him] to investigate unusual or serious crimes, in particular murder investigations in London or indeed anywhere in the world, if a UK citizen was the victim... Shortly after his transfer he arrived back at Acton (Met 'X' Division) as one of his first 'jobs' was to investigate an old murder in Ruislip. I had no input in this investigation, but if my memory serves me correctly the following took place:

In 1982/83 an aged US citizen and ex US soldier presented himself at Acton Police Station. He volunteered information about [the] murder of a female in Ruislip [Jean Townsend] some years previous. He had nothing to do with the murder directly, but one of his close friends, who along with him was based with the US Forces at Northolt Airbase, was responsible for the murder... The reason for the caller's information after such a long period was that his friend had recently died in the US, and he felt that the victim's family should know the truth. I recall that the 'File' from NSY was located and allocated to Nick and his small team. I also recall that they managed to trace relatives of the deceased, I believe a sister... [Jean had no sister, she was an only child.]

Apparently a US Soldier at Northolt was suspected at the time of the murder, and all were interviewed, but due to lack of forensic and witnesses no progress was made...

The email concluded, "Hope this is not a 'red herring'."

Trouble was, this story didn't tally with the Met Police embargo on the file. Why remain secretive if the most likely culprit was dead? [And if the police were protecting this suspect's relatives it would be simple to redact identifying details.]

In any case, in 1982 the officer in charge of the re-investigation was Tony Lundy, not Nick Carter. (Though Nick Carter might also have worked on it).

What was more, I could get no corroboration of this story from other sources. [Nick Carter, for example, didn't answer my emails.]

Finally, the assertion that: "a US Soldier at Northolt was suspected at the time of the murder, and all were interviewed" – clashed with a statement that Reg Hargrave had obtained.

During his investigation into Jean's murder, Reg talked to a Ruislip woman, Francis Burnett (nee Edmonds). She'd been the daughter of a Detective Superintendent John Edmonds, involved in the 1954 Townsend investigation. She gave Reg this written statement:

> I well recall that during the course of the police investigation, my father contacted the Commandant at the United States Airforce base at Victoria Road, South Ruislip... When he arrived home on the day in question my father, who was usually reluctant to discuss with the family cases he was currently working on, was clearly upset because the Commandant had refused to cooperate in the CID enquiries for reasons best known to himself. A short while after this, I remember hearing my father say that it had come to their knowledge that certain military personnel at the airbase had been sent home to the United States. According to my father, the military authorities turned down a request by the CID to interview personnel in order to eliminate them from the police enquiries. [Signed, 10 January, 1997]

Another rumoured American connection concerns the Scottish serial killer, Peter Manuel.

It's been suggested Manuel was in the Ruislip area when Jean was killed.

Manuel is known to have murdered seven women between 1956–58. It's suspected he killed at least eighteen people. He was hanged in 1958.

Hector MacLeod and Malcolm McLeod – respectively a solicitor and university professor – have written the definitive study of Manuel. They tell how:

In December [1954], Manuel drew attention to himself in a most bizarre fashion when he went to see the US Consul in Glasgow in connection with his American citizenship and told one of his far-fetched stories. At the meeting, he revealed that he had information about an important security matter. The American authorities were interested, so interested that they flew him to a US airbase near London to be interviewed by an FBI officer. The interrogator quickly realised he had no information but by then Manuel had had a day out and received the attention he craved. It is not known if the US authorities flew him back. One suspects he had to make his own way home.[64]

The airbase where Manuel was interrogated was South Ruislip.

Manuel was therefore in the area.

But that was three months *after* Jean was killed. At the time of her murder, Manuel was in Scotland.

Malcolm McLeod told me [email 6/08/2012] that he doubted any Manuel link to the Townsend case. He added that one connection in particular was spurious and came from a Scottish journalist, Bob Smyth, trying to "spice up" an article on Manuel.[65] But, as McLeod pointed out, "the dates don't fit."

[McLeod's book on Manuel was based on access to 29 police and judicial files at the National Archives of Scotland. In his email, McLeod referred to incongruities around the Townsend case. Concluding, "There is also the strange matter of why the Townsend case files are still inaccessible, of course."]

---

64   Hector MacLeod and Malcolm McLeod, *Peter Manuel. Serial Killer*, 2010, p62
65   Bob Smyth, "Was this pretty art student a serial killer's ninth victim?", *Mail on Sunday* (Scottish Edition), 19 February 2012

WE ALL WEAR A GREEN CARNATION

By late 1954 Liz and George Baron had divorced. But they kept friends in common, and saw one another, and Liz still frequented the Londoner.

Once, discussing her divorce from George Baron, Liz confessed:

Can I tell you all this?

But I don't mind saying this 'cause it's true.

I went back to him, as so many women do.

Because he took me one day to the Ideal Home Exhibition and decided he'd buy me a house.

And the house was just outside Windsor.

I moved in. And he didn't.

And then he went to Africa to dance with the Masai Tribe.[66]

And mother here [indicating herself] was left again without any money.

---

66 Baron had a great interest in African dance. In 1954, enthused by an exhibition of Kenyan dancing: "He declared that he intended to use the Kamba dance steps he had just seen in his upcoming part as Man Friday in 'Robinson Crusoe.'" Robert Edgerton, *Mau Mau*, 1989

Then one day, GB's father turned up with another guy with a lorry and they removed all the furniture.

And his father was very apologetic, but he was weak, you know?

And the kid was running round the garden, with his toys, and saying "You can't take this. You can't take that".

But they took it all.

I was lucky in that I had parents. Didn't want to go back to them, because they were quite elderly. They lived in Sutton. But I went back to them.

Abandoning acting, Liz trained as a nurse.

———

In the early sixties, after travelling to Africa to study the traditional Masai jumping dance, George Baron enjoyed a renaissance. He ran a theatrical agency from above the Londoner at 16 Irving Street, and appeared on TV, including in a series for Associated-Rediffusion, *Hooray And Co.* He also began working as a choreographer.

In December, 1965, this appeared in *The Stage*:

If there is a certain "Stars and Garters" [TV variety show] atmosphere around the Londoner Club in Irving Street, these days it is only natural, as co-owner George Baron is now responsible for staging the TV show and pianist Mike McKenzie [black jazz pianist and composer, who took over from Russ Conway at The Londoner and later featured in many movies] is, of course, one of its musical stars. For George and partner Paul Clay this is a return to the Londoner, as they had the premises eight years ago. Now back in harness after a period away from the business... George has opened an agency in addition to carrying on his production work and running the club. And if you noticed an unannounced gentleman in a number with Gary Miller and Ivor Emmanuel in last week's edition of "Stars and Garters" that was George getting the feel of the boards again.[67]

———————

The high point of George Baron's career was two years later, in 1968, as assistant choreographer on the movie *Oliver!*

Liz Baron:

> I saw him at the studios at Shepperton. I had a lot of friends in *Oliver!* – actors, dancers and singers. And I knew Ron Moody, who played Fagin. Lovely guy. Lovely guy. I used to take Jane [daughter from second marriage] when she was a little girl. We used to watch them filming and so on.

> And I must confess, in my tiny little way, I didn't realise how wonderful a dancer GB was until I saw him working in *Oliver!* at Shepperton.

> And one day I think we were sitting in the café – and he told everybody – he introduced me to everybody, including Ron Moody, as his wife.

> "Oh, this is my wife."

> And I was married to somebody else by then – do you follow me?

> You see, GB was a sort of romancer – and I mean that not in a "romantic" sense...

---

67   *The Stage*, December 2, 1965

And Sammy Davis Jnr was at the studio. He was there with Peter Lawford, making a film called *Salt and Pepper*.

And Sammy had this huge caravan at the studios and GB took me along, and Sammy came out of the caravan and GB said, "This is my wife."

I said, "ex-wife, actually."

———

Once, Ron Moody said to me, "Why have you two split up?"

I said, "It's a long story – I don't want to go into it."

And he said, "Oh, come on…"

And I said [speaking crossly], "Ron, he's gay for a start…"

He said, "Yeah, well you can…"

But it was just a bit of conversation in the restaurant – you know. Because people look at you and they don't know, do they?

What's gone on – or what's going on – or whatever.

I guess it's the way we were brought up: you didn't wash your dirty linen in public. You were a brave soldier – if you had an injection or anything you didn't cry – and I guess it's a generation thing.

———

After *Oliver!* George tried film production – but no luck.

Then the work started to run out.

By 1972, he'd moved to a council flat, 40 Gilbert House on the Churchill Gardens Estate in Pimlico. Here, he lived in a ménage-a-trois with Paul Clay and the younger Simon Austin. In the late seventies, the three men moved to 6 Bradman House, Abercorn Place, NW8.

By the early eighties George had also found a new girlfriend, Joan Elizabeth Cooper. She, too, moved into Bradman House.

Liz Baron:

> He rang me up one day, and he'd obviously been drinking, and he said,
>
> "Oh guess what, darling, I met this woman. She's got the same name as you."

———

Paul Clay died in October, 1982, at the age of 78.

In memory of his acting highlight – in Noel Coward's *Bitter Sweet* – green carnations were strewn on his coffin.

This after Coward's use of the imaginary flower as a queer emblem: "We all wear a green carnation."

Paul was cremated.

George was distraught. He put a notice in *The Stage* – adapting the Rod Stewart lyric, Stardust:

You wandered down the lane and far away.

Leaving me a song that will not die.

Love is now a stardust of yesterday.

The memory of the years gone by.

It was signed, "G"

Less than two years later, in January 1984, George too, died.

Liz Baron:

> I was directing an amateur play at Launceston. I had this phone call from [her and George's son] saying GB was dead.

> GB had been out celebrating on Burns Night. He went to see this Liz woman, drunk, and he fell down these cement stairs and was found, I believe, by the postman in the morning.

> He wasn't dead, but he was dead on arrival at the hospital.

However, George's death certificate says he died from a combination of pneumonia and bronchitis at St Mary's Hospital, Maida Vale. Also, his new girlfriend lived with him in Bradman House, and the flat was on the ground floor.

Still, a fantasy ending suits George Baron.

Liz Baron:

> GB was a fantasist. He told our son that when he died he didn't need to worry as he had a load of money stashed away, and the poor boy tried to find it. And I kept telling him it wasn't true – fantasy land.

Liz added,

> What a waste.

Then, after I heard... it was most peculiar, because I suddenly felt totally devoid of energy. I mean, me and the other actors, we used to have a little get-together after the show, but I couldn't go to it. I had to go home.

Liz thought she should tell their mutual friends.

I knew that Lionel [Blair] was in panto at Bristol.

So I rang the theatre and asked for him, and he got on the phone and the first thing I said, "Look Lionel, I think you ought to know GB's passed away."

"Well darling, are you out front? [In the audience]"

So I said, "No, I'm not. I'm living in Cornwall."

Then he put Joyce on the phone, and the first thing she said was, "Are you out front?" and I said "No." "Out front" – that was kind of the most important thing, you know. Because they lived, breathed and thought showbiz.

But they didn't go to the funeral or anything like that.

Liz added:

With George – I tend to believe with people like that the alcohol gets into the system even when they haven't been drinking that day.

It stays in the system. It does something to their brain.

In more carefree times, George and Liz (far left in the image) beam with fellow thespians at a theatrical agency. The figure looking down, above and second right to Liz, appears to be Paul Clay.

THAT POOR LITTLE BITCH IN HIS HANDS

A couple of months after my appeal in the *Police Pensioner* I was unexpectedly contacted by another ex-cop with a story to tell about the Townsend case.

He said he knew who the killer was. He asked for anonymity. The reasons will become obvious.

I interviewed him at length in his home. I've changed identifying details and refer to him as "Ray" – as in ray of light.

Ray came from a police family. His father was a police sergeant who fought in both world wars. Ray joined the Marines in 1938 at the age of 16. After the war he was a military policeman in Kenya. He then joined the civilian police and moved to the Ruislip-Northwood area onto a police estate. Ray's beats covered Ruislip, Greenford, and Ealing.

Ray:

> We had a lot of hooliganism. Plenty of that. And plenty of Irish trouble. And the Yanks were a pain. They were a bloody nuisance.
>
> When you [arrested an American serviceman], you had to have their liaison officer come down straight away, and then there was their welfare officer, and then the chaplain was there on their tail, and I thought blimey!

We used to say for Christ's sake don't dock a Yank, leave him alone. If they were fighting, let them sort it out – drop dead, both of them. Because when you interfered they all turned on you. They were very partisan.

It was mostly drink, the Yanks. The occasional fight over women. Local boyfriends found out about things, and went down and sorted it out...

Ray was candid about police corruption in the area. For example:

There was this Detective Sergeant. Percy Brown.

He'd been at Arnhem in the war. He was dropped at Arnhem. And he said. "We fired the last round and then I said, 'what we going to do lads?' And they said, 'We've got nothing to fire with, so sod it.' And they all stood up and put their hands up."

A very wise man! (laughs). He became a prisoner of war and then volunteered to join the Met Police and was brought out of prisoner of war camp straight home, because they were so short of policemen. A quarter of them had been killed.

So old Perce and I served together right from DC, Detective Constable, and I was a Sergeant when he was only a Constable.

But then he went straight through... he got into a Masonic lodge and went straight up the ladder. Woof! Every time I saw the bugger he had another rank. Woof! And when he came [to Ruislip] he was Detective Chief Superintendent. He lived over just the other side of our [police estate]. We met once a month regularly for years and years... He died a while ago.

And Percy was as bent as a nine bob note.

He was a good policeman. But if there was a couple of bob in it, Percy was there.

Old Perce...

227

He came in one day and said, my snout [informer] is in a bit of bother. Are you going to help out? Worth a couple of quid.

I was Station Officer at [location suppressed]. I said to old Perce, I said, "Well, what do you want?"

Well, he said, his driving license is out of order, and his insurance is a bit out of date. I want you to mark him up.

So the driving license was about a year out of date and on top of that he had an endorsement for 12 months' disqualification and that was still running.

He was still disqualified. And his insurance certificate was a cover note well out of date.

So I said, "You've got to be bloody joking. He's not covered in a million years."

I said, "Look at the loopholes you can get done with. You're a Detective bloody Inspector. What's your game?"

"Well," he said, "you put it through the books and nobody's going to bother about it."

I said, "you can get stuffed! On your bike."

He said, "Five quid in your pocket."

"I don't want it."

But he tried, old Perce. Everything was a joke for old Percy.

FV: What about black market – did you have to deal with that?

There was a hell of a lot of black market, a lot of that.

But most of our trouble came when the Hungarians came over.

They came over in a flood, when Russia invaded [1956] and they escaped from all the prisons and came over here.

And that's when they started smashing all our shop windows. That was your Hungarians. Pinch a car, smash a shop window, grab what's there, put it in the car, and just drive 150 yards round the corner, dispose of the gear, and then leave the car there. That's it.

They were a real problem, because we used to have fog in those days. Smog. They took advantage. Smashing shop windows. And then they didn't care who they hit with somebody else's car. They were a bloody menace, they were.

And fighting! Cor! You used to bash 'em, but they would struggle like mad.

FV: Why were there so many of them round that area?

They had a settlement camp for the buggers, an old army camp at Northolt. And they stuck them all in an abandoned army camp. They were all in one place, that was the trouble.

———————

Another thing was the toms [prostitutes].

We used to get the toms up all the time for the Yanks at Ruislip. We had a lot of trouble with them. Because in those days you only had two cells in Ruislip police station. Ealing only had four, and that was a major station. But the smaller stations, like Ruislip and Greenford, places like that, only had two. So if you were getting two toms in, who were going to give you West End addresses, you don't know where to accommodate them. You can't put two in the same cell.

And they would be crapping up the walls. That's what they used to do. That was getting their own back. Crap up walls. Lovely. Open the door at 6 o'clock in the morning to find your toms lying on the floor, state of undress, spewed up... Oh God!

You'd say "clean it up!"

"Clean it up your bloody self!" [laughs].

Oh God. Funny old days they were.

———————

And the suicide was phenomenal. The suicide rate in the early years, just after the war, was absolutely terrific.

Especially Ealing way, post-war Ealing, W5, that was a terrible place.

Every copper at Ealing did at least two suicides a week. And some of them were pretty horrific.

We had a couple of homosexuals locked together in a gas oven. Locked together. Both the heads were in the same oven, and they were frozen stiff. There'd been no warmth in the flat for a week. They'd been dead a week. And separating them wasn't funny either.

Refugees. Old people. All in bedsits.

All those old Victorian houses, they were all full up with foreigners. Bedsits. All bedsits. Hundreds and hundreds.

And all they had was a gas ring. That's all they had. They cooked on it, and kept warm by it. And died by it.

———————

But the main thing Ray wanted to tell me was the story of the Irishman who claimed to have killed Jean Townsend.

His first name was Brinsley... Mac... It's a Mac something. Something like MacDowell I think it was. It's an awful long time ago.

He'd been living in the South of Ireland before he came over here because I remember Ken [fellow officer] saying they went to the Gardai for information on him. It was in Dublin. He was a bloody nuisance over there as well.

At the time he was lodging just round the corner [from the crime scene], in Victoria Road. He had lodgings there. He'd been there for about six months. We'd known him for longer than that, from where he'd been before, in the W5 area.

But then he moved to South Ruislip.

He was just a labourer, roustabout. Odds and ends. Then we heard he'd got a job in the American Base, the PX, supplies.

The stuff in the PX used to come straight from America to the Base. Never used to go through us at all. And he used to be employed in the American PX as a labourer, moving the stuff about.

Now this bloke had an old van but whether they found it or not I never knew. Course it was never taxed or insured. And he'd been nicked so bloody often he'd dump the van in a side street, then come back when it was quiet and drive it home. He'd drive late at night, he'd drive this thing around. This is the information I got from one of the CID blokes.

FV: Oh, so he might have been involved in black market himself?

Oh well, undoubtedly that happened.

He was between 30-35 years old, and big. I was 16 stone in those days, so I was a big bloke myself. He'd be about a couple of stone lighter than me. About 13 stone. But he wasn't muscular. He was flabby.

He was a smelly bugger – I tell you that. I mean, a bit pongy.

He was a drinker and when he was drunk it caused his bloody rages. A pretty heavy drinker. He was known in Ireland for his drinking. And he had four or five convictions in Ealing alone. Drunk and disorderly, found drunk in the gutter. In those days if they were in the gutter, we used to take them in and put them in a cell. Nowadays of course they don't bother.

There were two Irish pubs in Ealing. One at Ealing Broadway W5 and one at Ealing Broadway W13. We [patrolled] the two and he used to come to either one.

One night he came over to the W13 one and got pie eyed.

[This was about five days after Jean's murder.]

I knew him because I'd nicked him once before – drunk and disorderly. This particular night I was called into the pub.

I was by myself. And when I went through the door he was waiting for me. He'd already wrecked the pub, he'd wrecked the bar. As soon as he saw me, he went straight at me.

As soon as I walked through the door he said, "I'm waiting for you..." and he came at me like a bull. I just went to one side and he went straight into the door. Crashed through the door. Great big brass handles on the door – went straight into him. Into his chest. And after that it wasn't too bad for me. Slowed him down a bit. So that's how we started.

We had a terrific fight and it went on for about quarter of an hour. Just the two of us. It spilled out into the street. There were about 30-40 people standing round gawping, enjoying the spectacle. We went through the side of a golf hut. There was a putting green at Haven Green, and – you know, a golf hut. We went through the side of that. And then we tore a park bench out of the ground.

It was cemented in, we rolled underneath that, and then it went up – straight out of the ground.

I got a nice fat lip out of it. Graze on my leg. Plus a nasty bruise on the back of my shoulder when we lifted that bloody seat...

And somebody told me afterwards that somebody took a delight to jumping on my helmet! Because that rolled off as well.

Finally, I got the better of him. I subdued him, and the booze got the better of him more than I did. He was well boozed. It impaired his fighting ability.

While I was fighting with him I dragged him down to the nick – from the Irish club to the nick was about two hundred and fifty yards.

I got him in the nick. Then I got him in a cell. And there was no-one to help me, because when I got there, there was only the station officer on duty, and no-one else in the nick.

So I had the job of putting him in the cell by myself. And I got him on the bench and I thought, well he'll be alright for a minute, and I made the mistake of just half-turning away from him to go out of the door.

I thought he was comatose, but he came alive like greased lightning.

He tried to get by – through me and out the door. Because he knew the layout of the nick, he'd been there before.

He knew it was straight through the cell door and straight to the street.

Well, another fight took place in the cell, and we were there for another five minutes just about.

I got hold of him again. I was 16 stone in those days so I had a few pounds to use, so I was alright.

And I got him back on the bench and he gave up, but there was a bit of blood around, but not much, and he was a bit bloody and so was I.

Anyway, I came out, shut the door. I went and saw the station officer.

"Have you managed to put him away?"

"Yes I have. Thanks for your help!"

He said, "You'll have to look after him. Look in on him every ten minutes."

So I went down the cell. I looked in through the hatch – I must confess I didn't go in – and he was up against the wall sitting down. I looked and he was alright. So I left him.

At five o'clock in the morning I'd cleaned myself up and I had no helmet. And, of course, my tunic was torn. So the station officer said, "You'd better go off duty."

Well, the station officer was supposed to have been looking in on the cell every quarter of an hour, twenty minutes.

Whether he did or not I don't know, but next thing we know [my wife] is getting me out of bed.

"You're wanted downstairs."

I went downstairs in my dressing gown and there were two blokes from the Yard.

Now, this was only half past ten, quarter to eleven in the morning. They must have put a bloody spurt on because they'd come from the Yard, and they were there in Ruislip.

I thought, "Christ, they must have got a move on."

They said this man was dead.

I said, "Oh well, fair enough. We had a good fight. But when I left him, he was alive."

They said, they'd got in the cell about half past eight, quarter to nine, and he was dead.

Well of course, in the old days if you had a prisoner in the cell that died in the cell, and you aspired to promotion, you could forget it.

Because that was the end of your career. Because you should have found him within twenty minutes of him dying at least. That was the time allowed.

Though... I'll be quite honest with you, the practice in the old days with dead prisoners was to write out a bail form, put it in his pocket, and go and prop him up against a bloody tree somewhere.

Bail him out, then lumber him out, so that he wasn't found dead in the cell.

Especially old drunks that you'd had for years and years.

You would put him in the van, take him down to Ealing Common, stick him up against a tree, and let somebody else find him.

In that case, if you're an aspiring inspector and you're stuck as a sergeant, you're going to get your promotion.

But if you were found with a body in your cell and it wasn't you that found it, that was it.

That was curtains. That was death.

They went away and then came back to me shortly afterwards.

They said "Well, it's under consideration for manslaughter and possibly murder..."

So I said, "Well right."

So I got my warrant card out ready, but they said, "Well we're not suspending you."

I thought. "That's bloody odd!"

I said, "Well if you're not suspending me, how come you're considering these charges?"

"Well it depends on the outcome of our enquiries."

Away they went.

And I went back on duty that night. Borrowed somebody else's helmet because mine was as flat as a pancake (laughs).

And I walked the streets.

About three weeks passed and W___, a bloke I knew, came in from Special Branch. He used to be a PC I knew from earlier on, and he'd gone on to Special Branch.

I thought he was doing a rubber heeling job on me, because he was in the canteen in plain clothes, and I said point blank, "You rubber heeling me? Let me know." He said no.

FV: What do you mean by "rubber heeling"?

Well that's policemen who checked on policemen – they crept round in plain clothes on somebody else's division, checking on policemen to find out if they were going over the side.

We used to call them rubber heelers.

So I said, "Are you rubber heeling me?"

He said, "No, I'm not." He said "I'm Special Branch, I don't do that. A4 do that."

If he had been rubber heeling me, he would have told me. We were friends. He wouldn't mess me about. There were no acts of confidentiality with us, at our level.

He said, "They've connected this bloke with the Townsend case."

And then that he was there "on observation."

But he didn't tell me what it was about.

Now all that time I was dragging this Irish bloke down to the nick, and while we were fighting, he kept saying, "I shouldn't have killed her. I shouldn't have killed her. I didn't mean to kill her. I didn't mean to kill her."

And he kept on saying this.

I didn't know what he was talking about, I thought it was just his drunken ravings.

And the last thing he said, when I left him in the cell, was, "It's all my fault. I didn't mean to do it. I didn't mean to kill her."

He kept saying that. I told the Station Officer, but he said, "Oh alright."

Like me, he thought it was just drunken ravings and let it go at that.

But it was continual, from the time I dragged him out from the old park seat and got him on his feet, and then got him up the road with his arm up his back, he kept saying it all the way along. He never stopped.

In fact, W___ told me later they were 100% certain it was him.

They were bang on, because of what they found back at his lodgings, and from what they'd heard from the people down there who knew about him.

Also, you see, they were looking for a bloke with an American accent, because Ruislip was crawling with Yanks. But maybe it wasn't an American accent.

Somebody had misheard it and thought it was an American accent, but it was an Irish accent. From a distance there's not much between the two. From a distance a Mick, a broad Mick talking, you'd think it was an American.

Anyway, I thought I could imagine that poor little bitch in his hands if he got worked up.

She wouldn't have stood a prayer.

————————

When those two blokes from the Yard didn't take my Warrant Card I thought, "Well…"

One of them was a Chief Superintendent, a CID Superintendent.

He'd been with me in Kenya. We were both coppers there. That was after the war.

He came up to me and said – well he called me by my Christian name, and I'm a bloody PC and he's a Superintendent… He said, "Well, Ray, it looks bad." He said, "You'll have to be careful."

Because I'd already been investigated for a murder in bloody Kenya. And he knew that.

But it all came to nothing. The affair in Kenya was in the exercise of my duty. We were armed out there, as you know.

When it happened in Kenya they said back off and leave it alone, and I did. I did just that. I didn't enquire, I didn't discuss it with anybody. I told the lads in the canteen, but as far as that lot's concerned you can forget it.

Then I heard that they'd written off this [Townsend] murder to this Mick.

And that it was classified.

And that's why they didn't prosecute or have a go at me.

The thing was, of course, he was never put on a charge sheet. He was never charged with drunk and disorderly. I didn't charge him – he wasn't in a fit state to charge because he couldn't understand the charge.

When you brought them in drunk, we used to throw them down the cell and once they'd sobered up, then we'd charge them.

But he was left there until he was fit to be charged and then he was dead.

So he was never charged. [So no paperwork.]

In the end I found out... they didn't tell me officially – never – but I found out through the grapevine – that they'd written it all off.

They'd written off the murder down to him, that's why I was never suspended and never charged.

Or even investigated – because, when I went back to the cell myself that night [after the cell death], blood was all round the walls.

I think he had batted his head against the wall, but that's only my opinion. I don't know whether he did or not – but there was certainly a lot more blood than when I'd left him.

So that was the end of that, and I got away with it.

But I tell you what: I was walking on cobbles for a long, long time [laughs].

———————

We chatted some more. Then Ray asked, "You want to see my little museum?"

He took me upstairs to a small room that was a shrine to his police career. Photos, certificates, trophies, a pair of handcuffs, and his old truncheon.

———————

Ray had nothing to gain by telling me all this.

In fact, quite a lot to lose. His pension for a start. But it seemed like a story he'd been wanting to confess for a very long time.

The story seemed plausible. It had a genuine feel of that rough and ready post-war policing.

But what had happened to the Irishman's body?

Ray:

> I went to the mortuary to have a look at him, he was well battered around the head. He mostly got that bashing round the head underneath that park bench, because he kept coming up and banging his bloody head. And I knew he was badly beaten about the head – but I rather fancy he was also smashing his head against the [police cell] wall. Unless I did finish him... If I did finish him off... I don't know...

After searching news reports and coroner's reports and indexes in the Middlesex area, for people of that or similar, name, or for any likely male aged around 30-35, I've been unable to identify anyone who died around then as described. However, the coroner's records in the London Metropolitan Archive are incomplete. Another factor may have been secrecy surrounding this death in custody: "they'd written it all off."

———

Ray's account told a believable sequence of events. About a believable culprit.

Ray could have made it all up. But why would he? His memory may have been occasionally faulty, but many details of his account were confirmed by cross-checking: dates, places, names – no anomalies. There was no element of garnishing – no recourse to a honed or hackneyed story line (unlike the Carlodalatri angle, see below). It all had that messy, ambiguous, unfinished, unsatisfying feel of "real life." What's more, Ray's wife knew the story too.

In fact, Ray's wife was concerned that Ray was incriminating himself. After I began the interview she asked me to switch my recorder off. She then asked whether I'd promise to protect Ray's identity. Only when I did, was I able to resume the interview.

The reported certainty of Special Branch officers was interesting: "...they were 100% certain it was him. They were bang on, because of what they found back at his lodgings..."

What had they found?

AS EASY AS WINK

Several things had puzzled the coroner and police in 1954.

Jean Townsend hadn't struggled. There were no signs she'd resisted or fought back. Jean's art college friend, Joyce Nunn, was adamant that if attacked,

> She definitely would have made a fuss. Before anything would even have started. She would have protected herself very quickly if she felt someone was moving on to her – it would have been all hell let loose.

That might suggest she was taken by surprise. And yet, on that patch of wasteland, as in Victoria Road, there was no cover. If anyone had approached she would have seen them coming and been on her guard.

So did she know this person or people? Or was there something about them that reassured her?

———

Then there was Jean's underwear: carefully removed, and piled beside her body.

The pathologist itemised three undergarments: "suspender belt, knickers, stockings." At the inquest, DS Richardson mentioned four: "knickers, suspender belt, panties, stockings."

That may have been a mistake. Or maybe "panties" referred to a device to secure Jean's discarded sanitary pad.

The coroner commented that one of the oddities of this case was that "none of [Jean's] clothing was disarranged except where the [underwear] was taken off neatly." Even Jean's discarded stockings were immaculate – apart from "a small ladder which a girl coming at night could have made herself."

Fifties' lingerie was fragile and intricate. The removal of undergarments on unlit wasteland[68] without leaving traces either on the body or the clothing would have been tricky.

This doesn't seem like a frenzied or excited action. Rather, deliberate and methodical. The assailant would have needed to separately unhook two stockings from the suspender belt, then roll them down and off the feet. Not easily done in a hurry leaving only a "small" ladder. Then unhook the suspender belt from under the skirt and remove it. Difficult on a prone body? And then remove the knickers (and "panties"?), and finally, the tampon. All that would have taken time – maybe ten minutes?

There is a ceremonial quality, suggesting the disrobing was an erotic end in itself. (Though the discarded tampon might indicate that having stripped Jean's corpse in preparation for a sex act, the killer's discovery that she'd been menstruating made him pause, or recoil.)

But there was another anomaly about the underwear.

Patricia Kemp, who'd seen Jean on the train the evening she was killed, made two statements to the police, on the 16th September, and 21st September. In both, she testified that Jean was wearing a black slip ["a black lace slip," "a black slip"].

---

68   The nearest lamppost was too far to give illumination and the night sky was overcast.

On the 15th September Jean's father identified Jean's clothing for the police. The police list catalogued: a white brassiere with a small rose pattern... a pink plastic headband... a "white nylon underslip." It did not include a black lace (over) slip.[69]

It's unlikely Patricia Kemp would have been mistaken about this garment. She was observant about Jean's appearance. And she made the claim in two separate statements to the police. So why was a black slip not among the items shown to Jean's father?

Had it been taken by the killer from the crime scene as a trophy?

Was this what the police later found at Brinsley McDowell's home, that made them certain he was the killer?

———————

McDowell's American connection was intriguing. "We heard he'd got a job in the American base, the PX, supplies."

Through online forums I contacted ex US servicemen and others who'd been at the South Ruislip base.

One was Dick Wilson. He was the son of Air Force Major-General Roscoe Charles Wilson. In June 1954, Major-General Wilson had become commander of the Third Air Force in the United Kingdom. His HQ was South Ruislip.

Dick Wilson emailed:

> My mother and I joined my father [in the UK] in June, 1954, so he would have been in command in September of that year...

---

69   These statements were among those that had leaked into the coroner's file housed at London Metropolitan Archive.

Dick recalled the Townsend murder – he was fourteen at the time – but could offer no direct information. He then – while reminiscing generally – wrote:

> There was a con-man operating in the area whose name I never knew. He wandered in and out of supposedly secure areas and talked to people he should not have met, and the police were very anxious to talk to him. He did things no spy would ever do, like play the quarter slot machine at the Officers Club with 5-Franc pieces – a tactic that considerably altered the odds in his favor, and gave the cops hundreds of copies of his right thumb print. He also picked up Lt. Romanovitch's car for her from a repair shop, and altered the bill by adding one pound to it. [Equivalent to about £17 today.]

Dick Wilson described Lt. Romanovitch as "a very attractive young woman" but would not be drawn further on the incident. In fact, he clammed up after realising there might be security implications to the Townsend case.

Before that, however, he'd clarified:

> I recall seeing an artist's drawing of the con-man, made from witness' descriptions. He was youngish, fair, and good looking. A Canadian or American nationality was most likely.

The recklessness fits Brinsley McDowell. The description doesn't.

But suppose this "con man" was not McDowell, but an accomplice of McDowell's? And suppose this person regularly serviced, or had access to, authorised cars on the base?

What a clever ruse: to drive stolen goods out of the base in vehicles registered to USAF personnel… and then transfer them to McDowell's battered van for distribution to local fences.

There was no better time and place locally to arrange such a transfer of stolen goods than around midnight on that deserted stretch of Victoria Road, at that feebly lit junction where Angus Drive began, and where Jean Townsend was killed. The spot was less than five minutes' drive from the USAF Base. It was isolated, with no overlooking houses, shielded from the main road. It was surrounded on all sides by wasteland.

Imagine an illegal transaction taking place. Suddenly, Jean Townsend appears.

Sees what's happening.

Hurries on... She has no reason to think she's in danger – just some dodgy men loading goods into a van. Maybe surprising and disconcerting – but why would they attack her?

But McDowell in his drunken state panics. He grabs Jean by her scarf. She tries to run. She screams. And the scarf is twisted tight – as suggested by Rex Lewis: "as easy as wink."

Jean is killed instantly.

Both men take fright. They argue what to do.

Brenda Thomson: "I am... of the opinion that the voices of the men had an American accent."

Two Americans? Or a Canadian and an Irishman? For most Brits, a Canadian is indistinguishable from an American accent. And, as Ray suggested, "From a distance a Mick, a broad Mick [Southern Irish accent] talking, you'd think it was an American."

———————

But then what?

The disrobing suggests a sexual motive.

But maybe it was meant to.

For was Jean's underwear removed to make her death look like a sex crime? Thus masking an illegal transaction – which might have led police to interrogate known petty criminals, rather than hunting a sex fiend?

That might explain why the disrobing was mechanical and tidy – it was a subterfuge to throw the police off the scent rather than satisfy a sexual impulse. (With the black slip stuffed by McDowell in his pocket as an afterthought?)

If that was the game, it worked.

Consider too, that after disrobing her, the killer/s pulled Jean's skirt decorously down to her knees – as recalled in Rex Lewis's detailed description of her body. And that her eyes had been closed – presumably by the killer. Rex Lewis: "Her eyes were closed… as though she was asleep."

Were these twisted gestures of atonement?

––––––––––

For my money, the Irishman, Brinsley McDowell, was the likely killer. A drunken black marketeer, gratuitously brutal, grabbing a potential witness by her scarf… Then (he or his accomplice) laying a false trail for the police before disappearing.

In which case it was, like so many crimes – like most crimes: random, sordid, and absurd – accidental. With no glamour or high-flown conspiracy, nor any particular meaning.

No scheming serial killer, psychotic club manager, sex-crazed designer or SM sex game gone wrong, no deranged aristocrat [see "The Carlodalatri Connection" below], and no American soldiers, or military or political dimension.

Just McDowell in a fix:

> I shouldn't have killed her. I shouldn't have killed her. I didn't mean to kill her. I didn't mean to kill her.

We don't know however, why Special Branch apparently became interested in this. Or why the discovery of McDowell's body in a blood-spattered police cell became so shrouded in secrecy his body was spirited away and Ray was let off the hook but sworn to silence.

Ray:

> Because I was told... warned by the [Police] Federation bloke, "Look – mouth shut – don't say anything to anybody." 'Cos he said "you're walking on bloody broken glass." And I obeyed that injunction. I kept... I made no further enquiries, I kept as far away... I had three kids to look after. I couldn't afford the push...

This was about more than coppers doing one another favours. Why the exceptional leeway given to Ray? Why was Special Branch involved?[70]

70　The *Daily Express* reported a conference on the Townsend case three days after the murder, held at Greenford Police Station. It was convened by the Deputy Commander of Scotland Yard, William Rawlings, and lasted over two hours. This report mentioned that, "Later, Detective Sergeant [in fact, the rank was Detective Inspector] William Heddon, wartime-colonel in the Eighth Army's special investigation branch, joined the conference." There was no comment about why Heddon's expertise was required. [*Daily Express*, Sept 18 1954]

The seasoned private eye and ex-intelligence officer Simon Fluendy, was pretty sure that given the degree of secrecy around the Townsend case file, there was a "national security dimension" involved. He thought maybe someone was being protected. When I speculated whether this might be a junior royal – I instanced Lord Snowdon – he thought that, given the concealment involved, it had to be someone "much higher up." Higher up than the Queen's eventual brother in law?

One reason for this inordinate secrecy may be that the Townsend investigation threw up embarrassing facts not necessarily to do with the murder itself. Facts connected to VIPs at the Londoner for example. Or maybe police intelligence about other VIPs in the habit of cruising the Victoria Road wasteland.

In any event, on the day the Townsend case file is finally opened, we may get to see those colour photos of Jean's body which the inquest jury "viewed through a box lighted from the inside." But we'll never get see any of the "missing" witness statements – or anything else that might have been artfully weeded.

———

Screen after screen after screen. Starting with those Heath Robinson contraptions of polling booth screens and sacking which trilby-hatted detectives erected around Jean's body.[71] Then that tarpaulin thrown over Jean Townsend's body to shield it from "the common gaze." Crafted lies and white lies designed to equally shield the police investigation from "the common gaze." The sealed case file. The secret session in a supposedly public Information Tribunal Appeal. The "closed annex" to

---

71 The reason they're all wearing that headgear in photos was explained by Rex Lewis. The reigning chief superintendent, "thought all CID officers should wear hats. Don't know why. He had a thing about it."

the Tribunal report. The vanished witness statements. All that ducking and diving and petulance from New Scotland Yard...

About my quest for information on the Townsend case, the Met Police scolded me by email that:

"The public interest is not what interests the public."

They would say that, wouldn't they?

PART TWO:

Other Connections, Other Theories

THE SWEETZER CONNECTION?

The year before Jean's death, on the day of the Queen's Coronation, 3rd of June, 1953, the heavens opened and the *Daily Express* gushed, "Despite the rain, defying the rain, singing in the rain, the People surged into London all day yesterday and equitably sat or lay down in its streets."

"BE PROUD" a headline shouted, "OF BRITAIN ON THIS DAY, CORONATION DAY."

Adding: "ALL THIS AND EVEREST TOO! BRITON FIRST ON ROOF OF THE WORLD."

Edmund Percival (shortly to be Sir) Hillary had conquered Mount Everest in the nick of time to anoint the New Elizabethan Coronation. A square-jawed hero for a perfect dawn and a New Jerusalem. The news was broadcast over loudspeakers to the three million onlookers along the 2 ½ mile Coronation route.

But there was another side to post-war Britain. A decadence invisible to the public "singing in the rain."

That is not an aspect of the fifties that emerges in official accounts or broadcasts of that period. No fresh-faced Queen gracing an Ideal

Home Exhibition. Rather a merry-go-round of self-consciously debauched intrigue going right up to the Palace gates, and even involving the Queen's allegedly randy consort, Prince Philip.

This secretive world was exposed in 1963 through the Profumo Scandal.

Centre stage here was the libertine osteopath, Stephen Ward, a habitué of the Londoner club and well known to Dennis Stafford.

Following the Profumo revelations Ward was framed as a pimp and put on trial. Then, with gentlemanly timing, this public school educated man did the decent thing, and swallowed a lethal overdose of Nembutal.[72] Lord Denning's Report then slammed the door shut through which the media and *hoi polloi* had caught a tasty eyeful of an alien and bewitching demimonde.

That glimpse exposed a now long vanished network of socialites, showbiz celebrities, gangsters and bohemians, commingling with naive relish.

———————

A vivid account of this "dark" British fifties is the previously cited, *Honeytrap: the Secret Worlds of Stephen Ward*, 1987, by Anthony Summers and Stephen Dorril.[73]

Honeytrap is about the Profumo Affair. But in telling the background and antecedents to that story, the book suggests an alternative history of the social and cultural elite of fifties Britain.

---

72   Although it has latterly been suggested that Ward was fed the overdose by an MI5 operative, Lee Tracey. See for example, *The Times*, December 1, 2013.
73   Updated and extended in 2013 as *The Secret Worlds of Stephen Ward: Sex, Scandal and Deadly Secrets in the Profumo Affair*.

Stephen Dorril, *Honeytrap*'s co-author, was one of the academics I consulted for this book.[74] He had never heard about Jean Townsend. But hearing my digest of the case immediately asked, "Was she one of Ward's girls?"

Stephen Ward would scour London for attractive young women. Pick them up and groom them. Then farm them out among his rich and famous acquaintances. Ward lived with two of these women, Christine Keeler and Mandy Rice-Davies. It's not clear what his motive in all this was. Probably not money. He was more likely to lend his "girls" a few pounds than take a percentage. And not sex. Some accounts suggest Ward was a voyeur rather than a player. His motive was social ambition. He was a snob and liked to be useful to VIPs.

> Ward's girls were... of a pattern. Most were long-legged and – with the odd exception, like Mandy Rice-Davies – ample-bosomed. They usually came from a lower-middle or working-class background. Ward would teach them how to speak and eat correctly, and even how to improve their sexual technique. Speaking properly was especially important, for Ward wanted his girls to be acceptable in London society. Like Professor Higgins, he taught them how to iron out their working-class accents.

> Girl after girl [came] off the Ward production line, little painted statues fashioned in coffee-bar conversations and late-night drives.[75]

Some of these women went into showbiz. Some married millionaires and aristocrats. Some did all those things. A few came to sticky ends.

---

74 I'd been intrigued by the dedication of *Honeytrap* to the situationist, Guy Debord. I guessed this was from the Huddersfield Polytechnic graduate, Stephen Dorril, rather than his Oxbridge/BBC co-writer, Anthony Summers. I also noticed that Dr Dorril was an expert in the British Intelligence services.

75 *Honeytrap*, op. cit., p32

But Jean Townsend wasn't one of Stephen Ward's girls. She wasn't pretty enough. And too serious – a career woman.

However, it turned out that Jean's closest friend in Ruislip, June Sweetzer, was one of Ward's girls.

When Reg Hargrave began his investigation into the Townsend case one of the first things he did was contact former neighbours from Bempton Drive and South Ruislip. In that way, Reg reconnected with his and Jean's childhood friend and neighbour, June Sweetzer.

They'd lost touch. June had moved to America at the end of the fifties.

She now lived in an affluent hamlet on Long Island's "Gold Coast". [With Mariah Carey as a neighbour.] Her married name was June Keller. She worked as an interior designer. Her husband was an architect.

June kept in contact with her mother. She came to the UK every year to visit her, generally fitting in a visit to the Chelsea Flower Show.

Reg was cautious. He guessed June might be reluctant to talk about the Townsend case. He contacted her as an old friend and neighbour rather than as an investigator. June responded. They met in London. June and her husband stayed with Reg and his wife. June relaxed and opened up.

But, Reg said:

> I always had that feeling that what she told me was restricted. Then, bit by bit she cooled towards me. Especially when I mentioned anything about Jean.

But before she cooled, June had let slip interesting information.

For one thing, she confessed that she and her then "boyfriend" had passed the crime scene on the night of the murder.

She'd never told the police this.

Reg Hargrave:

> June came home on that night. She told me, "We must have driven past there almost at the time she was murdered."
>
> That's the words she used to me.
>
> I said to her, "Were you interviewed by the police?"
>
> And she said she was, but she didn't tell them about that.
>
> And the reason was that she didn't want their enquiries to lead to her boyfriend.
>
> This boy came from a strictly orthodox Jewish family and his family would have disowned him. She was protecting him.

Whether or not that was the reason for June's silence in 1954, it meant the police were unable to interview two potentially key witnesses.

During the initial "honeymoon" period, June Sweetzer also told Reg some of her adventures in fifties London.

For example, that she'd allegedly been a lover of the then little-known actor, Roger Moore. [My email to Sir Roger went unanswered].

259

And that she'd been "a friend" of Stephen Ward. Ward, she said, had even painted her portrait.

Ward used to sketch and paint his "girls," as well as socialites and celebrities. While modest about his work (his sister in law, Kay Ward, told me "he had scant regard" for it, considering it "rather photographic," than "artistic,"[76]) he nevertheless memorialised a cross section of fifties' society, from good-time girls like Christine Keeler and Mandy Rice-Davies (nude reclining with legs up and peek-a-boo fanny), to Prince Philip (fully clothed and firmly seated). Ward didn't make portraits on spec or for strangers. He did it for social cachet, or for friends.

There was no cachet in portraying the unknown June Sweetzer. There must have been a bond.

June Sweetzer's model card, mid-fifties.

Details about June during the fifties are scarce. After art school she worked at a milliners. Then went into modelling. She modelled in London and Paris. A *Daily Mirror* reporter talked to her in 1952. He was intrigued by how quickly models changed costume. June explained, "We become jet propelled the moment the curtain closes behind us. We walk from the salon slowly, so slowly, and then as the curtain closes we suddenly whip off the dress, shoes and hat, and rush like mad to the hangar."

In early 2007 I contacted June Sweetzer by letter. I told her I was looking into the Townsend case. She responded by email. We exchanged further emails.

June commented that:

> Jean was an only child and tended to be quiet and a loner. She was more into drama than playing ball etc. I think Jean was shy over her appearance. Her face was long and slightly crooked, her bottom teeth came over the top teeth, so she hardly ever smiled, giving the feeling of being aloof.[77]

June made no mention of her fashion modelling, of Stephen Ward, or of Roger Moore.

Nor did she repeat that she'd passed the crime scene with her lover, in a car on the night of Jean's murder, and then concealed that from the police.

Rather, she told me she'd passed the crime scene on a bus on the morning after the murder. On that morning she'd bumped into Jean's father at the end of their road.

---

77   Email, 6 July 2007

We walked to the bus stop together and sat together on the bus. As we passed the open field the police had a tent [sic] up. We both commented on what it could be. Little did he know it was his daughter.

June said that when she went for lunch that day she saw the *Evening Standard* headline, "MYSTERY GIRL FOUND STRANGLED IN FIELD. Jet earrings are a clue." She guessed the mystery girl was her friend and "fainted on the spot."

MYSTERY GIRL FOUND STRANGLED IN FIELD
Jet earrings are a clue

But at that time, the victim was unknown. So why did June make such an immediate connection? Had she recognised the description of the earrings? Or seen Jean near the murder scene from her boyfriend's car the previous evening?

I wanted to interview June. But by now her mother had died, and she rarely came to the UK. She was reluctant to be interviewed in the US. We never met. She died in 2011.

After her death I had email contact with June's relatives. They confirmed there was indeed a picture of her by Stephen Ward.

Regarding the portrait it hung over the fireplace during their marriage until June's passing. It is my understanding that [June's husband] took it home with him after the funeral.

Further enquiries about the portrait have gone unanswered.

June Sweetzer told Reg Hargrave her reason for not telling the police she'd been near the crime scene was to protect her "orthodox Jewish" boyfriend.

Who was this boyfriend?

In 1954, June Sweetzer was listed in the electoral register as living with her parents in Bempton Drive.

In the electoral register of 1958 she turns up in Flat 3, 46 Upper Grosvenor Street, W1. She is living there officially with John V Marcus. [At the same time, she has a separate residence listed in the London telephone directory, Flat 32a, 29 Abercorn Place, NW8.]

John Victor Marcus (b. 1928, d. 1986), was the son of Lionel Leopold Marcus, founder of Marcus Estates Limited. John managed the company with his older brother, Ira Morley Marcus. Marcus Estates had extensive holdings all over London, and especially around Mayfair. When it was floated as a public company in 1962, it had a share capital of £1.5 million. [Today, around £23 million.]

John Marcus's and June Sweetzer's home at 46 Upper Grosvenor Street was grand. The building, converted into luxury apartments from the former residence of the socialite Mrs Simon Hartog, was owned by Marcus Estates. In Edwardian London it had been the setting for balls and parties attended by Prince George – later King George VI.

As you'd expect, this Mayfair address was sprinkled with titles. Apartment 12 for example (which John Marcus later moved into) was occupied by Ivan and Lady Edith Foxwell.

Ivan was a movie script writer and producer (*The Colditz Story*, 1955, *The Quiller Memorandum*, 1966, etc). In the 1950s his wife, Lady Edith (this title in her own right), was the aloof face of Pond's Vanishing Cream: "her delightful home forms a perfect background for her exquisite, peaches-and-cream loveliness." Lady Edith enjoyed a career as a socialite and club entrepreneur, "The Queen of Café Society" – and later, in the 1970s, "The Disco Dowager." For years she ran the Embassy club in Mayfair and was vaunted in gossip columns for her "hospitality." In the 1980s she had an affair with Marvin Gaye.

Lady Edith was also inside Princess's Margaret's libertine circle and close to the Duchess of Argyll. The Duchess, like Margaret, patronised the Londoner. Described by Dennis Stafford as "a right pervert" and branded a "nymphomaniac" by an outraged judge during a lurid divorce case, the Duchess had wrecked her standing in polite society. But Lady Edith stood by her.

In those days the friends lived next door to one another, for the Duchess lived at 48, Upper Grosvenor Street. [Number 47 being unoccupied – the numbers ran consecutively].

And on the other side of Number 46 was 45 Upper Grosvenor Street. This was the London home of Viscount Astor and his wife.

———

These coincidences of real estate and Profumo Affair psychogeography extended beyond Upper Grosvenor Street.

The Marcus family was Jewish. It was closely linked by blood and business ties with other Jewish property magnates, including Charles Clore.

Clore was fêted as "the richest man in England." His influence and prestige were enormous. His country residence was a few minutes from the Cliveden estate of the Astors – just over the River Thames – and Clore partied there with the Cliveden Set: the Astors, Stephen Ward, Jack Profumo... Clore's later life was a protracted "libidinous rampage," expressing a "virility and appetite for women [that] unnerved many of his social and business acquaintances."[78]

---

78   Cited in Richard Davenport-Hines, *An English Affair*, 2013, p165.

During the Profumo Scandal, Clore was anonymised as "Charles" in Stephen Ward's trial for pimping. It was alleged that "Charles" had paid for sex with Christine Keeler, and had also slept with Mandy Rice-Davies.

In 1954, the Marcus family and Charles Clore were central to a network of property speculators and asset strippers. The opulent life style of these Jewish entrepreneurs,[79] and their social connections, caused friction – and jealousy – in the City and elsewhere. Some of this was expressed as anti-Semitism.

Perhaps it wouldn't have done to get Scotland Yard connecting these august circles with the Townsend murder.

---

79   There's no evidence that the Marcuses were "orthodox" or even practicing Jews, though ethnicity may have been one factor in June's discretion about her boyfriend.

THE VASCO LAZZOLO CONNECTION?

Vasco Lazzolo: portrait of an artist as a young rake [Photographer unknown].

In 1963, press speculation linked the artist, Vasco Lazzolo, a close friend both of Stephen Ward and the Duke of Edinburgh, to the Jack the Stripper case. Some have wondered whether Jean Townsend's murder was a prequel to this case .

The Jack the Stripper serial killings are sometimes called the Towpath Murders, or the Nude Murders. They happened in the early 1960s. Women's bodies were found scattered around West London, stripped naked, on or near the banks of the Thames. There were at least eight victims. They were all prostitutes. None of the crimes were solved (see Jackie Cliff's take on this, Appendix, below).

Frances Brown, a prostitute, had been one of the Stripper victims. She'd previously testified during the Profumo investigation to having had sadomasochistic sex with Stephen Ward and Lazzolo.

Brown was one of Stephen Ward's "girls." He visited her Shepherd's Bush address for sex and also painted her portrait.

The Epilogue to Summers and Dorril's *Honeytrap* records that:

> Frances Brown, the prostitute, did not live long after testifying that she had been involved in a sex act with Ward and the artist Vasco Lazzolo. In November 1964, Brown's decomposing corpse was found on wasteland in Kensington, apparently strangled. On her forearm was the tattoo 'Helen', over a design of red flowers and green leaves, and the legend 'Mum and Dad'. A dustbin lid had been placed over her face.[80]

A society portraitist and socialite, Lazzolo hobnobbed with movie stars like James Mason and Dawn Addams, and billionaire playboys like King Faisal of Saudi Arabia. Then there was Somerset Maugham, Sam Goldwyn, Peter Ustinov... and Prince Philip, and his cousin, the Marquess of Milford Haven.

---

80   *Honeytrap*, op. cit., p241

Old friends recall Lazzolo as the man who introduced [amyl nitrate] poppers to fifties' London. They remain in awe of his sexual voracity. Whereas his friend and occasional partner on philandering sorties, Stephen Ward, was a casual pimp, Lazzolo was more full-on and better connected. Several sources have testified he provided sexual services to highly placed people, including at least one senior royal.

The son of a merchant sea captain, Lazzolo was raised in Liverpool. He studied architecture and then switched to painting at Liverpool Art College. After that, he began working as a commercial artist.

In 1938 he appeared in court after assaulting a model in his studio. He apologised and offered compensation. "Outside the court, short, stocky Lazzolo joined the model and they shook hands."

In February 1944, he was back in court. This time as complainant. A "Mayfair inventor", Arthur Stambois, had made an "abominable [verbal] attack" on Lazzolo at a tea party. This "went far beyond an attack on a man's moral character." What was more, Stambois had telephoned Lazzolo's then lover, Joy Frankau. [An actress, and the daughter of music hall comedian, Ronald Frankau.] He told her that Lazzolo was "a diseased pervert" and that the police were watching him. To cap it all, Stambois declared Lazzolo was "Leader of the worst set of people in London." He'd even yelled at Lazzolo in the street, and at a club, declaring that the artist was "a pimp and a pervert."

The inventor may have been wonky. But it seems his smoke had fire. In one magazine interview, Lazzolo mentioned that, "in his bachelor days he shared a flat with the Marquess of Milford Haven." An interesting flatmate.

David Michael Mountbatten, 3rd Marquess of Milford Haven, was the first cousin of Prince Philip, and a master-swinger.

The Marquess cut a lurid path through London Society in the forties and fifties, and his intimacy with Prince Philip caused tremors of panic at Buckingham Palace in years to come.

And:

In the mid-fifties, Milford Haven played host at specially organized sex parties in Mayfair. Selected men would be invited to the Marquess' flat at 35-37 Grosvenor Square. The evening would begin with card-playing and then, when the drink had flowed for a good while, girls would be brought in. Then the betting would be on the women, in games with names like 'Chase the Bitch' and 'Find the Lady'. Winners won the obvious prize – intercourse in one of the luxurious bedrooms.[81]

When Philip married Elizabeth in 1947, Milford Haven was best man.

Philip had, indeed, Found The Lady.

As a portraitist, Lazzolo's moment arrived in 1952. The January issue of *Picture Post* featured him sculpting a bronze bust of Prince Philip. He milked the story, complaining that Philip was, "Too good looking. Ugly persons with irregular features come out best in sculpture."

The same year, Lazzolo was commissioned to portray Philip in a painting.

---

81   Summers and Dorril, *Honeytrap*, p26

Clockwise from left.
Lazzolo (right) camps it
up as a French Foreign
Legionnaire. From a contact
sheet of Lazzolo making his
bust of Prince Philip, 1952.

In 1957 Lazzolo married an heiress, Leila Crawford. That set him up for the rest of his life.

Naturally, the couple had an "open marriage."[82]

Clement von Franckenstein[83] was a lodger in Lazzolo's former Chelsea studio, in South Edwardes Square. He remembers the arrangement well. Lazzolo would have every Monday night "off." Franckenstein and Lazzolo's wife would go out while, as Franckenstein put it, the artist, "brought his women [prostitutes] to the studio for a little light 'S&M' and Amyl Nitrate!"[84]

Not that "light."

When Franckenstein returned, there'd be tables and chairs overturned, empty bottles everywhere, discarded whips on the floor, and the fruity stink of poppers.[85]

After the 1970s Lazzolo became a tax exile, first in Jersey, then Malta. He died in Malta in 1984. The Duke of Edinburgh was represented at the London memorial service by his Private Secretary and Treasurer, Brian McGrath.

Lazzolo was a man with secrets. There was his extensive porn collection – hastily detached from his studio during the Profumo investigation.

82　Open marriages were the thing in those circles. Princess Margaret's marriage was famously "open," as was Antony Beauchamp's marriage with Sarah Churchill, as was Jack Profumo's with Valerie Hobson. Stephen Ward proposed one to Christine Keeler, "It would be ideal, an open arrangement with no jealousies or questions." She turned him down.
83　Clement George Freiherr von und zu Franckenstein, born 1944, educated at Eton, movie and TV actor, lives in Hollywood.
84　Email, 28 June 2011
85　Lazzolo had another lodger, an alleged prostitute with links to organised crime, who supplied him with women. This person currently lives with her husband, a convicted cop killer who, in the Dennis Stafford tradition, made himself a millionaire while behind bars, speculating on real estate. I wrote to her well-guarded compound in Kent, but got no reply.

And while frequently mentioned as a shadowy sexual enabler and fixer, he eschewed limelight and was difficult to pin down. He seems to have exploited his foreign name (albeit, innocently subject to misspellings), to cover his tracks. In phone directories and electoral registers Lazzolo (dis)appears throughout the 1950s and 60s at various London addresses as "John Lazlow," "Vasco Lazlow," and "Vaxo Lazzolo."

He equally used different personae for different situations. With the rich and famous he was suave and accommodating. But with a dangerous edge. A bit like the manipulative butler in Joseph Losey's movie *The Servant* (1963). With Frederic Mullally, journalist, writer, and man about town, and especially close to Lazzolo in the 50s, he was a roguish but dependable friend, one of the few who, like Mullally, refused to abandon Stephen Ward in his Profumo Affair troubles. Clement Franckenstein, meanwhile, warmly recalled an avuncular sex fiend with discriminating criminal contacts. A neighbour who knew Lazzolo in Malta recalled an impetuous joker who loved to terrify people with reckless boatmanship accompanied with braying laughter.

The model Jackie Cliff met Lazzolo in his later middle age living on the island of Jersey and knew him as part of a *menage* that involved Jackie and her boyfriend, Ted, and Ted's then wife, a stripper called Lana. This apparently ended with Lana's suicide.

Nowadays a footnote to the Profumo scandal, Lazzolo's reputation has faded, his online representation is minimal, and his painting oeuvre looks in retrospect mediocre and obsequious. But his influence remains tantalizing.

During my research I gained access to a private, and apparently unweeded, archive of Lazzolo material. As well as cuttings and correspondence and financial documents, there were numerous postcards and photographs that testified to his globe-trotting playboy lifestyle and frolicking with the high and mighty.

Left. Lazzolo, mid-1950s, larking with Thursday Clubbers. He's being pulled "reluctantly" towards a wicket by the actor Peter Ustinov. The portrait was taken by Baron. Its inscription: "To that great cricketer and sportsman Vasco, from Baron." Right. Lazzolo stuffs a freshly painted portrait of Prince Philip into his sports car, 1963.

There was no hint in the archive of Lazzolo's legendary porn collection. Except for one disturbing photograph of an unknown naked boy: pretty, blonde and freckle-faced, probably around nine years old. He lies in erotic languor on his side on the floor. He is feminized by squeezing his genitals behind his thighs, suggesting a prepubescent girl. His expression is uncomfortable. He seems defiant and watchful. The whited-out background suggests this image was taken in a studio. The boy's right hand rests on a sliver of broken mirror. The sliver is pointed at the boy, to form a sort of knife. I've shown a crop of that boy (his face) to several people from Lazzolo's circle. No one can identify him. One informant ventured he "looks aristocratic." The writer Anthony Frewin emailed, "There seems to be a knowingness in his eyes in advance of his years, like he knows something about whoever it is taking the photo."

Lazzolo's father – also called Vasco – was a sea captain of Italian descent, who settled in Toxteth, Liverpool. After Captain Lazzolo retired in the 1940s, he moved with his wife Bessie, to 10 Deane Way, Ruislip, just under a mile from Jean Townsend's home.

Lazzolo's sister, Kathleen, lived with them.

THE YOUNGEST SKIPPER OF AN OCEAN LINER.

The Ellerman Lines of Liverpool boast that they employ the youngest captain of a liner sailing out of any British port. The picture shows Captain Vasco E. Lazzolo, of the s.s. "Assiout," one of the company's largest boats in the Mediterranean service.

Left. Lazzolo's father circa 1906, as captain of the SS Assiout, "The youngest skipper of an ocean liner." Right. Captain Lazzolo's retirement house in Ruislip.

Lazzolo's mother died in April 1944. His father died in 1952. Kathleen continued living at the house till 1957.

Lazzolo was close to his family. He regularly motored down to Ruislip in his sports car.

The logical route from the Lazzolo family home to the Western Avenue (the A40) and so back to London, was along Victoria Road.[86] This passed the wasteland where Jean Townsend's body was found.

Lazzolo would have known that wasteland. It was locally notorious and frequented by his favourite sport and prey – prostitutes.

Is there a clue here about the sensitivity of the Townsend case file? Had Lazzolo, maybe with a celebrity friend in the passenger seat, been clocked by the police cruising the area? Not necessarily on the night of the murder, but around that time?

The police kept tabs on prostitution in the area and routinely arrested "toms." They never arrested punters. But they may have had intelligence about regular punters that featured in the Townsend file. Someone of interest. Perhaps someone of far too much interest.

---

86   In 1954, Lazzolo was living at 9 Bradbrook House, Kinnerton Street, SW1.

THE CARLODALATRI
CONNECTION?

Mollie Thurston in her twenties.

Reg Hargrave had a theory about Jean Townsend's murder. He became convinced that a certain Count Carlodalatri had done it. This Italian aristocrat was then assisted by people in high places to flee the country. I was dubious, but thought the story merited investigation. I present the facts here, as I found them, for others to decide about, or follow up.

On 26 January 2002, 78-year-old Mollie Thurston had participated in the BBC Radio 4 programme, *Home Truths*. This was broadcast weekly. It was hosted by the DJ John Peel. The show featured Peel's quirky interviews about unusual topics.

Mollie Thurston claimed on air that she knew who'd killed Jean Townsend.

It was an Italian aristocrat, Count Francisco (Frank) Carlodalatri.

John Peel (introducing the interview):

> [In the 1950s] Mollie [Thurston] was a clerk working with a firm of solicitors. She was also by her own admission an airhead. Albeit, an airhead with a heart of gold. Thus it was that Mollie befriended Frank [Carlodalatri], an odd, slightly sinister chemist who rented a room in Mollie's friend [Elena's] large apartment.

> Mollie: He was half English. And he hated the fact that he was Italian! He spoke beautiful English... His mother was an English aristocrat.

> [He was] a very dour sort of character. Not the usual bubbly Italian type of man. And not particularly attractive to look at. But I suppose I felt sorry for him, and he followed me around like a little dog around this flat... He used to take me out to dinner, most posh dinners, [and he] always came with flowers etc, a lot of hand kissing...

Mollie and Frank found common ground in a love of opera. But she added that Frank was "what my daughter as a toddler would have called an 'oddy bod'."

And, she said, "There was just that one thing," a gut feeling that stopped Mollie inviting Frank "home to Catford."

> I always left him at Charing Cross Station. A kiss on the hand and see me into the train and that was it.

Mollie then told Peel about an alarming experience during one of their dinners.

> Mollie: [Frank said], "Now you're a solicitor... I need to add a codicil to my will. I want to leave an annuity of £1,000 a year to any man who kills a woman."
>
> Peel: Oh my Lord!
>
> Mollie: And I said, "Now come on Frank. I mean, for one thing this man isn't going to be able to collect because this was still a hanging offense."
>
> "Well", he said, "I would just like it there."

Mollie fobbed off Carlodalatri's suggestion. Peel wondered why she hadn't been more alarmed.

Mollie then told Peel about her closest friend, Elena Shayne [born 1909], a dancer and novelist, who sublet a room in her Bayswater apartment to Frank. When Elena realised Mollie was dating Frank, she told her:

> "I'd rather you didn't, because there's something very funny about him. He tends to creep around the flat in the middle of the night, cursing women in all the Italian swear words under the sun, and when he's finished with the Italian he goes into English, and then he goes on to German! And we're getting a little bit cheesed off with him. We're always locking our doors at night and so on. And he's been picked up by the police and taken to Paddington Green police station for questioning. But I don't know what about."

Asked by Peel about the reason for this police interest, Mollie said that Frank had a habit of stalking women on tube trains. He would

THE CARLODALATRI CONNECTION?

often travel aimlessly on the Central Line underground (used by Jean Townsend) especially in the evenings. Here he would sit and ogle mostly women. "All he did was just sit on the train. He never read a paper, never read a book. He just sat there watching."

Mollie then talked about the Townsend case.

> Mollie: The only clue that they had – I don't remember whether it was in her hand or on the ground – was a button from an American serviceman's uniform."
>
> Peel: [Dubiously] Hmm...

Eventually, Frank told Mollie that he had to move back to Italy as his visa was running out. He asked Mollie to go with him. She declined, but accompanied him to Dover.

> That was the last time I saw him. But he used to phone me every Wednesday afternoon in my office. For many months. Then, suddenly, nothing. Nothing at all.

Meanwhile, however, Elena had found a locked wardrobe in Frank's former room. This she broke open. Inside, was an American serviceman's jacket – with one button missing.

> Peel [interrupting]: That is pure whodunit!

Elena contacted the police. They apparently confirmed he'd been questioned for stalking women on trains. But as for connecting him with the Townsend case,

> there was no talk of bringing him back for questioning. They must have thought that even if he did it they didn't have enough on him.

When Reg Hargrave heard about Mollie's claim he thought there might be something in it. Here, at last, was a plausible villain, and Carlodalatri's supposed connections with British aristocracy suggested reasons for secrecy around the case file.

He contacted Mollie through the BBC. They spoke on the phone. Mollie added details. Frank's father, Count Vincenzo Carlodalatri, was an Italian nobleman. His mother was nee Lady Nora Dickinson. Frank had been born in Rome, 12th of April, 1918.

It seemed that Frank had trained as a biochemist but never followed that profession. He had a connection, however, with a family-owned scientific glassware company. But mostly, as a man of means, he didn't work. He had died in Rome, in 1987.

Reg now located a relative, Pablo (aka Paulo) Carlodalatri – Frank's nephew.

Pablo was an architect with a side-line designing catamarans. He split his time between Rome and Buenos Aires. In Buenos Aires, Pablo had a reputation as a professional tango dancer and lyricist.

The Carlodalatri family owned a pied-à-terre in Wimbledon. Reg met Pablo there on the pretext of enquiring about Frank on behalf of Mollie, a former girlfriend. Reg didn't want to alert Pablo to the Townsend case, in case he clammed up.

Pablo claimed that Frank's mother was indeed a titled Englishwoman – "Lady Dickinson."

When told that Frank had run a business in London, Pablo laughed. His uncle was so nutty he couldn't imagine him running a business. Frank, Pablo said, had died after "an accident" in his Rome flat.

Reg went away and brooded. He thought Pablo was concealing something. He decided on a more direct approach. He wrote a letter:

Dear Mr Carlodalatri,

Re: Count Francesco Carlodalatri

You may recall our meeting at Wimbledon in February 2003 when you kindly provided me with certain information concerning the Count.

I mentioned at the time that a lady called Mollie had sought the information. What I did not mention, however, was that I was carrying out a personal investigation into the homicide in September 1954 of a young woman named Jean Townsend. That murder remains unsolved to this day...

Reg explained his connection with Jean and that he was pursuing a private investigation into her murder. He thought Mollie's allegation might have substance. And:

...there is just a possibility that the Police here may be forced into re-opening the Townsend case. In that event, there is also the possibility that they might ask the Italian authorities for permission to exhume the Count's remains to take a DNA specimen. I felt it only fair that your family should be aware of this possibility.

I trust you are keeping well.

Yours sincerely,

Reg Hargrave

———

No surprise this scared Pablo off. The tone and allegations are unsettling. The mention of exhumation and DNA testing must have seemed creepy.

Reg got no response to his letter. Or to subsequent approaches.

I doubted Reg's Carlodalatri angle. It was too pat. Like an Edgar Wallace yarn. The Case of the Crazy Count. The Clue of the Missing Buttons. As John Peel had exclaimed, "pure whodunit!"

In any case there was only Elena Shayne's word for a uniform and those buttons.

Elena was long dead.

Ominously, too, she'd been a novelist.

What was more, the story about missing buttons had migrated out of a different incident.

This was a report that a woman, Dorris Vennall, had been attacked in nearby North Harrow following the Townsend murder.

A man had followed her off a tube train, and as she was nearing home ran up and "grabbed her throat."

She fought him off. In doing so she tore four buttons off his "grey belted raincoat." She gave these to the police.

Her description of the assailant fitted Carlodalatri. Also, this man had previously been staring at her in the tube train, making her feel "uncomfortable." That was the behaviour reported by Elena Shayne.

The press in 1954 linked the Vennall attack to Jean's murder. The buttons then became fixed in folklore. In Elena's account they transformed into "American military buttons."

But I could find no contemporary reference to any buttons at the Townsend crime scene. (Nor did any of the ex-coppers I interviewed about the case know about any buttons.)

In any case, maybe Mollie Thurston was a fantasist…

In April 2007, I flew to Aberdeen to find out.

———————

I found Mollie in hospital, recovering from hypothermia.

A breeder and trainer of dogs, she lived alone with her hounds in an isolated cottage. One winter's evening in 2006 she'd tripped and became trapped under furniture. She couldn't move and began hallucinating.

"I'd see little Japanese men and women sitting and having a picnic. And I'd see a graveyard with bones, moving about. Then I saw a hedgehog sitting on my window sill."

Night came. She began to freeze. The dogs piled on top of her. Their warmth saved her life.

Mollie lived in Dufftown. [Self-styled, "Scotland's Whisky Capital", and boasting seven distilleries.] She'd been raised in Bath as the daughter of a wealthy factory owner. In the thirties she was a "bright young thing," a flapper and drifter. Her life changed in 1940 when she was drafted onto an assembly line in an aircraft factory.

During the war Mollie also discovered professional dancing. She hung out with American soldiers in Bath. They taught her to jive. Her flair for this got her into USO – the American version of ENSA – and she began giving shows to American troops. She found the best dancing teachers were black soldiers, and arranged private lessons.

> Until you jive with a black American you've never done it. Absolute wizard. But of course, you couldn't let any white Americans see you do it.

———————

In 1947, Mollie married,

> A group captain who turned out to be of the other persuasion.
> And I was an innocent little flower, believe me! So that was
> a fiasco.

After obtaining a decree of nullity Mollie moved to London. She secretaried for a firm of London solicitors. She carried on dancing and gave lessons. Meanwhile, she teamed up with another dancer, a friend from Bath, Lucy Thomas, AKA, Elena Shayne, Carlodalatri's landlady.

Elena's large apartment was in a now demolished mansion block in Clydesdale Road, near the Portobello Road. Mollie recalled meeting Frank:

> over lunch at the flat. He was tall and balding, handsome
> in an Italian way. He was well educated and said he was a
> biochemist. He seemed to have plenty of money. He used to
> take me to the Capri and all sorts of beautiful restaurants.
> Always gave me orchids.

Frank claimed he was importing scientific glassware from his family firm in Italy.

But Mollie was surprised when he told her he'd given up his office just off Piccadilly and sacked his receptionist. He then set up at a row of telephone booths by the exit to Charing Cross Underground Station. Frank had a business card printed with the phone number of one of these booths. The card said he was available for business between the hours of midday and 3.00 pm.

> And he used to go and sit there every weekday on a little
> campstool, reading papers and magazines, waiting for
> telephone calls.

Frank told Mollie that his mother was Nora Dickinson, a titled Englishwoman who had "died young." She was the sister of a Viscountess Davidson.

One evening Frank took Mollie to the House of Lords. He introduced her to his aunt, this Viscountess Davidson. Mollie recalled her as dignified and amiable.

Frank frequently told Mollie he was an anglophile. He especially loved English women. He thought them pretty. He had no time for Italian women, whom he denounced as "hairy creatures."

Then, "He asked me to marry him."

Mollie declined. She found him interesting but worried about his eccentricity and macabre streak. Particularly after that business about the codicil to his will offering £1,000 [in today's values, £17,430], to "any man who will kill a woman."

But they continued friends. She found him exotic and generous. He found her attentive and attractive. They may briefly have been lovers – though Mollie denied this.

When Frank eventually left England at the end of 1954, he gave Mollie his cherished Vespa motor scooter – one of the first imported into England.

———————

The crucial link in this story was Elena Shayne and her Clydesdale Road apartment.

Elena [born 1909] used several names. As a girl, she was Lucy Thomas. Elena Shayne was her pen name as a novelist. As a professional ballroom dancer, the dancing partner of her second husband, Paul Barêl [they married in 1947], she used her married name, Elena Barêl.

Top. Paul Barêl and
Mollie Thurston.
Bottom. Elena and
Paul Barêl.

Their original surname had been Barrell. Elena protested that being billed as "The Dancing Barrells" wasn't quite the thing. She convinced Paul to drop an "r" and an "l" and Frenchify the "e": Barêl.

When Elena became pregnant in 1947, Mollie took over as Paul's dancing partner. Mollie also became Paul's lover.

They were free spirits, post-war bohemians. Elena accepted the infidelity. Mollie became godmother to Elena and Paul's daughter, Pauline [born 1948].

———————

Like Mollie, Elena came from a wealthy family in Bath. She was the result of a fling between her posh mother and a socialist firebrand. This quasi-illegitimate status was known in the family and she was ostracised.

Even so, she had a privileged upbringing. As a young woman she went backpacking in France and Spain with her sister. They had adventures and close shaves – hiding their money in a Kraft cheese box.

Some of this went into Elena's novel, *Everyday*, published when she was 26.

The book was risqué for 1935. It tells, for example, how the first-person narrator visits a Paris brothel, and is fascinated by the prostitutes:

> ...they were better than the many girls I know, who do little but waste their own time and their parents' money. These [prostitutes] at least work hard enough for a living, and take a sporting chance of many terrors.

The book describes a "Nigger Dive" in Montmartre:

> The large low room was thronged with various races and a dense smell of smoke and men soon hung on what little air there remained to bless us. The walls were covered with

figures and Cubist designs, executed in yellow-brown and grey. The orchestra was grouped on a small dais before a velvet curtain much the same hue as the performers' faces.

...What music! In it stirred all the fierce feeling of an alien race, echoed in the shuffle of feet and the swaying of jerking squirming bodies packed close together on an inconsiderable piece of parquet squared in by tables. A negress in a backless white satin gown; dark shop girls and their French equivalent; great lusty negroes, clasping their arms all round their full, hot partners, as they moved to the ironic, rocking rhythm of those unseen players. I watched one couple progress round the room; they took ten minutes to pass by our table in an ecstasy of shoving, wriggling, quivering and leaping. The Beguine! What god invented it to be danced in his honour by black man?

There was a smell of sawdust somehow there. I breathed it in with all the other smells. These people Lived.[87]

––––––––

Like Mollie (and like Liz Baron), Elena's first marriage was to a homosexual.

This was during the war, to a naval officer, John Knott [name altered]. They were married by the Bishop of Bath. The Bishop knew the officer's orientation.

Pauline [Elena's daughter]:

He asked if they knew what they were doing. And in fact, the Bishop had a good point because John was so horrified at the

---

87   Elena Shayne, *Everyday*, Jonathan Cape, 1935, p172

thought of having to sleep in the same bed as my mother he rushed back to his ship and spent the night there.

The marriage was annulled. Nevertheless, they remained friends.

After the war, Knott worked in television. Pauline says,

He shared a flat in Maida Vale with his partner and all my childhood I had these two wonderful gay uncles who I adored – and their lovely flat.

Elena then married the conscientious objector, Paul Barrell. With Elena's money they set up a School of Dancing and Health Culture. This advocated "rhythm therapy," vegetarianism, "natural childbirth," and the wearing of loin cloths.

Also on the curriculum was "The therapeutic use of Ballroom and Latin American dancing."

RHYTHM THERAPY

"The instinct of the happy is to Dance"

. . FOR . .

• DINNERS   • DANCES   • MEETINGS
• REUNIONS   • FUNCTIONS

—Book our *CABARET*

✕

PAUL and ELENA BARÈL

Batheaston Cottage Studios, nr. BATH, Somerset

'Phone: Batheaston 8174

All London Enquiries for Dancers' Manipulative and Relaxation treatment etc., c/o 30 Cleveland Square, London, W.2. 'Phone PADdington 4358

RHYTHM THERAPY

• MATERNITY, FUNCTIONAL, and POST-OPERATIVE EXERCISE after Eeman and Stonefield methods, given by Mrs. Elena Barèl, M.M. Diploma, member Physiotherapists' Association. etc.

• NEW RELAXATION and CO-OPERATIVE HEALING (Eeman Method)

• FOOD REFORM

• DANCING used for HEALTH

MOST VALUABLE IN THE STRAIN OF MODERN LIFE

It went bust. The couple split up. Elena was forced to sell her portion of the family treasure and ended up in a caravan with "a £10 note and a child."

Elena's sister rescued her. She set Elena up in Clydesdale Road.

The two-floor apartment had five bedrooms and a view of All Saints Church. Elena decorated the place with her own paintings and the paintings of friends. People came and went. "Everyone had keys."

———————

In the 1950s the mansion block was surrounded by post-war dereliction. It was next to a bomb site and adjacent to prefabs. Next door was a basement brothel.

The bomb site was a place for Elena's daughter, Pauline, to play and make fires and bake potatoes – pincered in embers with metal coat hangers that burned her fingers.

Pauline was entranced by the nearby prefabs with their "white picket fences, marigolds and swings in the garden, and pussycats and things."

Her own mansion block was depressing. It had gaps in the stairs, bare light bulbs, exposed wiring. She recoiled at the "filthy blankets."

> I was very unhappy as a child in that flat. I would come home from school on the bus and have to stand on tip-toes to open the front door. It was dark and the light in the hall was always broken. And you had to go up and there was a half landing and you were afraid someone was going to pounce on you. And then you had to turn your back on a frightening dark stairwell and open your own front door – with my little heart going thud thud thud...

In the front hall was a grandfather clock, the only antique remaining from Elena's former life. She refused to attach it to a wall.

So every time someone had a fit of temper and slammed the door it crashed on its face, and by the time I inherited it, it was useless, broken in 17 places.

Elena had many subtenants. Often eccentric. Elena "always surrounded herself with weird people because they made her feel better."

Some were artists. Carl Davis, the American musician and composer, had the "Piano Room" for a time. Other tenants had the "Green Room" or the "Pink Room" or the "Back Room."

Another artist tenant was a sculptor, Denison Moore. "But he was always having depressions, so he didn't do much sculpting."

Many parties were held, some of them said Pauline, "pretty wild."

As well as being a landlady, Elena worked in the nearby Fraser's Antique shop. She was a soft touch and was always helping people out – therefore generally broke.

But a luxury she insisted on was eating out. Her favoured venue was the local Windmill Café. Holding lunchtime court there was the highlight of her day.

With her peroxided hair and genteel manners and posh accent, Elena struck people as a wealthy eccentric.

Pauline: "She was a born con artist. She lived in a fantasy world."

———————

Elena kept up her writing, covering envelopes, pads, diaries, and notebooks, and hammering her typewriter. However, to her literary agent's exasperation, she refused to have her work edited. She never had another book published.

Then, in 1956,

> She collected me from school one day. I think she'd got herself
> into some sort of difficulties [hinting at an argument with the
> brothel keeper next door, which had involved Elena trying to
> help out one of the girls]. We left everything behind. Except for
> my satchel. But I had my beloved Flanders with me, a strange
> little soft toy horse.

They went to Scotland, where Elena settled in a village and assumed
the name "Rose Kitten." News that she'd been published, and also
wrote poetry, leaked and she became a minor celebrity. *The Scotsman*
interviewed her and declared that "Meeting Mrs Barêl was like
meeting a bird of paradise amongst the pigeons." Pauline: "Needless
to say that didn't go down very well with the pigeons."

Elena died in 1984. Pauline remarked, "She wanted to be a household
name – and it destroyed her."

So it turned out that Elena was possibly a flaky witness. But Mollie
Thurston herself seemed credible. I believed what she told me about
Frank Carlodalatri. But Frank a likely suspect? Had there been a
cover-up motivated by Frank's aristocratic British family? In any case,
who were these aristos?

For clarification I emailed Frank's nephew, the architectural tango
dancer, Pablo. Like Reg, I got no response. I needed a way in – to
bypass Reg's lack of tact.

Then, one day, googling "Carlodalatri," I noticed that Pablo was trying
to sell family heirlooms: antique cameras and a solid silver cutlery set
made by the Austrian silversmith, Herman Ratzersdorfer.

FIFTY PIECES ASSEMBLED DURING 1812-1870. THE BOX WITH THE FLATWARE WAS GIVEN TO ME WHEN I WAS ELEVEN YEARS OLD BY MY ENGLISH SECOND UNCLE, FRANK CARLODALATRI. THE FLATWARE WAS GIVEN TO HIM BY HIS MOTHER.

Left. Pablo Carlodalatri in Tango flow with a glamorous partner in Buenos Aires. Right. Part of the Dickinson-Carlodalatri family treasure.

Masquerading as Herbert Butterworth, from the University of London, a collector of antiques, I emailed Pablo on the pretext of wanting to know more about the heirlooms' provenance. I also asked for details about the Carlodalatri family. Particularly about Frank Carlodalatri's mother, "Lady" Nora Dickinson.

Eventually, Pablo agreed to meet me at Terminal Four, Heathrow Airport, to discuss all this. Pablo was due to change planes there from Rome, en route to Buenos Aires – a regular commute for him.

At this point I revealed my true identity and interest. Pablo was more amused than annoyed. He agreed to meet me at the appointed venue, and be interviewed about his uncle.

Pablo was urbane, with a patina of old money. We chatted for an hour in a café, and then as he browsed in a WH Smith bookshop. He asked what to read on the flight. I recommended Simon Sebag Montefiore's *Young Stalin*. He then asked whether I might be interested in buying a rare edition of Voltaire's *Candide*, which he happened to have in his overcoat pocket, wrapped in brown paper (I'd mentioned that I collected illustrated editions of the book). It was a nice edition but too pricey for me.

Pablo told me that Frank's (and his own) money came from Frank's mother's side, as Frank's father, Vincenzo, had "not a penny." He thought that Nora Dickinson had died young, soon after Frank's birth.

He also confided that after returning to Rome from London, Frank Carlodalatri never worked or travelled again. He hardly went out and spent his time tinkering with antique radio sets, which was his hobby. He kept two large apartments (around 250 square metres each) in Rome. One was for him. The other was solely occupied by his 15 cats, and an elderly female "catkeeper."

Frank was a drinker. Pablo remembered his apartment littered with radio parts and empty bottles. Then, one day, Frank accidentally started a fire in the apartment. He was badly burned. He was moved into a hospital, diagnosed with Parkinson's disease, then lodged in a hostel. He died there of a heart attack in 1987.

After Frank's death his relatives tried to get possession of the cats' apartment. There was a court case. The judges decided for the cats.

Having told me all this, Pablo flew to Argentina.

———

But Pablo was wrong about "Lady Dickinson."

From documentary sources it transpired that Frank's mother, Nora Frances Margaret Dickinson, was the daughter of Major General[88] William Rice Dickinson.

She was born in England in 1877 and died in Rome in April 1952. She'd been wealthy – her father left his family [the equivalent today of] £1,376,400 and Nora collected a quarter of that. Nora in turn left all her jewellery and all the money that was in her Brighton, UK bank account, to her son, Francesco Carlodalatri (described as – at 33 – "a student"[89]), "and the rest of my property to my dear husband, Vincenzo Carlodalatri."

So Nora Carlodalatri was not, after all, titled.

However, through one of her uncles she was linked to a Willoughby Hyett Dickinson (1859-1943), a barrister,[90] QC, liberal MP, leader of the London County Council, and peace activist. In 1930 he was ennobled as the 1st Baron Dickinson. This Baron Dickinson fathered a son, Richard, and two daughters, Desiree and Joan. Mollie had talked about a Countess Davidson, as Frank's aunt. Was one of these daughters the aristocratic connection?

Like many patriotic upper-class women, during World War One Desiree and Joan Dickinson worked for the Red Cross. Desiree served on the front lines in France dealing with horrific casualties and seeing things the family later thought had traumatised her. Her son, John Butterwick, wrote to me these memories pained her so much she never talked about the war. He also recalled that having a "fine contralto voice [she] was much in demand to sing popular songs in the wards in the

---

88   Which was, however, an honorary rank – his last serving rank before retiring was Colonel.
89   When told about this, Pablo emailed: "As for Francesco being a 'student' at 33, yes, it was like so, he was like so. At that time I was ten years old or something like so and Francesco had, some how and not seldom, the attitude of a sixteen years old boy."
90   Willoughby Dickinson was one of executors of William Rice Dickinson's will, so the family tie was close.

evening." Desiree married an Eton housemaster, Cyril Butterwick. The wedding guests counted assorted Lords and Ladies, Hons and Sirs, MPs, Commanders and Dowagers. But Desiree herself had no title.

However, in 1919, her sister Joan married John Colin Campbell Davidson. Davidson was a Tory, a major political wheeler and dealer, Bonar Law's private secretary, and a close friend of Stanley Baldwin. During the twenties he became Tory party chairman.[91] Davidson was also an international businessman with vast family estates in Argentina. John Davidson was ennobled in 1937. From that date, his wife, Joan Davidson, nee Dickinson, became... Viscountess Davidson.

———

When in 1953-4 Frank Carlodalatri visited England, he fell for the upper-middle class, exquisitely English and un-hairy, Mollie Thurston. To impress her, he arranged to visit his not-so-near relative, Baron Dickinson's youngest daughter, Viscountess Davidson.[92]

I can see no reason why a Viscountess would entertain an undistinguished and barmy Italian and his English girlfriend in the House of Lords, other than a family connection.

---

91 This marriage was encouraged by Stanley Baldwin. He advised Joan's mother: "You are giving your child to a man with a mind as clean as the north wind... whatever life's sorrows may bring her, she will never have the bitterest grief a woman can have, in discovering too late those things in a man which make her life hell." Robert Rhodes James, *Memoirs of a Conservative*, 1969, p80
92 I contacted the descendents of Baron Dickinson. They had never heard of any Count Carlodalatri. Nor of Nora Dickinson. Nor of a family connection with Rome. Desiree Dickinson's unpublished (1980) family memoir recorded visiting Rome as a teenager. She didn't enjoy it. "The sad thing is that because of that grim fortnight I have never been able to revisit Rome and always had some alternative when [her husband] suggested going there."

So was this the missing link in a Townsend case "conspiracy"?

By the mid-1950s, Baron Dickinson's daughters were established upper crusters. Joan Davidson was Tory MP for Hemel Hempstead from 1937 to 1959. During WW2, "she undertook important and highly confidential work as a member of the Select Committee on National Expenditure – which sometimes came into conflict with Churchill." After the war, she was for several years the only female Conservative MP. In 1952, she was made a Dame of the British Empire. She went on to become Baroness Northchurch, a title she held in her own right. She died aged 91, in 1985.[93]

As far as I could make out the Dickinson clan were admirable. Like most families, they had secrets. Baron Dickinson's biographer commented that his diaries were censored by his family after he died.[94] Desiree's son, John Butterwick, wrote me that in her family memoir [which he allowed me to read] Desiree "sadly... left out... anything

---

93   As for Desiree, when her husband Cyril retired from Eton he become a director of Sotheby's, "concentrating on old silver." In 1966, Desiree was given an OBE for local community work. She took Cyril to Buckingham Palace for the ceremony. After she'd left her coat in the cloakroom she noticed Cyril, "half way up the stairs" to a viewing area. He waved. She entered a waiting room. Her name was called out unexpectedly. There had been an accident. In a corridor she saw Cyril, "being carried into a nearby bedroom..."
"[I]realised immediately he had died."
Desiree died twenty years later, aged 93.
94   Hope Costley-White, *Willoughby Hyett Dickinson: a Memoir*, 1956

remotely intimate."[95] But there was no hint that the family might collude in thwarting a murder investigation.

In short, it seemed unlikely that in order to save the Dickinson name from association with a sex crime, Viscountess Davidson, then in Churchill's cabinet, leant on the Met Police or MI5 to enable a murderous Italian Count – a somewhat detached relative – to scarper back to Rome...

———————

In any case, was Frank Carlodalatri a plausible murderer?

He seemed more comical than sinister. Mollie felt the same. That's why she stuck with him.

Then there was Brenda Thomson's report of an argument between two men. It's difficult to imagine someone as dysfunctional as Frank Carlodalatri colluding with another "person unknown" to commit murder.

Also, the logistics were against it. If he'd strangled Jean Townsend that September night, how did he get back to Bayswater from South Ruislip after the last train?

Mollie said he didn't own a car. So on his Vespa? Vespas were conspicuous and noisy in 1954.

Sometimes, you just have to laugh.

---

95   Desiree Butterwick, *A Happy Life* (unpublished ts), May, 1980

THE KROGERS OF CRANLEY DRIVE

Of the many rumours circulating around Jean Townsend's murder, the Kroger connection is the most outlandish. It casts Jean as the innocent victim of a spy drama. I've sketched it here because it gives some insight into the Cold War paranoia prevailing in our cosy suburb around that time.

In late 1954 a married couple were scouting South Ruislip for accommodation. They eventually took out a mortgage on a bungalow, 45 Cranley Drive.

They said they were Americans, Peter and Helen Kroger. But their real names were Morris and Lona Cohen. They were Soviet spies.

Peter Kroger had fought as a volunteer in the Spanish civil war. In 1941 he married Helen. After the war he worked in New York as a teacher. Then, in June 1950, he resigned his post. He and his wife then closed their bank accounts and cashed in their savings bonds. And disappeared for four years.

The next record of the pair was in London in 1954. They now had New Zealand passports.

Peter set up as an antiquarian bookseller. His shop was opposite Saint Clement Dane's church in the Strand.

In South Ruislip, the Krogers were known as cosmopolitan and convivial.

> Helen Kroger: "Everyone in the street liked me. All the children used to come and I'd give them a piece of candy. They all loved me."

The Krogers became especially friendly with a family across the road, the Searches. The daughter of this family, Gay Search, is nowadays a TV producer. She remembers the Krogers:

> My mum was very much in awe of Peter. And though she didn't want to disturb him, especially when he was working, she always loved to talk with him about art. And I remember her saying that in these conversations about painting he was describing things with his hands and she noticed his hands were very badly scarred. And it was apparently the Spanish civil war, because he fought in the International Brigade.

Gay Search was especially taken with Helen Kroger: "a rebellious adult," "wild and happy."

> Helen was the sort of creature we had never seen before. She wore trousers, which women didn't have in those days. She was loud, boisterous, very masculine.

———

Peter Kroger's book business did well. His colleagues admired him. One was Oswald Snelling. He enthused about visiting 45 Cranley Drive.

> Here you received good food, good wine, and the most wonderful hospitality. If, as you ate and drank, you also wondered how a naive bookseller like Peter Kroger could maintain such an establishment, unless he had private means

– well, you were entitled to. The man certainly knew books, and literature and history, too – far more than most of us – but the craft of bookselling needs much more than that.[96]

Meanwhile, what became known as the Portland Spy Ring, was in business.

Two British civil servants, Harry Houghton and his mistress Ethel "Bunty" Gee, stationed at the Portland naval base, had taken to photographing secret documents. They then passed the filmstrips to a KGB colonel masquerading under the name Gordon Lonsdale.

Every so often Lonsdale would motor down to South Ruislip. He would park his car in a street behind the Krogers' bungalow and walk up an alley to the back entrance. A local boy remembered the "strange American" "who used to park his Buick/Oldsmobile at the back of the bungalows in the next road." When the boy queried the "American" about this arrangement, he was given money to "guard" the car.[97]

The Krogers' job was to develop the Portland filmstrips and turn them into microdot images. These images were so tiny they could be hidden under stamps. They were then concealed under stamps stuck on parcels of books. As a bookseller, Peter Kroger sent these parcels abroad to "clients."

As their plot progressed the Krogers made home improvements. They expanded the cellar and lined it with concrete. They put wheels on the fridge so it was easy to move. The fridge was then placed over a trapdoor to the cellar. The cellar was full of equipment used to communicate with Moscow.

---

96   Oswald Snelling, *Rare Books and Rarer People*, 1982.
97   http://www.ruislip.co.uk/krogers-ruislip.html

———————

But the British secret service was on to them. MI5 began watching Harry Houghton, his mistress, and Gordon Lonsdale. They followed Lonsdale down to South Ruislip, and noticed where he went.

Now they wanted to spy on the Krogers. They approached Gay Search's parents. Without telling them what it was about they arranged to keep a 24-hour watch on the Krogers from a window in the Searches' house.

Gay Search and her brother were sworn to secrecy. They should not say anything at all to anyone about the strange people who came and went in their house.

The British agents watched the Krogers from the Searches' house for two months. Things got tense. Especially for Gay's mother.

Most days she dropped in on Helen Kroger, chatted and took tea. Then she'd go home. Here she made tea for the secret agents. A neighbour noticed, "that it was strange that the Searches had 'friends' staying for tea, but that the 'friends' were eating in the kitchen, and the rest of the Search family were eating [in the dining room]".

———————

When the police eventually arrested the Krogers, South Ruislip was electrified.

Gay Search said,

> I burst into tears and I ran upstairs and I collected everything [Helen Kroger] had ever given me. All the jewelry and scarves and things and I threw them in the dustbin. I just felt destroyed. It was the bombshell of my life.

The press talked about the Krogers' "House of Secrets." At the trial the prosecutor said:

> This innocent looking suburban house with no external wireless aerial, not even a television aerial, in which the Krogers had lived... [was] quite clearly a high-powered wireless station capable of transmitting to and receiving direct from Moscow, full of photographic equipment, all the equipment required for making and reading microdots and also for these code pads for coding messages... also possibly, in view of the money that was found there, the bank of a spy ring.

The jury got a guided tour of the bungalow. They saw hollowed bookends containing thousands of dollars, and a torch with a "false battery" containing a KGB expense sheet.

RONSON RONDELIGHT

For Father's desk! This good-looking lighter is specially balanced — can't be upset. One fuelling lasts months. As shown, 63/-. Other finishes from 52/6.

Santa sent a lucky lady

three flowers

FACE POWDER · LIPSTICK · ROUGE

Santa sent her beauty

Be a popular Father Christmas this season. Give her one of the gay, exciting Three Flowers Christmas beauty packs.

RICHARD HUDNUT · NEW YORK · LONDON · PARIS

In the Krogers' lounge was a Ronson cigarette lighter with a hidden compartment, and in the bathroom a tin of Three Flowers talcum powder concealing a microdot reader.

A local mystery was now solved. For some time, neighbours had been puzzled by interference on their TV sets. One recalls:

> I used to live in Ladygate Lane with my parents and like most people had a TV. ...we were experiencing very bad reception when the picture would completely break up. This occurred at regular intervals during the day. Of course we complained to the television repair man about this (a shop next to Ruislip Manor tube). He came round on a number of occasions but was unable to fix it. Later out of the blue two men in civilian dress knocked at the door saying they were from the GPO and asked more about the problem. My parents explained that it happened during certain times of the day. Having been told this they left and said they would return and look at the TV set when it was expected for the picture to break up. They duly returned and saw what was happening to our programmes. They both conferred with each shaking and nodding their heads. They never touched the TV set! They eventually left and my mother thought they did not "look like TV repair men, they spoke much too nice." About two weeks later the Krogers were arrested. From then on we had a perfect picture!![98]

The Krogers were sentenced to 20 years. But in 1969 they were released under a spy swap arrangement with Russia. Once in Moscow, they were awarded the Order of the Red Banner and the Order of Friendship of Nations and made Heroes of the Russian Federation.

The Krogers toast their freedom on the plane to Moscow.

Many people who met the Krogers commented how kind and thoughtful they were. Oswald Snelling wrote in his autobiography:

> Don't try to tell me [it] was all a front, that this very pleasant pair really cared not one jot about any of us who had made them our friends. They deceived us all, I know, but I believe they truly loved their fellow men, far more than most of us. They proved it time and again in both tangible and intangible ways. They did good by stealth, but they never 'blushed to find it fame'.

Someone else who fell under the Kroger spell was Dennis Stafford. The gangster befriended Peter Kroger in jail. After Kroger was released he sent Stafford a postcard from behind the Iron Curtain.

> Special Branch spent a fortnight examining it and then came to me in my cell and demanded to know if there were any secret messages of subversion. I wasn't very helpful, I'm afraid. I told them I wouldn't tell them anything even if he was going to blow up the Queen. Why should I, after what British justice had done to me?

Conspiratorial rumours have linked this Kroger story to the Townsend case. I found no sensible connection, but to give the rumours their due:

A key factor here is the time-line. Were Soviet spies already in South Ruislip in 1954? The allure of the area was the USAF Base, built in 1949 (not to mention the military aerodrome in nearby Northolt). As the American intelligence HQ for Europe, the airwaves would have bristled with interesting messages. After the KGB officer Gordon Lonsdale reconnoitred the area, he cited the "web of radio communications" as a draw, because, "I could think of no better place [to conceal radio transmissions to and from Moscow]. Detection would be almost impossible."[99]

45 Cranley Drive was an unassuming but strategic HQ. It was triangulated between the military Base, Northolt Aerodrome – and the Victoria Road crime scene wasteland – frequented by disreputable or furtive characters and frisky US servicemen on temporary French leave… A choice habitat for espionage?

The Portland spy ring was active from at least 1953. The Krogers moved into Cranley Gardens in "late 1954." They presumably would have been reconnoitering South Ruislip before then, and may have contacted other agents in the area.

So was Jean Townsend bumped off because she stumbled on something sensitive? That's some stretch! A more plausible connection might be

---

99 Gordon Lonsdale, *Spy. Twenty years in Soviet Secret Service. The Memoirs of Gordon Lonsdale*, 1965, p118

that information in the Townsend case file relates to national security and may touch on the early days of the Portland spy ring. It was said that what MI5 uncovered was the tip of an espionage iceberg. But other than that...

PART THREE:

Finding the Fifties: Snapshots

> "The formation of a concealing memory depends on the forgetting of other important impressions."

> — Sigmund Freud, *The Psychopathology of Everyday Life*, 1901

Trying to solve a murder mystery was one reason for researching the Townsend case.

But another mystery I wanted to unravel was the culture that created the fifties – the decade that Jean Townsend represented, that formed my generation.

In that way, this true crime foray was a kind of wild card methodology, a way of throwing things in the air to see how they might land – re-mapping the period through unforeseen sequences and lacunae, micro-events, historical "nonentities," erasures and ambiguities, and loose ends. In other words, a way of bracketing the usual suspects: the incestuous roundup of markers, celebs and events, clichés from Suez to Tommy Steele to John Osborne…

Or what Freud called, "screen memories."

TWO GIRLS

"Did you ever think about the fact that all the fabrics we wore in the fifties were stiff?" my friend Ronnie once asked me. I hadn't, but the minute she said it I thought: faille, shantung, felt, taffeta, pique. Nothing clung, or fell, or draped – everything was crisp.

Forties clothes were truly sexy – those swingy little dresses in soft, flowered rayon prints with shoulder pads had a jaunty, competent femininity. Fifties clothes were like armour. Our clothes expressed all the contradictions of our roles. Our ridiculously starched skirts and hobbling sheaths were a caricature of femininity. Our cinched waists and aggressively pointed breasts advertised our availability at the same time they warned of our impregnability.

In the daytime we wore tight, revealing sweaters, but they were topped by mincing little Peter Pan collars and perky scarves that seemed to say, "Who, me? Why, I'm just a little girl!" At night our shoulders were naked, our breasts half-bare, the lower half of our bodies hidden in layers of tulle. Underneath it all, our flesh, like our volatile sexuality, was "contained" by boned girdles and Merry Widows, in an era when "containment" was a political as well as a social obsession.

— Brett Harvey, *The Fifties: A Women's Oral History*, 2002

Jackie Cliff on Jean Townsend:

> ...we never spoke to each other. She'd see me, and I was a bit jealous of her really and I think she might have been a bit jealous of me, you know. The usual sort of thing: two girls...

Two girls.

What separated them?

First of all, looks.

Jackie was an effortless beauty. Her pictures seduce from every angle in any light. She hardly bothered with make-up – jiving up a sweat in the 100 Club in a baggy sweater with "Jackie" stitched on the back. No wonder Joan Collins gave her the evil eye.

Jean was plainer, but a perfect fashion plate even on a suburban train after an evening out. Plastered with that fifties layering of makeup commented on by the witness Patricia Kemp: "I noticed her because she was heavily made up," and the station porter that night: "painted eyebrows and a well made up face."

Separated by looks and style, but also by aspiration.

In the fifties a forensic marker for aspiration was spoken accent.

Accents then, summoned a now-redundant etiquette of intonation, elocution, affectation. Nowadays, it seems comical – the strangulated whinny of BBC announcers and mock posh cadences of landladies or sergeant majors. But in those days not to have a proper accent – one befitting your station – or prospects – was cultural suicide and social death.

Jean Townsend spoke posh. But Bempton Drive, South Ruislip, posh. Not the insolent camp, the West End swish of her boss, Michael Whittaker – his mastery of cut-glass drawl. Jean's dutiful Queen's English rather announced deference and willingness to please. A subservience to Whittaker's classy "class." An eagerness to "fit in" and "get on."

Whittaker was high camp. And camp then, as now, was a strategy – a play for domination. Camping is how speakers tell us how easy and familiar they are with the codes. Camp says: I have flair, I have mastery, I own this culture... As I glide and soar and dip and slip – in and out with nothing the slightest bit clumsy or vulgar as effort... The swing and swagger of cultural capital.

That is how the upper classes represent themselves as floating beyond social gravity. And how homosexuals learn to shuffle and fool around with signs and meanings like a reckless game of cards – accounting for their remarkable creativity.

For a dude like Michael Whittaker, Jackie Cliff's suburban Middlesex patois would have jarred as dull and vulgar. While perfect for the 100 Club and backstage at Murray's Cabaret Club, Jackie's under-elocuted tones would have seemed amiss in the Londoner. More native to the Londoner crowd's pretensions (brass name plate, cut glass decanters, grand piano, gangster overlord, queer manager...) were Lady Nora Royce Docker's arriviste bray, Jack Profumo's landed languor, or the RADA tinkle of his actress wife, (Babette) Valerie Louise Hobson.

1954 cosmetics ads – British and French.

The "two girls" equally represented opposed versions of fifties' womanhood.

Many popular images of 1950s women have a hermetic allure – crudely and blatantly fetishistic.

The philosopher Jean Baudrillard thought that one appeal of fetishism is its apparent magical integrity. Fetishism seems to conjure a secret "which radically excludes us in the name of its internal logic or perfection: a mathematical formula, a paranoiac system, a concrete jungle, a useless object, or, again, a smooth body, without orifices, doubled and redoubled by a mirror, devoted to perverse autosatisfaction."[100]

Fifties exemplars of womanliness often have that same internal logic, a perfection that excludes. They radiate an improbable blend of wholesome and erotic – radiant yet enigmatic sex appeal – slender necks and engaging lipstick pouts with haughty yet inviting gazes under arched eyebrows.

But however alluring, they are distant. Seductive but remote.

Seductive *because* remote.

That is because these images were mostly fashioned by gay men. They are "queer" images. They offer a male homosexual version of femaleness and femininity.

The photographer David Bailey:

> The whole thing of fashion [in the fifties] was sort of upper middle class, especially in Europe. Upper middle class gay men really ran the business. A bit less so in New York. In a funny way it was a kind of gay Mafia. In fact, [John] French [who Bailey was apprenticed to] sort of fell in love with me.

---

100 Jean Baudrillard, *For a Critique of the Political Economy of the Sign*, 1981, p67

> And, you know, I'm not against someone making a pass – I
> was rather flattered – but that was as far as it was gonna go.[101]

The photographer Terence Donovan also worked as French's assistant in the fifties. He reckoned him, "the most important fashion photographer in this country at the time, an extraordinary man. Couldn't actually open the lid of his camera. He was a marvellous sort of queen…" Adding, "At that stage in England all fashion photographers were gay." According to Donovan, in the fifties heterosexual fashion photographers were "unheard of apart from Norman Parkinson."[102]

Working with these gay photographers were gay designers, editors and stylists, and model agents. These men set the agenda for fashionability.

A prime example was Michael Whittaker ("Mr Fashion"): theatrical dandy, movie actor, designer of stage and movie costumes and bespoke garments for female stars, creator of fashion parades, active in promoting UK fashion worldwide, fashion commentator in the press and on TV, and from the mid-1950s proprietor of the leading model agency in London.

The gay agenda of men like Whittaker dominated the fashion scene. They knew what looked right and they set the tone and created the rules. Heterosexuals like Norman Parkinson had to fit with their remit, making female objects of desire demure, ambiguous or nebulous. Even cheesecake merchants like Walter Bird. Bird relished Jackie Cliff's womanly curves, but turned her (as she said) into "a girl who was like a nymph. A fairy or something."

---

101 http://pdngallery.com/legends/bailey/interview03.shtml <accessed 01.08.2014>

102 Michael Gross, *Model. The Ugly Business of Beautiful Women*, 1995, p165

The photographer, Juergen Teller, has commented:

> [Much fashion photography is about] gay people finding women sexy... which is sort of not sexy at all, at least to a heterosexual man... [The model is] so retouched, so airbrushed, without any human response at all, and, well, you don't really want to fuck a doll.[103]

Teller tells it in a nutshell: fashion (and commercial) images of fifties' women were crafted to make them look unfuckable. They look like dolls: fascinatingly, spookily, alien.

The gold standard for this unfuckability was set by Cecil Beaton's mid-1950s portraits of Queen Elizabeth II.

In his diaries, Beaton enthused about the Queen:

> serene, magnetic, and at the same time meltingly sympathetic... the dazzlingly fresh complexion, the clear regard from the glass-blue eyes, and the gentle, all pervading sweetness of her smile.

In Her Majesty's wake came all those "meltingly sympathetic" and clear-eyed ladies in page after page of ads for hosiery, electrified kitchens, and the Parisian New Look.

Trim, sedate, and forgiving.

That was essentially Jean Townsend's look.

As Liz Baron put it, Jean looked like "that type of woman that used to come to these [gay] clubs and would sit there and would know everybody, and they were almost in a perverse way revered by the gays."

---

103 Juergen Teller http://nymag.com/fashion/08/fall/49257/<Accessed 01/08/2014>

But there was another look – style-kit – available in those days to women. An aggressively hetero look that acted as a subversive under-the-counter style edging into cheesecake and soft porn. It was mainstreamed through Jayne Mansfield, Sabrina, Diana Dors, Jane Russell, and continental stars like Sophia Loren and Brigitte Bardot. Naughty verging on dangerous. Cleavage and thighs to die for.

That was Jackie Cliff's professional look.

Two types of fifties' womanhood: vertical and horizontal. Left. Barbara Goalen, photographer, John French, 1951-2. Right. Pam Green in Peeping Tom, *1960.*

Two celebrated fifties' models summed up the difference between these looks.

First, Barbara Goalen – the most successful and written-about fashion model of that decade.

Goalen was all haute couture and gracious put-downs. Wasp-waisted and delicate, an English rose, poised and electric: she was Mayfair and *Vogue*. She stood for what Jean Townsend aspired to. [Jean worked with her at several fashion shows with Michael Whittaker, who counted Goalen a friend.]

Then, another sort of model: Pamela (Pam) Green.[104]

Pam was Soho and *Men Only*. Saucy and available: a slut in scanties.

While Barbara Goalen's figure, 33-18-31, murmured, "good breeding," Pam Green's 37-23-36 bragged, "good breeder!"

Jackie Cliff knew Pam Green professionally: "She was like the Jordan of the day, and she had the biggest thingies, they'd come right out, and a tiny little waist. And the men used to think it was wonderful – they used to say, 'Pamela Green!'"[105]

Goalen was well known to the author, Frederic Mullally. She moved in his Mayfair circles.

When I mentioned her he sat up and his eyes sparkled. "The minute she walked in a room... That woman she had such... such fucking style!"

---

104 Pam Green's archive is extensive and excellently preserved by Yahya El-Droubie, a writer and designer who befriended Pam in her later years – she died in 2010. Yahya gave me complete access and allowed me to quote from Pam Green's unpublished autobiography. I also tracked Barbara Goalen's private archive to the basement of her son, Rupert's, house. However, Rupert balked at the last moment and insisted on censoring "personal" material. This bowdlerised Goalen archive is now in the V&A Museum.
105 Like Jackie, Pam Green had started modelling while a fashion student at art college.

Another witness to the decade, the journalist Douglas Sutherland, swooned in print:

> Barbara [Goalen], perhaps more than anyone else I have ever met, had that natural grace of movement which is almost animal. It was impossible for her to come into a room, sit in a chair or, I truly believe, ride a bicycle – surely the most inelegant of all female actions – without a distinctive elegance and poise. That she was to become the leading model of her time was as inevitable as night following day...[106]

Goalen's career ended in 1954 when she married an Old Etonian millionaire stockbroker called Nigel. Nigel objected to chaps ogling his wife. Goalen gave up working to swank around Mayfair and Malta doing what rich people call charity work.

In the same year that she and Nigel exchanged vows, Goalen made headlines refusing to model lingerie.

"It simply isn't done, you know."

On the other side of the divide, 1954 was when Pam Green began touting sets of postcards of herself around Soho newsagents.

Lingerie was the *most* she ever wore. Sometimes too, it was dishevelled, or artfully torn. Sometimes, Pam was starkers.

The pictures were by her then lover, Harrison Marks. Pam helped print and glaze the postcards and packed them in cellophane bags and generally did the business. In 1955, her first book came out, *Pamela: A Portrait in 58 Studies*.

---

106   Douglas Sutherland, *Portrait of a Decade: London Life 1945-55*, pp110-111

With Harrison Marks, Pam then launched *Kamera*, a soft porn mag. It cost half a crown. It was a sell-out. In 1959 came a movie, part filmed at the Spielplatz nudist camp. When the movie opened at the Cameo Moulin in Great Windmill Street the queue was so long police had to cordon the street off. Pam remembered, "I cut the tape, and was given a bouquet of flowers shaped like a windmill." The movie was a hit. The debut of the UK soft porn movie industry.

A sub-genre of the Pam Green look was the curvy corpse.

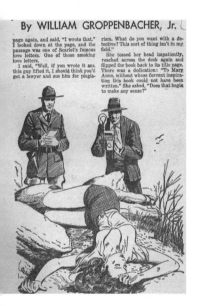 

Left. Private Detective, *1951. Right.* Detective Tales, *1948.*

Left. Mystery Magazine, *1954. Right. The real thing: Betty James, murdered by Raymond Barker in 1953.*[107]

While Barbara Goalen wouldn't have been seen dead as a corpse, Pam Green was a dead ringer for the role. The film director Michael Powell thought so. He cast Pam in his classic of murderous voyeurism, *Peeping Tom*, 1960. [Her only appearance in a mainstream movie.]

Green plays a busty beauty being photographed in a soft porn photo session – wearing lingerie selected by Powell from Green's extensive wardrobe.

Then her character is murdered by the deranged serial killer.

Pam Green:

> Having seen all the Hammer Horrors, where there was Eastman Blood all over the shop; this story was different. I

---

107 TNA: CRIM 1/2390

had been secretly hoping that my end would be bloody, but I was told that after my last line, the camera would cut away to a shot of a policeman looking down at me with the brilliant dialogue, "She's dead"...

Not even one drop of blood would come my way.

In the movie, Pam's last words to the killer as she sinks onto a bed in a "revealing" shortie negligee are:

"Are you safe to be alone with?"

A long pause as she lies against the pillows.

"It might be more fun if you weren't".

We don't get to see Pam's corpse. But we deduce it as an afterglow of her previous sensuality.

There's much talk about Powell's cult movie: "male gazes" and all that jazz. Pam's comments in an unpublished memoir are blunter:

On arrival at the studio... I found the red corselet and the shortie top had been put out for me in my dressing room... I was to put them on for a special shot that Powell wanted... I stood on the set and Powell looking through the back of the camera, told Otto to light me. Four Brute arcs [9000-Watt cinema lights] were arranged to light me, still looking through the back of the camera, Powell asked for more light, the image was not bright enough. Otto took a reading on his meter, the movie camera was in position; Powell was not satisfied, still more light.

Then he asked for the Fresnal lens to be taken off one of the Brutes, Otto protested, "No Michael, it is too dangerous." Powell took no notice and had the glass taken off another

Brute, and yet another. Bill, checking my make-up, warned me, "Don't look at the lights Pam," and then turning to Powell, "for Christ's sake, you'll blind her."

I felt my skin beginning to burn, red patches appeared on my arms and shoulders. I tried not to look at the blaze of light coming from the four naked Brutes burning in my face.

Powell watched my discomfort with a slight smile on his face. Eventually the shot was over and the Arcs quickly killed. Bill came hurrying over to me; first he took off the false eyelashes, then in the make-up room cleaned my face of all make-up. "That shot should never have been permitted." I didn't know that a bare Arc could blind; I had felt it more of a trial of strength between Powell and me...

Next morning when the alarm clock went I knew. I tried to open my eyes and found I couldn't: they were badly swollen. I was helped down to the waiting car by a shocked driver when he saw my face. Bill, awaiting me in Make-Up looked grim, by now I could just see out of tiny slits. Seizing my arm he guided me onto the set. Powell was there; Bill dragged me up to him. "Look at her face, will you." Powell turned, glanced at me and said, "Make sure that she is ready and made up for 9 am."

"I can't put make-up on her as she is." Powell shrugged his shoulders, "That is your problem, just see that she is on the set by 9," and walked away.[108]

———————

Barbara Goalan, too, was punished for being beautiful. But through the post, rather than on set.

108   Pamela Green, *Never Knowingly Overdressed*, nd [Unpublished autobiography]

In interviews Goalen came over bland. Everything in her world was just fine and everyone was just lovely.

Except for one interview, where her guard drops:

> Q: Did you make any enemies?

> BG: Does one ever know? I hope not. One doesn't know. I didn't find anyone vicious. The only vicious people I have ever come across are the ones who write one vicious letters. I think they are, absolutely, the scum of the earth. I don't see how people can write to people they have never met, and whom they can never see, and say the terrible things they do and pretend they know you so well.

> They write things which are completely and utterly untrue. It is horrifying. These people are really beastly. I think they must know what they are doing, too. And they're such cowards; they always put false addresses or something. I wrote to one address and it turned out to be a pub, needless to say. How I should have liked to have met that woman! I wish you would put something, because I feel strongly about this. I think they cause such a lot of un-happiness. One knows they are cranks and one should feel sorry for them, but if one's at all sensitive, they are just terrible.

> It is so terrible to feel so strongly about someone you have never even met. This letter I had was so full of utter, utter hatred. Quite extraordinary.[109]

---

[109] "Talking Freely, Barbara Goalen interviewed by Tom Greenwell", *The Bed Post. A miscellany of The Yorkshire Post*, edited by Kenneth Young, 1962

WASTELAND

Jean Townsend's body being discovered on wasteland resonated in 1954. The location had exotic cachet. Wastelands, usually associated with bombsites, were an institution, a state of mind. They were all over post-war Britain. Foreigners were astonished at their persistence into peacetime.

In 1953 the *Daily Mirror* reported that such areas had become bizarre tourist attractions where "foreign visitors... flock in coach loads." It claimed there were at least 150,000 of these "desolate acres, rotten with decay and disease." It was rumoured that criminals hid out there. Hooligans supposedly formed "bomb site gangs" to waylay passers-by.

Wastelands spelt dread and enchantment. Reality suspended. Anything might happen.

James Donald, trying to recall his special "Inner London" of that period, wrote that:

> What flashed up was an image of the bomb sites that had littered the London landscapes of my 1950s childhood...

> Although part of a familiar and mundane landscape, the accidental memorials, like all ruins, had something of the sacred about them. Maybe that is why they signified, for me, less mass destruction and loss, than mystery and possibility...

In 1954, South Ruislip was criss-crossed with wasteland areas: bombsites or stray fields between newly built estates. Lovers loitered there. Kids played there. Families picnicked there. I have these family snaps taken a few months before Jean Townsend's killing about a hundred yards from where her body was found. They were taken by my "Auntie" Iris. The occasion was a surprise picnic. Mum and Iris had bunked off work and stolen me from school. It was summer and the place was bright with daisies and buttercups. For years after the murder I was conscious as I traversed this area by foot or bike, of doing something slightly irreverent and weird – of animating and commemorating the ground and its pseudo wildness, as a metaphor for Jean Townsend's body.

fantasies about what lurked there, and about the adventures that could happen there... strange enchantment...[110]

---

110   In *The Cambridge companion to the Literature of London,* (Ed) Lawrence Manley, 2011

Philip Oakes reminisced:

> On Sunday mornings we took long walks through the empty streets of the City, pausing by bomb sites to stare through the charred sockets of windows and trace the configuration of vanished offices by the veining of flues and the bleached and bold patterns of wallpaper, stamped by lost filing cabinets and calendars turned to tinder.[111]

Rose Macaulay's 1953 classic, *Pleasure of Ruins*, mused on "the startled ecstasy," the "melancholy splendour" of "wrecked cities." The text's origin was the London Blitz. Macaulay's London apartment was bombed in 1941 while she was away. "I came up last night... to find Lux House no more – bombed and burned out of existence, and nothing saved. I am bookless, homeless, sans everything but my eyes to weep with..." Macaulay also explored the eeriness of a wasteland London in her 1950 novel, *The World My Wilderness*. Here, the bombed-out city is a fairy-tale dystopia overrun by spivs, outcasts and revolutionaries.

In September 1954, *Men Only* ran a piece, "Britain's Bombed Sites Today. How Our Scars Have Blossomed."

This boasted how bombsites had become nature reserves and gardens and cafe terraces. One picture was captioned, "A girl gathers flowers in the ruins near St. Paul's." Another showed city workers sunbathing on a bombsite in King William Street.

But one hundred yards from King William Street in Budge Row was another bomb site. In late 1953, the decomposed and rat-gnawed body of William Pettit was found there. Pettit was a murder suspect. The first to have his face flashed on British TV. He'd stabbed his lover, Rene Brown, in the chest, in Lover's Lane, off Chislehurst Common.[112]

---

111   Philip Oakes, *At the Jazz Band Ball. A memory of the 1950s*, 1983
112   Pettit had been an aspiring actor. He had a walk-on part in George Bernard Shaw's 1945 movie *Caesar and Cleopatra*. His parents defended him at the inquest. They said Rene Brown, a married woman, 18 years older than

A girl gathers flowers in the ruins near St. Paul's.

London never had this before!—an outdoor restaurant on Ludgate Hill.

owers of the itzl A City gar-n started by the rewatchers of oldsmiths' Hall.

pping drinks der a coloured nshade, you rdly notice the d Bailey loom-g in the back-ound.

Men Only, *September 1954*

Pettit, had corrupted their son. "One second she could be like a lover, the next like the devil." Brown's husband said his wife had felt "sorry" for Pettit. She wanted to "save" him. "She was one of the sweetest women in the world." About the forensic finding that his wife had sex shortly before she died, Mr Brown said, "There was talk of recent intimacy before she died. That is a mistake. My wife radiated purity of soul. Her qualities were almost nunlike." At the inquest Pettit's father declared: "I will never believe my boy killed her. If you killed a fly in my house he would look at you in horror." He further claimed the Browns had been manipulating his son into "sabotaging" the cars of neighbours they disapproved of. At this, Mr Brown began laughing. Mr Pettit shouted, "There is no need to laugh, Mr. Brown. It is not a laughing matter." Adding, "The last person who had his car sabotaged was 207, Westmount Road." The coroner interrupted, saying that this had nothing to do with the case.

FIRST MURDER HUNT ON TV
Screen flashes wanted man

90-SECOND DRAMA

For kids, bombsites were excitingly dangerous. [I once fell onto a pile of shattered glass in a bombsite, gashing my wrist vertically, millimetres from a main artery, the 4-inch scar a permanent reminder of near death.] DC Measham's *Fourteen, autobiography of an Age-Group*, quotes Laura, aged nine, visiting her grandmother in London:

> We decided to go over to the bomb site where all the kids go to play. As we was walking down the road my mum called out "be careful". "All right," I answered back. When we got there was thousands of kids there all like little flies climbing over treacle. They all called out, "Hello Laura," for I knew nearly all of them.

> About half an hour later someone called out, "Look that wall's going to fall any minute!" Everyone stopped what they were doing and looked. A wall that had been left standing was swaying dangerously. "Run for cover," they all shouted and belted off down the road.

> As my friend and I ran, we tripped over some rubble. Just as we did the wall fell and covered us. All I can remember was a pain and then I went unconscious. Next thing I knew was I was lying in hospital with my head and arms bandaged up and a pain in my side every time I breathed. The first thing I said was "Margy", for that was my friend's name.

> "She's in the next bed," said the nurse. When I looked she had two broken arms and legs and her head was bandaged up as well. When I looked back again, my parents were there and they tried to comfort me, but they couldn't.

Just below the Townsend crime scene, across Angus Drive, was another, triangular patch of wasteland. Here, a gang of older boys truanting from my school made a secret base: a hole in the ground camouflaged by brushwood. In this hideout they read soft porn mags, larked about, and smoked Woodbines. Occasionally they masturbated. One of them astonished me by winding a string of chewing gum round and round his erect penis.

Bombsites could trigger mayhem. The movie *Hue and Cry* (1946) climaxes in a bombsite setting, with a battle between schoolboys and assorted spivs and crooks. "Frequently shot from either above – looking down, for example, into bomb craters and smashed up ceilings – or from below – looking up through the lattice of beams and rubble to the now clear skies – the film's scenes of ruin and debris evoke a strong sense of vertigo."[113] In the Ealing Comedy *Passport to Pimlico* (1949) unsettling a bombsite reveals treasure which subverts the established order and detonates comic revolution. And in one episode

---

113 Cited in Leo Mellor, *Reading the Ruins. Modernism, Bombsites, and British Culture*, 2011. Mellor describes post-war bombsites as representing imaginary zones, "from which forces would emerge to destroy society – but a space also ripe for redemption and rebuilding."

of the popular *Quatermass* TV series, (1953-59), excavation of a bombsite unearths an alien space ship, causing uncanny vibrations and madness, unleashing poltergeists and hallucinations, and triggering mass psychosis.

In real life, in 1954 a 1,700-year-old Roman temple of Mithras was unearthed at a bombsite in central London. 10,000 people flocked to see this shrine to the God of Light. So many that the archaeologist in charge, William Grimes, panicked. He closed the gates and called the police. People were upset, shouting, "What kind of show is this?" "We came to see the ruins and the ruins we will see!"

The sinister aura of these wasted places was milked in Ex-Superintendent Robert Fabian's lurid memoir, *London After Dark. An intimate record of night life in London*, 1954. In "The Blitz-Site Murder," the very wilderness speaks and nails a killer.

> The weeds that had grown up in the blitz site were dead now. The woman who lay among them was dead too, but more recently. Blood from her crushed forehead still shone wet.

Two children find the body:

> "Look Arthur!" shrilled little Terry Cordner, "a lady's legs!" Dark blood dappled the weeds. Police hurried from the city's C.I.D. headquarters...

A suspect's clothing is matched to the crime scene: "Brick-dust, cement-dust, charcoal, clinker and withered... willow-herb weed or knot-weed..."

> The dead, unheeded flowers of a city blitz-site had, it seemed, left their Judas-kiss upon the hem of a murderer's garment!

> Two months later he was hanged.

NO WAY BACK

South Ruislip shopping parade in the mid-fifties. Today, many suburban niceties like the stately trees that shaded shoppers have gone.

Kiddies Korner was a toy shop run by two elderly spinsters, selling Dinky Cars, magic sets, and stink bombs, etc. Next door, the hardware shop, Skinner and Parker, sold weedkiller. This was useful for making bombs.

Boys mixed it with sugar, adding a dash of sulphur. It flared up a treat. It also went bang when hit with a hammer. However, for a real bomb, like the IRA used, you needed a detonator. We used to steal these from sheds along the railway line. (They were used as signals in foggy weather.) But none of us could figure out how to adapt them. We had to be careful robbing these sheds. Queers went up there. They paid small boys half a crown to wank them off. Better than bob-a-job.

These pictures show the shopping parade outside South Ruislip underground station, where Jean Townsend started her last walk home. It's the mid-fifties. We check the cues: an almost car-free road, length of skirts, width of trousers, how people stand or arrange themselves walking along... Summoning tones of voice, common understandings, turns of phrase...

We've lost the codes now. No way back.

So we recreate the post-war-fifties period through current fantasies.

TV dramas and biopics set in that period are too brilliantly lit and chic and over-designed. They miss the cigarette fug and coal dust smog, the mend-and-make-do of most things, the smell of soot and taste of tapioca pudding and lard, and all those dowdy grey costumes and dingy brown and cream paintwork.

Tellygenic fifties' fashions, too, are overly tailored and crisp. In those days only Yanks dressed like that. Hollywood actors, or American servicemen with wallets ostentatiously bulging in back pockets in Ruislip Manor High Street.[114]

---

114 Even the most fashion conscious in the 1950s patronised second-hand clothes shops. Jackie Cliff:

> The best place to get clothes in the fifties was a secondhand dress shop, bottom end of Portobello Road. It was called Marie's Dress Agency. [The shop had been going since the 1940s. Norman Collins mentions it in his novel, *London Belongs to Me*, 1946.] It was wonderful for day and evening clothes, and shoes and bags and gloves, and even hats.
> Marie, who owned it, was this really huge lady – about 20 stone. So fat she always sat on a chair. A real old cockney lady. She was helped by Ethel – as skinny as Marie was fat.
> Some days the shop was just packed with young models and showgirls and rich ladies selling garments and furs to Marie.
> I loved the atmosphere and stroking the satins and silks and evening clothes. Also trying on the long furs fashionable then, especially white fox wraps – some of them had fox heads on.
> Then there were snow white furs with satin lining. Long satin gloves kept in a case on the wall.
> Little Ethel would be zipping us up or doing up little hooks and eyelets on dresses. She'd also help us on and off with satin shoes, sometimes in the same material as the dresses or coats.
> We always bought our underwear from Marie's. See-through stockings and satin suspender belts. No tights then!
> Marie's was a hub of gossip, especially for getting a nightclub job. And we always asked Marie what she thought we looked best in. Marie, who couldn't wear any of it herself, always seemed to know what looked best.

Plus, actors' faces today don't fit: they are too self-knowing, smug, narcissistic, too comfortable in their skins and familiar with their own orgasms to approximate their fifties' originals – unenlightened, dutiful and frigid – remember frigid?

———

One reason the 50s are intransigent to memory is that between that decade and the present, the brash and bright 1960s intervened, and still casts its brilliance backwards.

Men weren't allowed in Marie's shop. They stood outside and peeped in through the window, and the girls made faces at them. Sometimes, girls went outside in a satin evening dress to show a man who would be waiting outside – in case he fancied buying it for her. Or else the men would sit in cars outside.

One dress I remember was purple velvet. It had a low-cut sweetheart neck with small points all round with sequins on. It had a tight skirt to the ground with a slit in the front. It had shoes to match – stilettos with black sequins – and gloves to match.

Another was what I called the Diana Dors look. A mermaid dress in white lace with long lace gloves. I wore a wig with this dress and a fur stole and diamante bracelet and necklace. And black high-heeled stilettos. Very, very high.

Shepherd's Bush Market was another place for clothes. There were several stalls run by cockney women. Some of their clothes came from Paris fashion houses. There were also fur coats and jewels. The clothes were in big heaps, with some hanging up, at the back of stalls.

The stallholders were always middle-aged or older women. They had loud voices and cackled like witches, and they wore fur coats and diamond rings and swore a lot.

I always wondered how they got hold of these amazing clothes. French ballgowns, long coats, and gloves and bags. People would go through the piles like it was a jumble sale. On a summer's day the clothes smelled of hot satin and hot smelly fur coats – like the jungle.

I had a one-track mind in those days: to put my hands into silks and satins, chiffon-bows, sequins, lace nets, leather handbags, silken evening bags with beads… Often it smelled of gone-off perfume. All that made me happy.

So we're now prone to re-imagine (and mask our incredulity about) the 1950s in the enlightened glow of the 1960s – the 50s configured as a kind of gauche anticipation of the 60s.

Hence the blurb for a 3-part TV series, accompanied by a book, *The Fifties and Sixties: A Lifestyle Revolution*, 2001, by Miriam Akhtar and Steve Humphries. This advises that "the fifties" were a "trailblazer for [1960s] youth, hedonism and modernity": a rehearsal for more liberated times just around the corner.

We forget that nothing in the fifties looked forward to the sixties. How could it? The sixties hadn't happened.

In fact, the tone of the fifties – culture and behaviours and attitudes, harked back to that unstable and malevolent interwar period – the 20s and 30s.[115]

You can see that hangover, for example, in casual reading matter.

Take what most people were entertaining themselves with. It wasn't *Lucky Jim* or *Look Back in Anger* or James Bond. More like ad hoc miscellanea sedimented in sitting rooms of seaside boarding houses – the detritus of rainy afternoons – distillations of average taste. There you might find an uplifting tome from Lord Bertrand Russell or HG Wells' *History of the World*. A stray Dickens or du Maurier. But mostly, stuff like "Sapper"'s Bulldog Drummond adventures, John Creasey's Toff books, or Sax Rohmer's Fu Manchu series. Greased and creased and stained pages, cracked spines and tattered covers.

Most such are never read nowadays. Or are unreadable. They seem musty and opaque. Uncomfortable. Even sinister.

115　Rather than the decade "the fifties", it makes more sense to think loosely about the "long fifties": between the Labour landslide of 1945, and three cultural shocks which broke the mould of post-war Britain: the *Lady Chatterley* obscenity trial in 1960, and then, both in 1963, the Profumo Affair, and *Please Please Me*, the Beatles' debut album. After that, the "fifties" were done and dusted.

There was often another book in those motley collections. A text we've equally lost the plot of: JW Dunne's *An Experiment with Time*.

Dunne's book was serious. It had a writing style to suit. Cool, dry and matter of fact. But the message was fantastic. Dunne said that dreams foretold the future. Time, he explained, was not a continuum, it happened all at once. We humans, stuck in our mortal frames, were only privy to small slices of the stuff. But asleep and in our dreams, we could access the totality. See the past and glimpse the future. What was more, Dunne said we could participate in this Experiment by making dream journals and checking them against future events.

Experiment with Time was full of reassuring diagrams and calculations. An engineer's instruction manual for the uncanny.

This perplexing nonsense was first published in 1927. The year of the first Nuremburg Rally, and when Stalin finally took control of Russia. A time of utopian spectacles, mass sporting events, totalitarian parades, and Busby Berkeley spectaculars: fashioning and sculpting, The People. A time of missionary nudist camps and Esperanto, of mystical jokers like Gurdjieff, the quixotic missionary Albert Schweitzer, and the preposterous Satanist, Aleister Crowley...

A time of cranks.

A period fascinated, for example, with "death rays." In development by inventors or government funded. Rays that might melt aircraft, neutralise poison gases, or create a "teleforce" "based on an entirely new principle of physics that 'no one has ever dreamed about.'"

The *New York Times* reported in 1924 that:

> The inventors of a "death ray" multiply every day. To H. GRINDELL MATTHEWS and Professor T.F. WALL have

been added two other Englishmen, **PRIOR** and **RAFFE**, and **GRAMMACHIKOFF**, a Russian. Herr **WULLE**, "chief of the militarists" in the Reichstag, has informed that body that the Government has a device that will bring down airplanes, stop tank engines, and "spread a curtain of death."

By the fifties, post-Hiroshima, death rays were for real. Eisenhower's *Atoms For Peace* speech in 1953 was replayed by documentaries in the USA and USSR showing atomic radiation zapping diseases and creating giant tomatoes. In 1954, three movies mined the topic. *Godzilla* starred a rampaging dinosaur created by radiation. *Them!* featured ants turned into man-eating monsters by radiation. *The Atomic Kid*, starring Mickey Rooney, showed how fallout could enhance your sex life and trigger jackpots in Las Vegas casinos.

There was equally a fascination with X-rays. In the fifties, X-ray machines were a feature of beauty salons, used to zap unwanted body hair. And a routine gadget in shoe shops was the fluoroscope (or pedascope), to show the fit of shoe and foot.

In a rare warning, Katherine Williams, "an atomic expert," told in the *Daily Express* how, "according to a survey little boys in the London suburbs had a wonderful game running from one shop to another looking at their feet through the X-ray machines. And there were some mothers who took their children from one shop to another and one X-ray machine to another, to get a proper fit."[116]

There were two such shops in Ruislip High Street. Through their X-Ray devices I'd peer at my skeletal foot and toe bones wiggling. Radiation was cool.

---

116   *Daily Express*, March 27, 1957

Another interwar overhang of popular culture in the 1950s was an equally freaky modern way to look "inside" people: psychoanalysis.

The 50s was when Freud's occult theories became "scientific" and institutionalised – especially in America. And "The Unconscious" (as a substantive entity – a noun rather than an adjective) became common sense.

Freudianism had become the bedrock of Broadway and Hollywood plots from the 1920s: Eugene O'Neill, Tennessee Williams, Alfred Hitchcock – even Rodgers and Hammerstein. Movies, plays and novels were steeped in Freudian motifs: repressed desires and hidden motives, irrational complexes and compulsions, fetishistic drives, ambivalence, catharsis, phobias, perversions, fantasy-work… and – as with JW Dunne – the meaning of dreams.

By the 50s, artists, playwrights, screenwriters, producers, and actors were habitually undergoing psychoanalysis to harvest "unconscious desires." This opened plot lines hitherto forbidden. The Id was mined and explored – constructed as dramaturgy and an agenda for art. It was the chic thing: to grapple with inner demons and taboos through adventures of self-discovery on a couch.

In the UK, where official shrinks snubbed Dr Freud, they still dabbled in "subconscious" motivations. When Raymond Barker murdered his lover, Beatrice James, in 1954, but claimed he could not recall the incident, a psychiatrist at Brixton Prison, "gave Barker a form of anaesthetic [in order to create] what was known as an abreaction, that was, a re-living of the repressed incident by means of the gas. This was administered at first lightly and then more deeply to the point bordering on actual unconsciousness." No memory surfaced. Conclusion: Barker was insane.[117]

---

117   TNA: CRIM 1/2390

Psychoanalytical folklore at Brixton Prison ("abreaction", "repressed incident") was apace with how Freud's insights had permeated by the 50s to ad agencies hawking "motivational research."

This Madison Avenue schtick was supposed to trigger "unconscious" or "subliminal" responses to ads, and therefore manipulate consumers. In fact, this was a conversation between Freud-savvy designers and a Freud-aware public – to get the joke or the point you needed to appreciate that a car that looked like a rocket or a lipstick was a "phallic symbol." You needed the vocabulary.

Lipstick ad, 1954, magazine cover, 1954

This pop Freudianism peaked in the mid-fifties. In 1955, a series of DC comics titled *Psychoanalysis*, launched: "case histories" as story lines – uncanny escapades. Equally, *The Strange World of Your Dreams*, solicited readers' dreams for scenarios while name-checking Sigmund Freud and Salvador Dali. And the rhetoric of psychoanalysis was

Left. The Strange World of Your Dreams, *1953. Right.* Psychoanalysis, *1955*

increasingly used to dramatise crime. Murderers were now not simple criminals, but elevated to "psychopaths," incarnations of the "Id": an unchecked Unconscious raging out of control. The unaccountable features – the loose ends and enigmas – around the Townsend case, provided a perfect Freudian case study, a convincing modern mystery.

THE FACTS OF LIFE

I learnt the "facts of life" from a school friend as we were walking through the playground to the school gates at the end of one day. I was 14. It was a shock. I couldn't believe it. Nor could the next boy I passed this information to. The mechanism of this reported "sexual intercourse" seemed outlandish and preposterous.

And yet, we were not innocents – rather accomplished masturbators, excited by budding bosoms or exhibitions of girlthigh – girls in those days practiced gym with skirts tucked into uniform knickers. We also gorged on cheesecake cleavage in "adult" magazines and confidently sang ditties like, "Lady of Spain I adore you, lift up your skirt I'll explore you..." But sex itself – how to do it, what it was for, what went where – was a blank spot – and that sort of (wilful?) ignorance was a dominating theme of post-war British culture.

This is plentifully shown in Simon Szreter and Kate Fisher's oral history, *Sex Before the Sexual Revolution* (2011):

> The great majority of respondents emphasised that they had not been accustomed to seeing unclothed or partially clothed bodies in any context when growing up. There were also few opportunities for casual observation of the human body outside the household. Respondents presented themselves as immersed in a culture which encouraged them to think of their own and of others' bodies as, above all, private and personal. Parental training taught that bodies were to be kept

to themselves and not foisted upon others or displayed in any way, starting with careful regulations in the home.

They quote Bryan, son of a Welsh miner:

> When my mother... had, my youngest brother, Mrs Ransome used to come and look after us kids, you know. Mum was in bed, and she used to bath us y' see, And I wouldn't undress; I wouldn't strip off "Come on", she said. "I got boys of me own", she said, "Come on". (laughs) And my mother used to say, "Don't be so silly, Bryan". I said "No, I'm not going to undress in front of her".

And Hubert, the son of an estate agent:

> I was put to bath with [my cousin]. Both together, but she had a big sponge strategically placed. So I said, "What does she want that for?" They said, "Well boys and girls are different", which I found hard to believe, I've forgotten what happened. I know the sponge was not removed anyway.

And Horace, son of a professional soldier:

> I shall always remember... when I was 16 or 17 I came downstairs with me trousers on. Just me vest, vest and trousers. And he [father] gave me such a clout. He knocked, me from one side of the room to the other: "You dare expose your body to your mother."[118]

In that virgin space flourished crackpots and alarming nonsense.

---

118 pp271-273

The 1950s saw the *Kinsey Report* published. But that modern and luminous approach took another decade to permeate. Kinsey in the 50s was known mostly through hearsay and confused notoriety – extending from tabloid scares and sneers, to the desks of the Home Office. Witness this handwritten cry from Sir Austin Strutt, Home Office Assistant Secretary – part of a discussion about whether the Female Volume of the *Kinsey Report* should be referred to the DPP for prosecution.

Reluctantly, Sir Austin thought not, but only because a successful trial would be unlikely. Meanwhile, he made clear his objections to the book. For example, about Kinsey's section on teenage petting. This might be taken to imply:

> ...that the more a young girl allows herself to be lasciviously mauled, the better her chances of a happy marriage. There can be no doubt that this and similar passages will give great offence to many people in this country and it is impossible to be sure that it will not encourage some youngsters to excess...

And:

> Much of the chapter on masturbation is hardly edifying...

Finally:

> The worst passage in the book, to my mind, is the statement on p327 that present methods of simple and rapid cures for the principal venereal diseases make their spread through pre-marital coitus a relatively unimportant matter. Fear of disease is perhaps the most important factor in restraining many young men from promiscuous immorality – at any rate it is the factor on which the armed forces principally rely – and to remove that deterrent gratuitously... seems to me to be monstrously irresponsible.[119]

---

[119] TNA:HO 302/10

Probably the most popular sex manual in the 1950s was the *Encyclopædia of Sex Practice*. The first volume of a trilogy, this went through many editions from the 1930s to early 1960s. It was over 800 pages long. It was supposedly authored by a committee of sex sages: Drs Norman Haire, L Willy, A Vander, O Fischer, and R Lothar, "and others." If you thought about it – and it seems not many people did – these combined surnames suggested: Hairy Willy Fisher – a bit of a Lothario.

The book was in fact ghosted by Arthur Koestler, using the pseudonym, Dr Costler. The additional "authors" were Koestler's little joke.

In his autobiographical *The Invisible Writing*, 1954, Koestler explained how he hacked the work out "at a rate of about four thousand words a day," condensing "a dozen or so standard text-books and reference works."

This was a book that in purporting to explain sex, rendered it clear as mud – with illustrations as bewildering as the text.

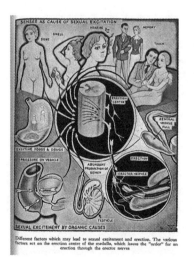

Different factors which may lead to sexual excitement and erection. The various factors act on the erection centre of the medulla, which issues the "order" for an erection through the erector nerves

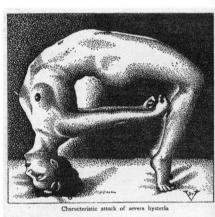

Characteristic attack of severe hysteria

Two illustrations in Koestler's sex manual.

Also muddy were some curious censorship trials.

> The early 1950s... saw a sudden recrudescence of obscenity prosecutions: during 1953 alone 197 prosecutions were instituted in respect of allegedly obscene publications... in 1954 [there were] five major obscenity prosecutions: Werner Laurie for Margot Bland's *Julia*; Secker & Warburg for Stanley Kaufman's *The Philanderer*; Hutchinson for Vivian Connell's *September in Quinze*; Heinemann for Walter Baxter's *The Image and the Search*; and Arthur Barker for Hugh McGraw's *The Man in Control*.[120]

Reading those books now would hardly raise an eyebrow, let alone rate a cockstand. They are sedate, earnest – aimed at an "educated" readership. For example:

> "Let me see you," she said, and she ripped the shirt away as if the fabric had been a spider web. Pietro gave a pant of anger as she laughed at him. Then his hand jumped out and he split her shirt open with a jerk and then the storm in his blood burst and he flung her down on the bed of grass. She kicked at his face and her heel smacked his lips on his teeth and then he threw himself down between her legs and tore the skirt away and saw the animal black hair on her belly and felt her lunging under him like a wild mare.[121]

At the trial of this book, the Recorder, Sir Gerald Dobson, thought it, "Repugnant to every decent emotion which ever concerned man or woman." The publisher, Hutchinson, and the printer, were each fined

---

120 PR MacMillan, *Censorship and Public Morality*, 1983
121 Vivian Connell, *September in Quinze*, 1952

£500 [today, around £8,700]. Katherine Henrietta Webb, a director of both companies, was fined an additional £500, or six months in jail.

———————

Less "literary" writers were equally targeted.

The most prolific pulp author in fifties Britain was Stephen Frances, aka Hank Janson. Janson began publishing in 1946, with *When Dames Get Tough*. He was soon knocking out a thriller a month. By 1954, it was reckoned Hank Janson sales were over five million.

In December 1954, Frances was sent for trial at the Old Bailey on seven counts of having written obscene books authored as Hank Janson. Frances' defence was simple. He denied he'd written the books. To prove that he had, the prosecution compared the use of certain words in books Frances admitted having written, with the Janson texts.

Words compared were, "animal," "skin," "biting," "breasts," "writhing," "body," "moist" – and so on.

The prosecutor's office produced a breakdown for the jury with lists and tables: pages of pulp surrealism. Eventually, perhaps sensing the absurdity, the judge terminated the trial on a technicality. Frances was acquitted.

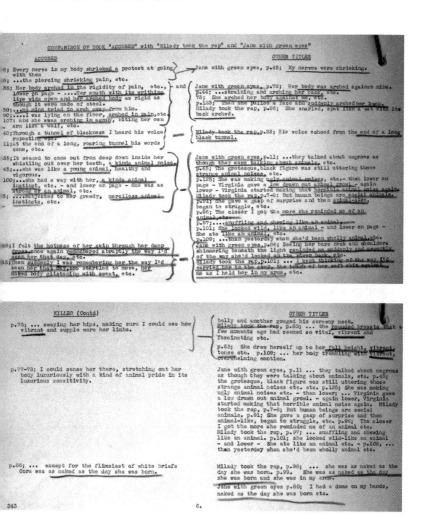

Regina v Frances, Exhibits, deposited in The National Archive. CRIM 1/2515

As for cinema, in the 50s the chief British film censor was Arthur Thomas Levi Watkins. Watkins wrote plays under the pseudonym of Arthur Watkyn. [That "y" being an antique flourish, befitting a poetic Welshman.]

One of Watkyn's plays, *For Better – or Worse*, was a hit. A comedy about the post-war housing shortage. It ran for 500 performances in the West End. In 1954, it was made into a movie starring Dirk Bogarde. But it was granted a certificate only after the producers had removed the expletive "bloody" from the script.

In September 1954, Watkins received complaints about an American movie, a 15-minute one-reel full-colour "glamour" production, called *The Body Beautiful – How to Get It – How To Keep It*. This came from Roadshow Attractions. Its producer was William Merle Connell, a veteran of skinflicks with medical sub or pre-texts.

The Body Beautiful showed many bodies. Some were indeed beautiful. Some were partly naked. One was being sensuously massaged.

Thousands had seen this film. It was being screened in two venues, The Tatler Cinema in Charing Cross Road, and the London News Theatre in Oxford Street.

Watkins rang the manager of the Tatler. He demanded to see the movie. Immediately!

The manager, Mr Holdsworth, hailed a taxi and took the movie reel in its aluminium canister to the Soho offices of Mr Watkins. Watkins projected it privately. Then announced, "This film can't be shown in its present form. Take it off at once!"

Mr Holdsworth returned to his cinema. He took down posters for *The Body Beautiful*. Then phoned the London News Theatre to tell them the film had been banned.

That evening people were shown instead a silent movie from 1914, Charlie Chaplin's *Caught in a Cabaret*.[122]

Such censorship bespoke a passionate voyeurism. A theme played out by those gimcrack screens erected round the Townsend crime scene, and in mainstream cinemas by Alfred Hitchcock's 1954 *Rear Window*. The impulse to look – and its official denial.

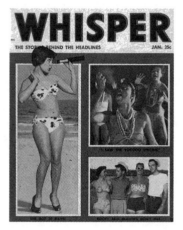 

---

122   There is a collection of censored play scripts kept in the British Library. These display the scribbled blue crayon misgivings of censors who vetted proposed stage plays up to 1968 – when censorship was abolished. Among the 1950s items we can find *Who Goes Bare?* in verse, proposed by Dickie Ray Productions, "When the wind blew her skirt about balmy/ And there between Dublin and Ould Galway Bay/ was that dear little spot Killarney." Or Dudley Harcourt's *Lady for Hire – A Melodrama*, with stage directions: "He sits at the back of the settee and runs his hands lightly over her body, caressing her as the curtain falls." But the curtain never fell on this scene, as its performance was forbidden. [Lord Chamberlain's Plays. LC Plays 1900/1 – 1968/34. Plays submitted for licence 1900-1968]

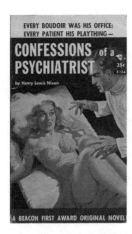

Left and previous page. Three publications from 1954.

The impulse was candidly expressed in a popularised case study, *Long Journey: a verbatim report of a case of severe psychosexual infantilism*, by Harold Kenneth Fink, 1954:

Session 120. Tabooed Impulses

At sixteen I'd buy *It*, *Peek*, *Keyhole*, and other such magazines, and hunt for public library medical books on women in various positions on the examination table, babies being born, and the like. The nudist magazines were the best, since they showed the pubic hair and breasts. But some, because of censorship, had the hair removed, scratched out. I didn't go for them; they seemed so weak!

And:

Session 60: Peeking Pleasure

Because of my dream yesterday I want to clean up this problem of voyeurism so I can enjoy real dates more.

When I feel frustrated I still like to go out and watch windows at night. I never feel satisfied with looking, so I keep on doing it, hoping to see something better. I always want to see more of the girl than I do.

I wouldn't want to lose the fun of watching women strip, for that would make marriage commonplace. With street-walkers it's no fun, because they're paid to peel. I sometimes drive to a college sorority house where the coeds never close their blinds. But they make me mad, for they have the trick of removing skirt, blouse, and slip, and then turning out the light while removing panties and bra. When the light goes on again, they're in charmless, baggy pajamas – stolen from their brothers' backs – patting grease on their faces.

One Saturday night I went with a group of guys to serenade girls under their windows. The gals leaned out in various attractive stages of undress, and one of them threw out a pair of panties. The lucky fellow who caught them pinned them on his wall, boasting that he'd return them for her autograph some time. I can just see him facing the house mother with that story!

I prayed that no one would ever catch me watching windows. If I didn't stay in my car I'd hide behind a tree or building. But the fear of being caught added to the suspense and excitement. If I ever get caught you'll bail me out, won't you? Tell them I'm your patient and I can't help it.

Even in exam week I was unable to keep away from house-watching, getting home at two a.m. I once carried field glasses on such a trip, but felt so guilty about the habit that I left them on purpose in a cafeteria.

I guess if I were married, I wouldn't think anything about undressing, since I could watch all I wanted.[123]

---

123 Harold Kenneth Fink, *Long Journey: a verbatim report of a case of severe psychosexual infantilism*, 1954, p183

It wasn't just "psychosexual infantalists" baffled or frustrated by what they saw – or failed to see. Husbands and lovers might be equally puzzled.

For clarification they could turn to Art – to flourishing genres of surrogate erotica.

Like the professionally sanctioned amateur competition photography, rife with female nudity in mythological or arty settings. There was also a genre of nude photobooks supposedly aimed at amateur artists. For example, John Everard's *Artist's Model*, 1951. (A successor, *Second Sitting*, came out in 1954 and featured Pam Green.)

Everard's books specialised in studies of naked women doing everyday things: brushing their hair, mopping the floor, reading a book. All these women were comely, and all were unclothed. Genitalia and pubic hair were crudely airbrushed as blurred or blind spots. In a cursory nod to possible objections, male and child nude studies were included. Also, creakily pompous "introductions." "The object of these poses is to supply the framework on which artists can hang the necessary garments…"

Nude women were a staple of popular photo annuals, whose respectability was sanctioned by officious commentaries. This image, Nymph, *1954, by Walter Bird, appeared in* Photograms, *which featured two introductions, by Bertram Sinkinson. FRPS, FIBP, FRSA, and RH Mason, MA, FIBP, FRPS. Jackie Cliff commented on one of her sessions with Walter Bird, that he turned her into, "a girl who was like a nymph. A fairy or something."*

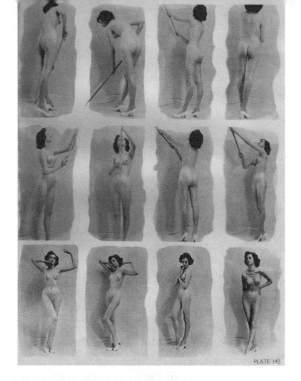

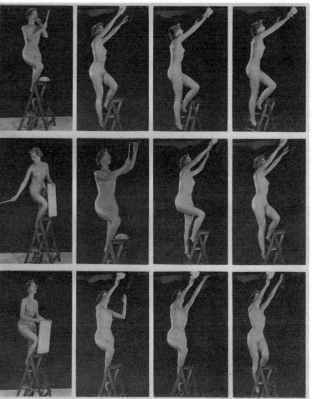

Two pages from Artists's Model *by John Everard, FIBP [Fellow of the Institute of British Photographers]. The model in the top image is doing housework; in the image on the bottom the model appears to be changing a light bulb.*

Much fifties erotica was sold in a quintessentially fifties institution: "surgical" or "men's" shops.

These places exuded the same "private" and masculine aura as barber shops, (where men bought condoms). Their displays were minimal like undertakers' windows, but instead of black they gleamed white and antiseptic. You'd see a rupture truss or elasticised stocking with a few primly posed "dirty" books in a pristine setting. You could never see inside these shops from outside. (Another fifties "screen"?)

On an online forum about Stockton on Tees in the fifties, Maureen Walker recalls a surgical shop "that we used to walk past quickly giggling as we went. It… sold surgical appliances, some of which looked a bit rude to naive young girls!"

The comedy writer Denis Norden told how, as a young man in the fifties, he was lured by a theatrical production company, International Masterpieces Incorporated, whose "London Offices were in the back room of a Surgical Appliances shop in the Charing Cross Road." Here, Norden was invited to script Babes and Boobs, starring Fifi La Tush.[124]

There was no such shop in Ruislip High Street. But nearby Harrow was a tad more cosmopolitan. And here, off the main shopping parade, was a "surgical supplies" retailer, baffling schoolkids with a window display which included an artificial leg, medical textbooks, and – centrally placed, *A History of Spanking*.

---

124   Denis Norden, *You Have My Word*, 1989

SCREEN MEMORIES

As with our schooldays, the memories we retain from our childhood family life of the 1950s are frequently quite simple ones; the wonderful smells of mum's roast dinners and freshly baked cakes; the cosy nights we spent by the fireside listening to the wireless as dad snoozed in his favourite armchair and mum rolled a fresh ball of knitting wool from a skein stretched between a child's tiny arms; afternoon tea at auntie's, patiently watching the clock as mum caught up on all the latest gossip; Sundays spent at granny's, with talk of drawing rooms and parlours and aspidistra plants; an ashtray in every room and ticking clocks all over the house; rooms filled with brown wooden furniture and comfy armchairs stacked with lots of cushions, all engulfed in a heady mix of musty smells sweetened with furniture polish. Homes were so very different then...

— Paul Feeney, *From Ration Book to ebook, The Life and Times of the Post-War Baby Boomers*, 2012

Many histories and memoirs of the 1950s are sentimentally soft focused. This sidesteps the violence and menace of the decade – and its excitement.

Even as a kid you registered grown-up terrors like the Red Menace, the H Bomb threat, the Malayan Emergency, Mau Mau barbarism, the Korean War, the Cold War, the Sex War, the Hungarian uprising...

Then all those executions by hanging, suicides by gas…

There was this dread around.

The everyday – casual and routine – violence a child encountered or witnessed was remarkable. Some of that is relayed in Jackie Cliff's account of her South Ruislip childhood. Ten years later when I was growing up in the same area, the Bug Hutch Saturday morning children's cinema was still going – punches still flew there – and occasionally knives flashed.

In those days practically every boy owned a knife. It was what boys did. Played conkers, collected cigarette cards, stuffed marbles and elastic bands into trouser pockets, wore school caps askew Just William style, and carried a knife. Mostly just a pen knife or Swiss Army. Sometimes a sheath knife. But if you didn't want to be messed with it was a flick knife.

Cheapo flick knives were side opening. More reassuring was an Italian stiletto. This shot out front-ways with a chunky click as it locked for business.

There were even flick knife guns. These were made in Naples and sold for 35 shillings in London suburbs, about two months' pocket money, a sound investment.

FOR SALE— IN LONDON

A flick-knife gun and flick-knives are shown in this picture of a London shop window yesterday

To sample knife crime in 1954: in May, 73-year-old Amy Katherine Lloyd, a "Boy Scout's badge secretary," was found dead in her hallway with 20 stab wounds to chest and throat. The culprit was 17-year-old Boy Scout Barry Musson: "His dark hair was heavily greased and well brushed." The jury was told that Musson "was very anxious to obtain badges for his distinction as leader of the Kestrel patrol," and when this was denied, became enraged. [Guilty and detained "until Her Majesty's pleasure."]

In June, six-year-old Wilfred Schofield was found "stabbed to death on waste ground near his home." Police concluded that "Wilfred might have died as a result of injuries received in a game played by other children... horseplay rather than a malicious or deliberate attack by someone with evil intent." Tommy Bamber, ten, eventually admitted stabbing Wilfred while playing cowboys and indians. In the coroner's court Mrs Bamber sobbed, "My son is innocent." [Verdict: misadventure.]

In October, nine-year-old Christopher Greetham was stabbed in the throat while playing on a riverbank. Christopher staggered to a doctor's house and gasped, "A man has stabbed me. Am I going to die?" The police received an anonymous postcard: "Dear Cops. I the likely boy stabber, trust you have success in your investigations, but you won't find the knife I used on the riverbank. If you don't get me I may give myself up, but don't bank on it. I am 23 – Potential killer." Peter Watson was later arrested and charged. He said the card was, "a bit of fun." [Found unfit to plead and imprisoned.]

We can find appalling stories like these in any year of any decade. The point is how they were reported and dealt with – reflecting the casual carrying of knives, and a nonchalant acceptance of knife crime.

In February 1954 the Court of Appeal made a judgment about a stabbing at Tredegar Grammar School. It said the school was not liable to pay damages after a 13-year-old pupil had been stabbed in the leg with a sheath knife in the school playground during a "fracas."

The boy's leg had to be amputated.

The school banned boys from "wearing sheath knives" [in scabbards] after this stabbing.

The QC who was speaking for the victim argued that: "Sheath knives should have been banned earlier. They were dangerous things which boys might be expected to put to improper purposes."

Lord Justice Maurice: "Do you say that every parent who allows his boy to go out with a sheath knife is guilty of negligence?"

GG Baker: "Yes, if he allows his boy to play with the other boys."

Lord Justice Maurice: "I should have thought that it depended on the kind of knife, the age of the child and of the circumstances."

GG Baker: "If the boy is wearing one, in the street today he may be committing an offence under the Prevention of Crimes Act."

The Master of the Rolls then quipped, "It is fortunate that fashions have rendered unnecessary the use of hat pins."

The court was also told that every time they went camping the boys of Tredegar Grammar would bring all their equipment into school including knives, and that a senior master "sometimes cleaned the knives."

———————

There were also guns around. Trophies from the war. Gradually these disappeared. In 1952, the *Mirror* campaigned for readers to hand in their guns to police stations or the local vicar, "No questions will be asked."

When 12, I went for a time to Roman Catholic school in Uxbridge. The place was ruled by Teds.

One morning, one of these Teds walked into class holding a service revolver. The teacher jumped up.

Ted: "Naah… don't worry, mate, I just wanna sell it."

He then informed the class that the asking price was £5.

We rushed up and clustered round, handling the weapon.

I thought it just the ticket: its weight and how the chamber spun, and its masculine whiff of oil.

This would see off bullies.

That night I asked my mum if I could have my birthday present in advance. Also, could it be exactly £5?

Suspicious, she grilled me at the kitchen table. I told her. The upshot was she took me out of the school and gave the headmaster an earful. But the other upshot was – that there wasn't one – no one else was told – no complaint made, the police not informed – nothing was done. It wasn't exceptional.

EXODUS

One classic riff about the UK 1950s is that the decade inaugurated mass immigration. And that you can't understand the mentality of that period unless you take account of this immigration. Nowadays that's a cliché, what everyone knows, common sense. Taught in schools, researched in universities, discussed on TV.

But I recall something different. That the existential reality for most people in Britain then was the opposite of immigration – it was mass emigration.

As a child, it felt like an exodus, a loss. Kids regularly disappeared from school desks. My best friend, Peter, vanished to Australia. My girlfriend

Diana, sexy in a tutu in her living room, also vanished. "For Sale" or "To Let" signs were common in our streets. Our next-door neighbours in Dudley Drive – who had habits my French mother sniffed were "so English!" – like putting a spoonful of disinfectant in their children's bath and sprinkling lettuce with sugar, took their habits to New Zealand. After demob, my uncle Pierre studied child psychology at Birmingham University, then took his wife and three daughters to Cape Town. After my Scottish grandfather died my French grandmother left South Ruislip for New York to become a dietician…

Deansfield Junior, c.1952. Like most of our classrooms, this was a prefab featuring a map of the world showing the extent of the British Empire, proudly shaded red. I am far left. Peter, my best friend, is next to me. A stalwart giant, Peter used to protect me from bullies in return for telling him stories during playtime. One of the girls in this picture delighted in exposing herself to boys. When the classroom was deserted at lunchtime boys crept in there with her. She'd lie on her back on a desk and lift her frock and pull her knickers down while we marvelled.

I wondered whether that displacement had affected Jean Townsend and her circle. I asked Reg Hargrave for his perspective on the Ruislip neighbourhood. He emailed: "As to the residents of Bempton Drive and neighbouring streets I cannot recall a single instance of post-war emigration."

Instead, Reg claimed to recall "large numbers of Jamaicans arriving."[125]

He forgot that the family just over the road from him had left for Canada. That one of his closest friends in Bempton Drive also emigrated to Canada. That June Sweetzer, his and Jean Townsend's childhood friend and his next-door neighbour, had emigrated to America at the end of the fifties. When challenged, Reg also remembered two aunts and their families who'd made the journey to Australia. Oh yes, and his local Ruislip barber…

Reg's amnesia is a cultural habit. Today no one remembers the people who left. Or why they left. Or especially, how many left. They have been obliterated: culturally cleansed and ritually forgotten.

―――――――

But is all that just anecdotal? Or local? What were the facts?

They're hard to fix. Because at the time no official statistics were collected, and no precise studies made. The only full and reliable account is *British Post-War Migration*, by Julius Isaac.[126] Published in 1954, this roughly covers the period 1946 to 1952.

Isaac was deliberately conservative in his estimates. But he shows that between 1946-1951, 871,000 emigrants left via what were classed as

―――――――――――――――――――――――――――――――――――――――

125   But the only black faces for miles around in those days were American servicemen.
126   Julius Isaac, *British Post-War Migration*, National Institute of Economic and Social Research, Cambridge University Press, 1954

long sea routes.[127] Also, that between 1951-1952, a further 322,000 emigrated the same way. Additionally, between 1946-1951, 6,150,000 British nationals left on short sea routes.[128] [129]

So if we revise the figure down for returnees and so on, around five million emigrants between 1946-1952? But even that figure is incomplete. For example, it doesn't account for the 100,000 war brides – which Isaac says is "a conservative guess" – who left the UK for America and the Dominions.[130]

Then there were the child emigrants still being sent abroad by Barnardo's and The Salvation Army etc. [A practice only stopped in 1970]. Nor do the figures include emigrants leaving by air. Air passengers were not counted at all in those days. Isaac comments, "A substantial number of emigrants went by air to the United States, South Africa, India, etc."[131]

Isaac concludes, "Notwithstanding a large margin of error in the above figures, they clearly indicate that the volume of emigration from Great Britain... is much larger than is generally realized."

In fact, by these calculations and from other sources the number of people leaving the UK from 1946 to 1952 could be in excess of six million. A substantial proportion of the UK population, which in 1952, was 50.2 million.

---

127 Ibid. Table 6
128 Ibid. n4 p30. This figure includes citizens of the Republic of Ireland.
129 Short sea route destinations were mostly to mainland Europe. Many emigrants used Europe as a staging post to more distant places. Others were going on holiday or visiting relatives.
130 David Reynolds, *Rich Relations. The American Occupation of Britain, 1942-1945*, 1995, gives approximate figures of 37,879 British war brides shipped to America up to 1950, and 40,353 to Canada up to March 1948. This doesn't include women who married other nationalities.
131 Isaac, op.cit., p35

What's more, emigration didn't dip after 1952. Far from it. And if we calculate for the "long fifties" – 1946-1963 – we may be talking in excess of ten million.[132]

And for every family that left, many others considered it. A Gallup poll in 1948 concluded that up to 42% of Britons wanted out. By March 1951 it was reported there were around 1,700 enquiries a day about emigration to Canada.

———

Historians of that period seem unaware about the scale of this emigration. In *Never Had It So Good*, Dominic Sandbrook comments that emigration has generally been more characteristic of the British experience than immigration.[133] But then parks the insight to dwell on the more familiar topic of immigration. Questioned by email Sandbrook admitted his sources were books on immigration (which are legion): "I'm not aware of any books specifically on emigration."

Sandbrook, like other commentators, also tends to trivialise the post-war emigrants. Implying their leaving wasn't such a big deal, and may even have been a blessing. Britain was better off without what he caricatures as Colonel Blimps escaping the socialist welfare state, congregating "on the [ex-colonial] veranda at sundown with their gin and tonics and copies of the *Daily Telegraph*." [The public-school Oxbridge educated Sandbrook no doubt prefers a tipple of Sauvignon as he scans *The Guardian* in the back garden of his Chipping Norton semi.]

---

132 The total population of the UK didn't dip over those years, no doubt due to the postwar baby boom.
133 For example, in *Never Had It So Good*, 2005:
If we look at the wider picture [of migration] the British experience is better represented by Ford Madox Brown's Victorian painting, The Last of England, showing a mournful couple being carried away across

A similar stereotype appears in *Austerity Britain* 1945-49, (2007) by David Kynaston. This time the emigrants are resentful *Evening Standard* readers, "malcontent" Kensingtonians, "for whom Derry and Toms [a posh department store] was almost a second home." Kynaston [Wellington College and Oxford], suggests that "most" of these rentier types, resisted the temptation to flee rising prices, Labour government taxation and the dearth of servants. The insinuation being that those who did succumb to emigration were well-heeled "malcontents."[134]

Betka Zamoyska's, *The Ten Pound Fare. Experiences of British People Who Emigrated to Australia in the 1950s*, (1988), is based on primary sources. It gives a different picture.

> Lots had little or no money, not even enough to buy the cheap ship cigarettes. Only a few were fully trained in good trades; quite a lot were semi-skilled or had no skills at all. Most of them did not have any job fixed up for themselves...

This source also commented:

> It was always very distressing watching the final farewells when the ship left Southampton. They used to play 'Hearts of Oak' and other traditional old songs over the tannoy and everyone was weeping; a lot of them felt that they would never again see the loved ones they were leaving behind. Australia really was a long way away in those days and it felt almost as if the migrants were going off to a different planet. The types that were prepared to go, especially those with hardly any money, were very enterprising people. It took a lot of guts to leave behind all your home ties, knowing that you'd got hardly anything to fall back on.

---

the Channel to exile, than by the famous photographs of bewildered West Indians holding their suitcases at Tilbury Dock.

134 David Kyanston, *Austerity Britain*, pp260-261

And a welfare officer recalled that many relatives of departing emigrants didn't even have the fare down to Southampton.

> There were always a lot of people weeping at Waterloo [station]. Some of the passengers looked completely stunned. You know - We've made this big decision and here we are at last - what's going to happen?'They were probably quite frightened.[135]

Such people are blanked in David Kynaston's, *Family Britain*, 1951-1957, (2009), which explores the everyday life of ordinary Britons. In 754 pages, Kynaston doesn't once refer to emigrants or to emigration.

Instead, he focuses on the experiences of immigrants – Caribbean especially. He rightly details the prejudice many suffered and acknowledges their endurance and initiative. But typically overstates their contemporary cultural as well as demographic presence. Away from the metropolis, in the suburbs and provinces, "coloured" people were rarely seen, and immigration hardly a contested issue.

But Kynaston claims that, "By the autumn of 1954 it was obvious that the number of West Indian immigrants was rising sharply..."

Obvious to who?

Home Office figures show that by 1951 the Caribbean ethnic population in the UK was around 28,000. In 1954, 11,000 newcomers arrived. By 1961 the total was 209,000. Figures dwarfed by the emigration statistics.

Historians like Kynaston are creating a screen memory, a mythology

---

135 Betka Zamoyska, *The Ten Pound Fare*. p37. The book records more in the same vein, pp. 47-49

initiated by writers like George Lamming in *The Emigrants* (1954), and Colin McInnes in *Absolute Beginners* (1959) – texts elevated to prophetic status.

————————

Which is not to deny the eventual extent of Caribbean influence on the UK. More a question of assessing the prevailing mood of the 1950s without retrospective blinkers, or homilies.

For example, the Notting Hill race riots of 1958 are often celebrated as epic and seminal, a cultural turning point.

When they happened, politicians and leader columns protested, the police clamped down, and magistrates handed out exemplary penalties. But many Britons were indifferent. In those routinely violent years, only 12 years after the end of a world war and the revelation of Nazi concentration camps, with armed insurrections raging in Cuba, Algeria, Kenya, Malaya and Cyprus – punch ups in W11 could be side-lined. The media was more exercised by two dogs, Belyanka and Pestraya, shot into outer space by the Soviets. And two days after the Notting Hill disturbances, front pages switched to a raid on the Ebury Street home of movie actor Michael Wilding: stolen gems, a missing deed box, and Wilding's housekeeper locked in a wardrobe. The arraignment of racists was shunted to page five of the *Daily Mirror*, next to a picture of Zsa Zsa Gabor's "heavenly body" promoting her new movie, *Queen of Outer Space*.

————————

Harold Macmillan famously quipped that:

> Europe is finished, sinking. If I were a younger man, I'd emigrate to the United States.

Geoffrey Gorer's forensic snapshot of the British fifties, *Exploring English Character*, (1955) comments:

> It seems possible that voluntary emigration may have attracted those with the greatest amount of social aggression, the greatest urge to mastery, leaving a stay-at-home population with less free energy and more internal conflict, in "this country of ours where nobody is well."[136][137]

In *Quatermass and the Pit* (1958-9), Professor Quatermass is puzzled. The Britain he thought he knew is cracking up. Haunted by an unidentifiable catastrophe rooted in a prehistoric past. People are going crazy. Her Majesty's subjects ventriloquized by a vanished civilization – an alien species. This species had wanted to found a new colony on earth as their old world perished.

A crisis of dislocation, loss and anxiety.

Britain was being hollowed out. Shrinking. And its remaining citizens began a furious game of Make Believe: refuge in withdrawal and escapism.

Each to their own means. Matching the British split between the public schools and the unschooled.

So an influential slice of the elite took to libertine carousing as if no tomorrow – gambolling with pantomime debauchery. Like the frenetic partying of Michael Whittaker, Stephen Ward, Baron Nahum, Milford Haven, Princess Margaret...

Or the society gynaecologist, Dr Edward Sugden.

> Sugden's main line of business, in the fifties, was as an abortionist. [Abortion being illegal before 1967]. In the fifties ...several sources confirm, [that] he was performing ten to fifteen abortions a day, at one or two hundred pounds a time.

---

136 WH Auden's phrase.
137 Geoffrey Gorer, *Exploring English Character*, 1955, p292

Among his long-standing friends had been the Messina brothers, the notorious Sicilian pimps. When Messina prostitutes got pregnant Sugden dealt with the problem. None of this bothered his friends in the fifties... for Sugden gave just the right kind of parties.

Sugden held his most exotic parties at a place known as "Teddy's Hut" which... "was next to the sewage department of Windsor Castle. The Queen had allowed him to build a bungalow on the banks of the Thames, and he enclosed it completely with a very high fence. Every summer Teddy would open the bungalow and everyone would go down... We would take off all our clothes when we got there, and didn't put them back on until we had to go back. People tried to bore holes in the fence to see what was going on..."

Sugden had an:

"unlimited supply of girls... because the actresses and models in London came to him for their abortions and then he'd ask them down to Windsor."

Dr Sugden squared things with the local police and invited one officer to visit. "We asked him in and gave him some whisky... He was lying on the grass watching the naked bodies cavort about when one woman popped her head up and said 'Hello!' It turned out that she was his daughter."[138]

As Dennis Stafford said of the Londoner clientele, "It was very open in those days, you know? They were all at it really."

That was the upper-class version of going AWOL. The lesser classes escaped by adopting an infantilised popular culture.

To sample just the year of Jean Townsend's death, 1954:

---

138 *Honeytrap*, op. cit., pp52-53

The mawkish *Oh Mein Papa* was Number One in the British Hit Parade for nine weeks; BBC radio's *Goon Show* was launched – a bonanza of quaint goofing and funny voices; the 39-year-old comedian, Norman Wisdom, whose comedy was all about dressing and cavorting like a toddler, got a BAFTA award as 1954's Most Promising Newcomer to Film; the biggest box office movie in the UK was *Doctor In The House*, which depicted the National Health Service as a gigantic boarding school; and then there was *The Belles of St Trinian's*, yet another boarding school metaphor for the state of the nation – in this case naughty schoolgirls swigging gin, betting on horses, and flashing knickers.

Jolly japes and desperate laughter. Bottoms up.

Here is a different account of a boarding school of the period, from DC Measham's *Fourteen, autobiography of an Age-Group*:

Geraldine:

I was at boarding school and after lights out you're not allowed to talk if you were caught you'd get the slipper. One night we were telling ghost stories to a weak girl and with torches shone in different colours, water pistols sprayed at her, and there was a terrific din going on. Matron had been in twice already, but this time she came in telling us to put on our slippers and dressing gowns. We were all wondering what was going to happen, when Matron said, "All right, march over to the Head's house."

We had to pass the boys' dormitories to get to the house and slowly all the boys' blinds were up and faces peering through them. The headmaster and mistress were told why we were there and the headmistress who had something against us girls said "cane them." The Headmaster who liked us better than the boys said, "no, give them the slipper."

But as usual Mrs Stevens won and told us to line up, Mr Stevens walked out of the room as the first girl bent over. She got it nine times and came back bawling her eyes out, then Mrs Stevens said, "Give it to them more and harder."

I was trembling when it came to my turn, but I walked up to where matron was standing, bent over, gritted my teeth, shut my eyes and – wham, the first one. I thought if I counted maybe I wouldn't feel it so much. I got sixteen and one or two others got eighteen.

We walked back to the dormitories, some crying, some swearing and some trying not to cry. I was trying not to cry, but as soon as I got into bed I burst into tears. Matron came in with glasses of lemonade and handed them round, saying how sorry she was and that she didn't want to cane us but she couldn't argue with the headmistress.

We all had stripes on our backsides the next day and all the boys kept teasing us. We wanted to write about it to our parents, but were forbidden to.[139]

Disconnection, denial, displacement, flight, detachment, absence, paralysis…

Different ways to leave a place.

---

139 DC Measham, *Fourteen: Autobiography of an Age Group*, 1965, pp 64-65

AMOROUS FIXATION

The 19th century French psychologist, Alfred Binet observes that "for fetishists, the sense perception of the loved object is a source of pleasure superior even to sexual sensation". The fetish is not to be confused, he states, with the stimulation sought by a mere jaded sexual appetite in need of unusual excitants. The true fetishist seeks and prizes a particular species of stimulus because it gives him pleasure "in itself, and for itself." The fetish is not only a means to sexual arousal, but is an end in itself. Amorous fetishism is a form of adoration; its origin lies in a "purely cerebral" need which is incapable of satisfaction in a directly physical way. It is the need, and the pursuit, of beauty.

—Vernon W Grant, "A Fetishistic Theory of Amorous Fixation," *Journal of Social Psychology*, 1949

This book has its roots in frustration with the jobsworths of New Scotland Yard. Anger that these people can get away with it, just as Jean Townsend's murderer got away with it. Jean Townsend was effectively buried twice over. Her ashes interred by her parents in a crematorium wall. Then, her case buried by the Metropolitan Police. Her short life extinguished, local reputation trashed, memory obliterated.

But to take this investigation as far as it could go – further than mere professionalism or indignation, further than the police or anyone else on the case had managed – needed a "hidden" motive. Or not so hidden motif. What does it take to become a detective? More than a calling – more like a talent: for voyeurism.

Curiosity is never pure, never idle. What's more, research – the game of prying, uncovering, disentangling, revealing, has ambivalent and sensual undercurrents.

Which brings me to a key puzzle of the Townsend case: that inexplicably neat pile of discarded underwear...

"Her knickers, suspender belt, panties, stockings and right shoe were by her feet."

Left. From The Teaser, *published in Paris by Olympia Press, 1954 [Edited by Alex Trocchi]. Right.* Elle, *September 13, 1954.*

For most men, women's lingerie is ambiguous: a baffling female technology. In popular entertainment, lingerie departments in stores are where men get lost and humiliated. As a transliteration of nakedness, a surrogate skin, clingy and silky, lingerie's fetishistic textures screen and suggest forbidden visions – a threshold which can also be a point of crisis, of embarrassment and emergency, where you let your slip show or knickers get in a twist: cue defensive laughter. As such, female underwear features in schoolyard jokes and in small talk as innuendo and smut.

This was especially so in my 50s boyhood when elaborately arcane and "technical" looking lingerie attained space-age sophistication – a site of feminine wiles and technical know-how, forbidden or inaccessible – resistant? – to men. Many ads and cartoons featured "scantily clad" women in solipsistic reveries before looking glasses or basking with girlfriends in mutual admiration and esoteric rituals. This lingerie also aped and mocked in its small scale and daintiness, and its sexual charge, the robust and humourless technology of men: suspension bridges, car bodies, rivets and screws.

American girdle ad, 1955

From left. A police "prosecution card" featuring an offensive postcard. This postcard was prosecuted once in 1953, twice in 1954.[140] Another version of the same joke, but this postcard was prosecuted ten times from 1951-1954 in places ranging from Grimsby to Ottery St Mary.[141]

Lingerie in the fifties also stood for a generalised voyeuristic censorship – the fraught and spitefully enforced prurience of that period. The impulse to gaze, thwarted – intensified – by its proscription. All that eye-catching eye-trapping erotic gadgetry: mysterious complication and looped seduction and layers of delicious shame.

---

140 British Cartoon Archive, University of Kent, ref: CP/0960
141 British Cartoon Archive, University of Kent, ref: CP/0673

As conveyed in this psychoanalytical session, published in 1954:

Session 11: Escape Through Sex

Before analysis began, everything connected with a girl seemed wrong and secretive, something that mustn't be seen or discussed. I couldn't understand a man daring to be a lingerie sales clerk. They leave slips, bras, panties, and night gowns right in the window for everyone to see. I'd watch those passing by to see if they blushed as much as I did. Some would stop to look, others pretend not to notice, but no one seemed anxious. I used to long for a chance to gaze at all the pretty things, and imagine how girls looked in them. But didn't want people to notice me doing it.

If I don't run a Chicago bar after college, I'd like to buy a lingerie shop in L.A. or Hollywood. Then I could work with filmy flimsies all day long, and no one could say anything wrong about it, since it was my job.

Marg [sister] would leave her scanties on the chair, which I though was very bold, for someone might steal them while she was at school. I couldn't imagine how Mom and Marg could dare put their intimate things on the clothesline in full view of the whole neighborhood, and I'd try not to look at them. Everyone would know what they wore next to the skin![142]

I may have become an infant voyeur in my mother's favourite art gallery, The Wallace Collection. Here, in her arms, I discovered – with according to her, the excitement I greeted big red London buses – the elegant rococo peek-a-boo of Watteau, Fragonard, and Boucher:

---

142   Harold Kenneth Fink, *Long Journey:* 1954, p31

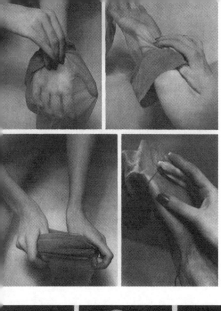

From John Everard's Artist's Model, *1951. Left. Nylon stockings being manipulated prior to being slipped on. Right. A lesson in applying make-up.*

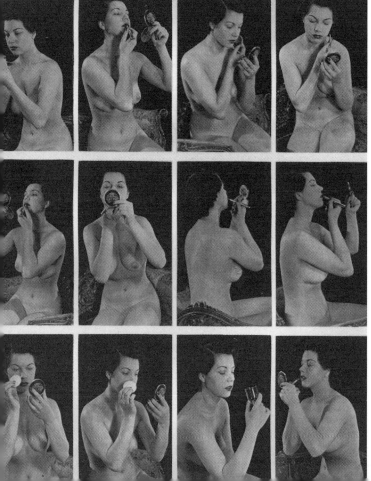

swellings and bunchings of flesh and ruched petticoats, orange storm clouds, swirling and vaporous tit and bum shows. Closeness was a woman on her own, in lingerie or dishabille, and in a reverie, by a pond, before a mirror – if only I was there, in that arcadia, what a place to be!

And as a boy, lucky devil, I often found myself exactly there – snug in my mother's boudoir. For I was regularly privy to her dressing up and making up as she changed out of work clothes, or into a glamorous outfit for a night out. That was our special time together. Moments when I sat on her bed, while she chattered at her dressing table, staring at her face in the mirror – with that hard, cold, abstract scrutiny women have at such times, like examining a lunar surface, or an author proofing a text.

A voyeur, too, notices everything: the smudge of ginger armpit stubble and white curvature of underarms, arranging her hair under a net. Her manipulating female things with uncanny dexterity: pots, jars, tubes, flacons leaking exotic odours, tiny nail scissors curled like lips, luxuriantly swollen cotton wool puffs loaded with sweet smelling powder, lipsticks arranged by shade, mascara pencils, eyebrow tweezers… And how her foundation cream was briskly smeared, whereas perfume was artfully dabbed, and lipstick levered over lips that pouted, then pursed…

All this time, she'd gossip about how Iris had upset the supervisor at work, or the promising letter Papa had received from France about a job. Or about how *Paris Match* had reported that Errol Flynn had shaved off his moustache and settled in South Kensington with his beautiful young wife Patrice Wymore and their white poodle Fubar…

I imagined she must be like this in the company of other women, with Iris maybe, in a powder room, or like the pretty dancers in Westerns chattering secrets as they prepared to can-can their knickers and petticoats to assembled cowboys.

Above all, I witnessed the rituals of lingerie: how knickers are stepped into: tentatively, one foot at a time, and then briskly seesawed until a superfluous flick of the waistband. How an embossed rubber corselet when unhooked and peeled away exuded her warmth and left intricate swirls indented in her freckled skin.

And the business of how nylon stockings are unrolled then stretched round fist and forearm, and then levered between thumb and splayed fingers – with toes pointed and a foot slithered through as the nylon is coaxed and unwrinkled and smoothed: shin… calf… knee… thigh… up to the suspender belt dripping ribbons and clips…

All such intimacy, transposed to a scene of brutality and a public arena like Jean Townsend's wasteland death, was unthinkable – travesty and violation beyond belief.

APPENDIX: "THEY KILLED THIS GIRL WITH AN OVERDOSE OF PILLS AND FROM MAKING HER INTO A HORSE."

At the end of one of our interviews Jackie Cliff told me there was "something else" she wanted to tell me about, something that had troubled her for years. It was about the identity of the serial killer known as Jack the Stripper.

It's a bizarre story, and not linked to the Townsend case, but it was told in good faith. It's also more credible than the theories cooked up by the Met Police. So here goes – some bonus sleuthing...[143]

---

143 There's an interesting contrast to the Met's attitude to the Townsend case file and the numerous "Jack the Stripper" case files.

In 2006, the writer David Seabrook published a book on the Stripper murders.

Jack of Jumps was extremely detailed. It drew heavily on Met Police files. Page after page of Seabrook's book was filled with digests and glosses, and sometimes even apparently unedited transcripts, of police reports and autopsies, police photographs, witness statements and surveillance reports, etc.

This was because Seabrook had been given complete access to all twenty-six police files on these cases – only forty years after the crimes were committed. In his Acknowledgments, Seabrook was grateful to the Met Police for access

Jackie Cliff:

> I want to tell you about something else that happened. This
> was at the beginning of the sixties. That's a bit – a shady part
> of my life...

> I was still living with my gangster [Frank Melito] off the
> Portobello Road.

> There was a hairdressers in the Portobello Road that all the
> girls went to. In those days it was these great big beehives. It
> took ages to make one.

> I had one of course. We all did.

> There'd be a whole row of us in this hairdressers shop, all
> having these things done. They were doing them all day.

---

to the relevant files. He commended "the kindness of the Metropolitan
Police," and especially thanked "Mr Capus [Head of the Records
Department] and his colleagues Andrew Brown and Alan Oakley for their
assistance in making the [MEPO] files available to me."

Seabrook added, "These files are [now] closed to public inspection: David
Capus of the Metropolitan Police Records Management informs me that
they will remain closed for '100 years from the date of the last active minute'
[of the investigation]."

I thought I should talk to David Seabrook. But before I could, he died
suddenly, of a heart attack, aged 48. Instead, I contacted several of his friends
and colleagues. It seemed that Seabrook had indeed enjoyed unrestricted access
to the Stripper files for several months. He regularly went into a police station
to look at them, and made copies.

I was also told he'd been given a file of 80 crime scene photos.

I was shown a copy of this file. The images showed the "comical" ways the
killer had posed the corpses. There were also nauseating close-ups of wounds,
and so on. This file convinced me that Seabrook had indeed enjoyed carte
blanche with Stripper case material.

I quizzed the Met about the difference in policy between Seabrook's access
to the twenty-six Stripper files and the embargo on the one Townsend file.

I contacted David Capus, Head of the Met Police Records Department, who
Seabrook had thanked so warmly.

Capus eventually – reluctantly – claimed that Seabrook's access had been
through a rogue policeman, "a senior member" of "an operational unit within

The man who owned this hairdressers was David. It was called David's.

We used to go there for – it was called, a comb-out. You had to get rid of all the lacquer and then have this comb-out. It was hell really – but we had to have it.

I noticed there were strange things going on down below.

This David used to go downstairs and then come back up looking strange.

There also used to be a girl sitting right by the door.

Every time I went she was there. She had a beehive: hair that had been dyed blonde and then bright red.

---

the Specialist Crime Directorate." Capus denied this was a policy decision. He added, "It is not possible to state why and under what terms this access was permitted as no records were made."

No records?

But it seems that Capus was playing the fool.

For Seabrook's access had, almost certainly, been directly granted and managed by Capus and his team. It's possible that the initial permission had been granted by the unnamed "senior member." But physical access must have been organised and managed – over several weeks, maybe months – by Capus and his team. And if no records had been made about this access, that, we might conclude, was the responsibility of David Capus.

Finally, in relation to the closed Townsend file, Capus asserted that the reason he couldn't discuss any missing material from that file was because "this may prejudice future investigation."

Same old yarn. But in other correspondence (see above) Capus at least seemed to have confirmed there were indeed documents that went missing – or were extracted – from the Townsend file.

Now it's feasible that the Stripper files were undervalued because the police considered the players in these murders – the victims and assorted pimps, punters, pushers, and addicts – as "lowlife." You certainly get the idea – from various sources - that the Met investigated these killings of "toms" [police slang for whores] holding their noses. The privacy of the toms and their associates was not worth protecting.

Whereas, something about the Townsend file was – and is.

She was the thinnest person I'd ever seen in my life. She must have been an anorexic. She was also very, very tall, and she used to look at me with these great big haunted eyes. She used to freak me out. She never smiled, just this deadpan face.

I lived in Lancaster Road, just round the corner from there, so I was always popping in to have my hair done.

I was stripping at the Georgian at that time.

One night, we heard there'd been a murder.

And then another one.

Then there was another one.

And this was the Towpath Murders. About 1962.[144]

The police were everywhere. All over Soho – asking all the girls if they'd seen anything strange to go and tell. Well, I'd never seen anything particularly unusual but then I wasn't really in that league. I was a stripper and working at the Georgian. Once a night at 11 o'clock there was a cabaret. Then I'd go home.

One day I went into the hairdressers to have my thing done and this strange creature – she used to make me feel peculiar – followed me into the street.

She had a big tin of pretzel biscuits – I'll always remember – and she walked along right by me she said, "Hello. Would you like a biscuit?"

---

144 Also called the "Jack the Stripper Murders," and "The Nude Murders".

I said, "No thank you." She opened the box and said, "Oh go on, have a biscuit."

I said alright and started to eat a biscuit. Then she said,

"Can I come back with you? I want to tell you something."

I asked her what she wanted.

I was very nervous of her.

She said, "Please, we can have some biscuits at your place."

And because I was a bit silly really... I suppose I thought, "Poor thing, she needs a friend."

So I took her in and we had the biscuits, and a cup of tea.

Well, the following day, she was waiting outside where I was living.

She said "Can I come in?" and I asked what was the matter.

She said, "I've got to talk to somebody. I've got to."

I had loads of drinks in there, and I poured her a great big whisky, and she drank it. She looked awful. She looked like a... I can't explain it, really – she was so thin – a living skeleton.

And she said to me "I've got to tell somebody. We did it. We did it."

So I asked what it was that she'd done, and she said, "We did them murders."

I asked if it was the Towpath Murders, and she said, "Yes."

I asked her to tell me what she'd done - my heart was pounding and I thought maybe my boyfriend would be back soon and I had to get her out, quick.

Maybe she was a joker – I didn't know.

Anyway, she sat there – I can see her now – and said, "My boyfriend, he sells pills."

387

I said, "Where's your boyfriend?"

"He works in the garage round the back of the hairdressers.

"I get the girls and he gets the pills, and we sell them where we live. They come back to our home."

"He doesn't like thin women, he likes plump ones. So we give them free pills so he can have a go with the fat ones."

And then - I'll never forget this: she pulled up her clothes and she didn't have any breasts at all. She was totally emaciated. She said,

"Look at me. Look. You look at me – what would you do? I love him so much, I'd do anything to keep him. And I get him these girls."

"But once," she said, "We were doing this thing with one of them and he was riding her like a horse."

And it was an accident. They killed this girl with an overdose of pills and from making her into a horse.

And they put her onto the top shelf of this wardrobe, then moved her onto this big mantelpiece – so it must have been one of those big old London houses – and laid her there.

Then they put her in the boot of a car, and they dumped her.

She said, "Then we wanted to do it again.

"Well, he did, anyway."

And they kept doing it. They couldn't stop it.

She said, "So then we had to dump the bodies but it's alright because he works in a garage and he could always get a car out."

And she said, "I want him to love me all the time."

I asked her what she was going to do – what would happen.

And she said she didn't know.

Then she was gone.

Well, when my gangster [Frank Melito] came back I told him.

He said. "Don't you ever, ever mention that again. Don't you mention a word of it, because you'll get into trouble."

FV: What was her name?

This woman was called Tina Barrington. Her boyfriend, the killer, he was also called Barrington. That was his surname, but everyone just called him Barrington. She took his surname as hers. Barrington... I never found out his other name.

He was black.

I couldn't keep this to myself. I was so worried about it.

So I made a phone call, not saying who I was, and I said about the hairdressers shop. I didn't want them to think it was me, or for her to know it was me.

I did this anonymous sort of thing.

The next day, the place was raided and what they found downstairs was a torture chamber place. Some of the girls having their beehives done were using it.

As to this Tina Barrington, after the raid I never saw her again. Ever.

And I always still think it was true. They never found who did it. A man committed suicide in a factory about it. They said it was maybe him and dropped the case.

But I think it was just the girlfriend and this guy Barrington. Nobody else was involved. Because she said he had to have a plump woman – he liked them plump.

And all she was – was ribs.

I felt very sorry for her. And I can never, ever forget her bright red hair. Oh, and her face was all pitted: acne and pock marks.

And she looked like a drug addict.

How plausible was Jackie's Stripper story?

The hairdressers, Dave's, was at 339 Portobello Road. The owner was an Eastender, David Monjack. He ran the shop for 44 years, commuting from Bishopsgate – and later, from Golders Green. He died in 1995, aged 78.

The ground floor of Dave's was for men. The first floor was a ladies' salon, with a separate street entrance. At one point this was called "Vicky's Salon." It was run by different women, including, occasionally, Monjack's wife. Monjack, too, sometimes dressed the women's hair.

From left. Dave's hairdressers, 339 Portobello Road, around the time of the Stripper murders. The building in 2009.

In an interview, David Monjack's daughter told me she was unsure why her father chose to be a barber. The profession hadn't been in his family. Nor did she know why he decided to trade in the Portobello Road – he lived the other side of London, some 10 miles east.

She said he thought Portobello a "posh" area, so business might be good.

But it was hardly posh immediately post-war, when he set up there.

She also said – unprompted – "I think there were lots of gangsters in the area – maybe I shouldn't be recording that... I think there was – I don't know how you'd put it – a lot of mischief at the time."

Adding, "He didn't get involved – my mother was very much of a coward – but I think there was quite a lot going on in the area."

Asked about the male clients, she mentioned, "a lot of these wide boys," qualifying that "wide boys" was a polite description.

"I know there was a lot of things going on."

Monjack also drank with "the guys" at a nearby pub.

Monjack looks an unlikely brothel keeper. Pictures show a bespectacled man in a white coat. His daughter says he was homely, keen on Wimbledon, and an amateur tennis player.

So what of the supposed below-stairs brothel?

Jackie mentioned a downstairs space from which Monjack would emerge, "looking strange."

That suggests a basement. But there never was a basement to the shop.

However, Monjack's premises backed onto the secluded Golborne Mews.

In this mews, behind Monjack's salon, was a brick-built extension. It was accessible from the downstairs salon through a door set in the back wall. Another door from this extension gave onto the mews.

At the back of the upstairs ladies' salon was a door onto a terrace overlooking the mews. This terrace was the roof of the extension.

The extension was an enclosed chamber, about a third the size of the downstairs salon. It was partly separated from the salon by a small yard. It was solidly made, with 9-inch thick brick walls.

Could this mews extension, rather than a basement, have been a "torture chamber"?

Planning applications[145] suggest that, having been connected to the ground floor of Dave's, the extension was "blocked off" around 1980. The extension was then bought by the occupants of 6 Golborne Mews, demolished, and converted into a large double garage in 1984.

According to a local greengrocer, in 1964 – the year of the Stripper murders – the dwellings in Golborne Mews were mostly used for storage. So – no potentially nosy neighbours. The mews became gentrified from the seventies, after the junkie rock guitarist, Paul Kossoff, moved in. Today, the mews is a quaint cobblestoned reservation, invisible from the Portobello Road, and occupied by media types.

When I went there in 2009, the ground floor of Dave's hairdressers had become a chic cafe. The first floor was now an apartment.

A few old timers recalled David Monjack. They said his shop was a local meeting place – as you'd expect from a hairdressers. They lamented a vanished village atmosphere, one muttering about "coloureds." They became guarded when I asked about villains. One Asian couple who ran a nearby grocery refused to talk to me. No-one recalled a police raid.

---

145 Lodged at the Royal Borough of Kensington and Chelsea Planning Department.

AS EXISTING

Top. The only image of the original structure, from a 1984 planning application, shows a door exiting onto the mews under a high tessellated balustrade concealing the terrace above. Bottom. Two views of the mews in 2009, showing the wall-length white door of the 1984 garage, topped by the now foliaged terrace.

Everything else Jackie had told me concerning her life and about the Townsend case had proved correct. I was able to corroborate people, times and dates from other sources. So I believed she'd told me her Stripper story in good faith.

I wrote to her for clarification about Dave's. She replied that, "after the raid" Monjack sold his shop to a man called George, a developer who "had properties turned into bedsits."

Jackie moved into one in the Oval: "a hovel."

Jackie concluded, "David was a workaholic. He was a Jewish boy and did wonders with the beehive comb-outs. He was good looking and fun... Women of the night came to Dave's for comb-outs especially from the Bayswater Road. Tina sat in a chair right by the window all day, every day."

———————

The Stripper investigation had been extensively reported. I was also able to indirectly access the police files through David Seabrook's promiscuous citing of them in *Jack of Jumps*. I cross referenced these accounts with what Jackie had said.

The alleged killer, who Jackie referred to as Barrington, had, she said, worked in a garage:

> So then [reporting Tina's conversation] we had to dump the bodies but it's alright because he works in a garage and he could always get a car out.

And, "He works in the garage round the back of the hairdressers."

During the investigation, the police were looking out for a garage. After analysing microscopic globules of paint on the victims' corpses, forensics had decided they'd likely been stored in – or passed through – a place where cars were spray-painted. It was also thought that maybe the killer was a car mechanic.

But where was Barrington's garage?

From Jackie's description, it had to be in nearby Chesterton Road.

In the early 1960s there were two car hire companies in Chesterton Road, Dorfman Hire, at number 2a, and Townman Hire, at number 20. Neither was a garage.

But by the junction of Chesterton Road and Ladbroke Grove I noticed a small stand-alone lock-up garage and workshop, Kleencars.

Among other services, Kleencars today advertises car repairs, rust repairs, and spray painting. Though the frontage is small, Google Earth shows an ample footprint with an open area behind.

No one locally recalled the street in the early sixties. The electoral registers showed a rapid turnover of residents. "Barrington" also drew a blank. Nor could I find property records for the lock-up.

But it's unlikely this lock-up ever served any other function. It's also likely (from aerial photos and ordnance survey maps) that it's been there since at least the early sixties.

It looks like another lock-up garage in Hammersmith, Wimpey Autos, which the police turned over in connection with the Stripper case.

Suspect garage in the Stripper enquiry, 1a Barb Mews, Hammersmith.

The lock-up garage around the corner from Dave's salon.

As well as minute particles of paint, "...fragments of coal, coke dust, coal" dust had been detected on the victims' bodies.

Jackie: "And they... moved her onto this big mantelpiece."

When I queried the mantelpiece Jackie said,

> I can remember [Tina Barrington] saying they took the [first] body from the top of the wardrobe or in the wardrobe – [then] they put it on the mantelpiece – so it must have been one of those big old London houses – and they left it on there till they could dispose of it.

Such Victorian mantelpiece shelves could be around 80 inches – over 6 feet long – and quite deep enough for a body.

Mantelpiece: coal dust?

Now consider how these women were killed.

Graphic descriptions (lifted from the police files) are in Seabrook's *Jack of Jumps.*

Common features included strangulation, probably with some sort of "ligature."

"Asphyxia due to pressure on the neck."

"Asphyxia due to pressure on the face and neck."

"Asphyxia due to strangulation."

It seemed that some of the victims had attempted to remove this "ligature" while it was suffocating them.

This caused additional bruising around the neck.

Another feature of these killings was that teeth were removed from some victims.

From *Jack of Jumps*:

> Four of Helen Barthelemy's [Victim number 3] teeth had been removed. Not knocked out, since there was no bruising of her lips or gums or injury to her tongue. Not extracted by dental means, since no dentist could be traced who had treated her...
>
> *Removed.* [Seabrook's emphasis]

How were the teeth removed?

Inspector John Du Rose, who was in charge of the case, recorded in his memoir, *Murder Was my Business*, 1974, "...strangely enough, there was no indication that the teeth had been dislodged by a blow."

Seabrook records about Margaret McGowan, aka Frances Brown [Victim number 7]: "Her lower jaw was missing three teeth, yet how and when they disappeared could not be determined."

And Bridget O'Hara [Victim number 8]: "She had a dental plate for six teeth that were missing from her upper jaw." A witness is quoted:

"She always wore her dentures even when in bed and only took them out to clean them." When her body was found, "her dental plate was missing."

It's been suggested the killer had a tooth fetish, or was collecting trophies. A common crime thriller scenario. That would suggest the teeth were deliberately, ritualistically, extracted.

However...

Jackie Cliff, citing Tina Barrington:

> We were doing this thing with one of them and he was riding her like a horse.

Jackie reiterated:

> They killed this girl with an overdose of pills and from making her into a horse.

A horse?

More information wasn't available. In the heat of Tina's confession it's understandable Jackie wouldn't have been asking for details.

But the "horse riding" references suggest a sexual ritual.

Such a ritual might be accompanied by appropriate "gear."

Was the "rider" using some sort of bridle on these women?

Something around their throats like a throat latch [a "ligature"] that could be tightened? Something at the same time clamped around their mouths like a bit, that might have loosened and forced teeth from sockets – and caused abrasions and bruises, in the way described?

Inspector Du Rose noted that, "Some [of the victims] had injuries and very slight bruising as though pressure had been directed in the region of the nose and mouth."

A bridle improvised by the killer? Or from a fetish outlet? (There were several such outlets in London at the time.) Maybe a version of the "scolds' bridles" used in medieval times to silence nagging wives?

If that seems far-fetched, consider the police theories.

Du Rose was convinced he'd identified the murderer, who then committed suicide. The Inspector's memoir states, "Because [the murderer] was never arrested, or stood trial, he must be considered innocent and will therefore never be named."

Du Rose cited scruples about the shock such a revelation would cause "the killer's wife and relatives."

Seabrook was less squeamish. In *Jack of Jumps*, he tells us this suspect was "a 45-year-old Scot named Mungo Ireland of 132 Tildesly Road, Putney."

Seabrook also pointed out – citing another policeman who worked on the case – who was fuming over Du Rose's alleged incompetence – that there was only circumstantial evidence linking Mungo Ireland to the Stripper murders.

Indeed, he had a solid alibi for at least one of the killings.

Even more outlandishly, the police at the time also theorised that the killer was suffocating his victims with his penis while having oral sex.

Seabrook is incredulous, and gleefully recounts that concerning the "ligature" marks on the victims,

> ...the means of pressure, [the police] concluded, was not a ligature, but rather the killer's penis. That's right, the penis itself was the killer, choking these women as they fellated this man. In his investigating officer's report William Baldock

states that the marks on their faces seemed consistent with "the slight bruising such as would be caused by the face being pressed, from the back of the head, into a man's lap or on his knees", and this obstruction prevented them from reaching the obstruction in their throats.

Furthermore,

According to Baldock, lack of teeth, allied to the difficulties experienced in manipulating the jaw "when the mouth or throat is fully occupied", would have prevented the victims from biting the murder weapon.

Du Rose put it more delicately in his memoirs:

[the killer] knew that these women set no limits to the sexual acts in which they would allow their clients to indulge. In obtaining satisfaction he became utterly frenzied and at the moment of his orgasm, the girls died.[146]

---

146 Du Rose's prose is as clunky as his detection:
It would have been easy to assume that the man we were hunting was a man carrying out a personal vendetta against prostitutes because he had caught [a venereal] disease. That was never my view. Early in the inquiry I became convinced that the killer was a man in his forties with extremely strong sexual urges which, perhaps because of his age, were not easily satisfied normally. It was probably this physical difficulty that took him away from his wife and into the twilight world of the prostitutes.
The Inspector continues:
One could postulate a theory that had this man been caught after the death of the first prostitute, and the circumstances of the sexual act had been revealed in court, the jury might have brought in a verdict of manslaughter or even accidental death. But when he continued to indulge in his particular perversion, well knowing that

Finally, what about the mysterious Barrington?

There is an intriguing passage in Seabrook's book. He reports that, at one point, a black man came under suspicion:

> He was Jamaican and his address, 7 Craven Hill Gardens, matched that of Von Barrington Adams, a Jamaican man in his early twenties. Registered unemployed,[147] he worked in the evenings as a disk jockey at jazz clubs, and for a few months during the winter of 1963/64 he conducted a casual affair with Helen Barthelemy [one of the victims].[148]

Seabrook records that:

> Barthelemy's ex-boyfriend Von Barrington Adams underwent several interrogations. He was in bad health at the time, still suffering the effects of a car crash in March, when his white Mini went into an obelisk. Barthelemy and three other passengers all escaped pretty much unharmed, but Adams, who was driving, remained in hospital with a fractured skull and other serious injuries until 16 April. He hadn't driven since the accident and police confirmed that his vehicle was a write-off by visiting a garage to inspect it on a dump.[149]

---

the girl concerned would die, then he must have recognised that he was fulfilling himself as a murderer. [John Du Rose, *Murder Was my Business*, 1974, pp102-103]

And so on. Curiously, the copy of Du Roses's autobiography in the British Library has been defaced. The only defaced book I've found in over 50 years using that library. And only the "Jack the Stripper" chapter is damaged. One of the victim's faces, Hannah Tailford, is angrily scrawled with blue biro. An image of the Inspector has its eyes scribbled out with red biro. The marks seem childish. But not arbitrary. A commentary on Du Rose's divinations?

147 It would have been simple in those days to claim unemployment benefit while working in a garage.

148 Seabrook, op. cit., pp189-190

149 Seabrook, ibid., p195. Von Barrington Adams is now deceased.

It was also said that Adams had been "at home with his white girlfriend" on three dates crucial to the Stripper killings.

But note that there was apparently only Von Barrington Adams' and his (unnamed) white girlfriend's word to say he hadn't driven since his crash. Or that he was at home on those dates. And while his own car was a write off, did he have access to other cars?

———

Jack of Jumps also records that in January, 1964 a certain "L. Piggott, was treated for Gonorrhoea at St Mary's Hospital, Paddington."

The police discovered that "L. Piggott" was a pseudonym for Von Barrington Adams.

A wacky sense of humour?

Lester Piggott was the most celebrated jockey of the day.

ACKNOWLEDGMENTS AND SOURCES

Thanks first to all my interviewees, especially Reg Hargrave, Amelia Windsor (AKA Jackie Cliff), Liz Lockyer (AKA Liz Baron), Anne Graham, Dennis Stafford, and "Ray" (pseudonymous ex-policeman). Reg Hargrave generously made his research on the Townsend case available. His efforts in demanding an Information Tribunal review supplied chinks of light from the hearing. As well as giving three interviews, Amelia Windsor provided written notes. (Amelia's boyfriend, Ted, added background). Then Frederic Mullally, Gwyn Robyns, and Mollie Thurston. Mullally made his papers, scrapbooks and address book available. He also drew "kinship" diagrams of London clubland, explaining links between clubs, club proprietors, pub landlords, and their clientele. Gwyn Robyns had been even better "connected" in the 1950s than Mullally, and over a vegetarian lunch and then tea with carrot cake in her Oxfordshire cottage, confided indiscretions about the great and good, from the Churchills to Mountbattens. Anne Graham generously donated her large stash of Whittaker related papers and art works.

Many others contributed interviews and source materials for this book.

For Ruislip in the fifties and contemporary recollections of the Townsend case, thanks to Bryan East, "Triton," Catherine Wenger nee Erritty (re Eileen Erritty), Bill Gurney, Sheila Kingdon (formerly Wright nee Tustain), Peter Beckwith, Pat Ainsworth, "Eveyln," Fred Stevenson, Allan Amott. For Jean Townsend and June Sweetzer at

Ealing Art School, special thanks to Joyce Hill, nee Joyce Nunn. For additional information: Sylvia W, Michael Searle, John Daniel, Derek Hunt, Winifred Speers, Sean Kelly. For Bermans: Margaret Brice (Pankhurst), Tessa Nelson, Ellie Baker. For the South Ruislip USAF Base: Dick Wilson, Mary Lutz, Janice Zabel, John McDaniel, Daphne J Gilbertson.

Other primary material came from June Sweetzer, AP Barel, John Baghurst, Jim Thurston, Kay Ward, Gay Search, Rupert Goalen (for Barbara Goalen), Yahya El-Droubie (for Pam Green and the cheesecake trade), Jenniffer Tish (for David Monjack), Elaine Gafney, and Anon (a bookie who ran his business in the fifties from the Londoner premises but declined to go on record).

For additional information on Michael Whittaker my thanks to his godson, Alistair Cameron, his former business partner, Michael Guest, and former fashion model Juanita Stickney. For Elena Shayne (source of the Carlodalatri story), her daughter, Louise Baghurst. Pablo Carlodalatri on the Carlodalatri clan and his uncle, Count Francesco (Frank) Carlodalatri. For the Dickinson angle, Richard Dickinson and John Butterwick obliged with family memoirs. For Vasco Lazzolo, thanks to Clement Von Franckenstein and anonymous sources. Also helpful for Lazzolo were David Arrigo, Jane Howe and, especially, John Hoare. Special thanks to Sarah Young, who helped me extend my Lazzolo research to Malta.

Additional sleuthing was undertaken by Simon Fluendy, Ron Delves, Anthony Frewin, and Debby Jones. Filippa Harrington-Griffin was my research assistant for the Whittaker research. Stephen Dorril provided valuable contacts and advice (suggesting I advertise for information in *The Police Pensioner* – I'd never have thought of that). I've noted in the text some of the academics consulted. Informal discussion and additional context was supplied by, among others, Paul Tickell, Malcolm McLeod, Christopher Breward, Adrian Woodhouse, Duncan Campbell, Andrew Orlowski, Chris Horrocks, Laurence Gane, Alex Seago, Nigel Pittam, Clive Soley, Nick Hurd MP, and Mark Field MP.

Among my ex-police sources, I'd like to thank informants who contributed off the record, as well as ex-Detective Chief Superintendent Rex Lewis, ex-Detective Constable James Shortt, and Colin Searle. Thanks, too, to the editors of *The Police Pensioner* and the Ex-CID Officer's Association.

Bob Dickinson mined material within the BBC archive. Gloria Fulvia transcribed interviews with speed and precision.

London guides, commercial, trade and street directories, showbiz directories and *What's On in London* were useful. The research was speeded by the Times Online Archive, the Guardian and Observer Historical Archive, UK Press Online, British Newspaper Archive, LexisNexis, and UK Newstand, the online The Stage Archive, online Who's Who and Who Was Who, Dictionary of National Biography, and Burke's Peerage (supplemented by printed biographical sources in the British Library).

Other important databases were Ancestry.co.uk, Findmypast.co.uk, UK INFO and UK INFO-POWER 2000, 2003, CD ROM people-finders, Companies House Webcheck, Land Registry Property Search, and the now defunct friendsreunited.co.uk.

Online forums gave me leads, especially, E-Goat: the Unofficial RAF Rumour Network, http://pub1.bravenet.com/forum (Third Air Force HQ South Ruislip), Ruislip Online, and Gay News. Facebook too, was useful for contacts – before it got privacy minded.

I consulted private archives on Michael Whittaker, Vasco Lazzolo, and Pam Green.

Also consulted were The National Archive at Kew (TNA), US National Archives (NARA), Colindale Newspaper Library, Victoria & Albert Museum (includes the Theatre and Performance collections, initially lodged at the Theatre Museum), London Metropolitan Archives, City of Westminster Archives Centre, Hillingdon Local Studies Archive, Kensington Local Studies and Archive, London School of Economics (Wigg Papers), British Airways Heritage Collection, the British Red

Cross Museum and Archives, Uxbridge Gazette, and the valuable Hans Tasiemka Archive.

The most useful general libraries were the British Library, Kingston University library (online resources), the libraries at Senate House, University College, LSE, and the BFI, Westminster Reference Library, and University of the Arts, London, Library (Chelsea & Central St Martins).

I owe a debt to biographies and autobiographies plundered of people both central and peripheral to the Townsend case. Works directly used or quoted are cited in the main text or notes. Other useful works were:

For showbiz: Barbara Windsor, *All of Me*, 2000; Danny La Rue, *From Drags to Riches*,1987; Leslie Phillips, *Hello*, 2006; Damon Wise, *Come by Sunday: The Fabulous, Ruined Life of Diana Dors*, 1999; Joan Flory & Damian Walne, *Diana Dors*, 1987; Jonny Whiteside, *Cry. The Johnnie Ray Story*, 1994; Robert Hofler, *The Man Who Invented Rock Hudson*, 2005. For the police: Martin Short, *Lundy*, 1991; Barry Cox, John Shirley, Martin Short, *The Fall of Scotland Yard*, 1977. For crooks: Wensley Clarkson, *Hit 'Em Hard, Jack Spot, King of the Underworld*, 2002; Michael Connor, *The Soho Don: Gangland's Greatest Untold Story* [Billy Howard], 2003; (and, of course Dennis Stafford, *Fun-Loving Criminal*, see main text). For the sex trade: Paul Willetts, *Members Only: The Life and Times of Paul Raymond*, 2010; Peter Henderson, *A Picture of Loveliness. George Harrison Marks Biography*, 2009 [privately printed]; Pamela Green, *Never Knowingly Overdressed*, nd [unpublished autobiography – see notes in main text]. Then the photographers: Tony Armstrong-Jones and Antony Beauchamp; Baron, [Nahum], *Baron*, 1956 [posthumously published autobiography]; Horace Roye, *Nude Ego*, 1956; Louise Baring, *Norman Parkinson: A Very British Glamour*, 2009; Fredric Woodbridge Wilson, *The Theatrical World of Angus McBean*, 2009; Adrian Woodhouse, *Angus McBean: Facemaker*, 2006. Artists: John Moynihan, *Restless Lives: the Bohemian World of Rodrigo and Elinor Moynihan*, 2002 [depiction of two of Jackie Cliff's patrons and their milieu. John Moynihan was the Moynihans' son and close friend of Jackie's boyfriend, Keith Critchlow]. Designers: Norman Hartnell, *Silver and Gold*, 1955; Charles Castle, *Oliver Messel: A Biography*, 1986. Various short biographies and folders from V&A Library and Archives, and the National Portrait Gallery, were useful for lesser known figures like John Everard, Walter Bird, Ronald Cobb, David Hicks, Pietro Annigoni, Feliks Topolski, John Ward, Norman Hepple.

My thanks for permission to reproduce images from sources cited in the captions. Additional images courtesy of Reg Hargrave, Liz Lockyer, Amelia Windsor, Anne Graham (Whittaker Archive), Frederic Mullally, Molly Thurston, Jennifer Tish, Yahya El- Droubie (Pam Green Archive), Anon (Lazzolo Archive), Andre Barel.

Finally, special thanks to my literary agent, Leslie Gardner of Artellus Ltd, for unfailing support and encouragement, and much shrewd advice.

ADDITIONAL BIBLIOGRAPHY

A partly annotated list of useful contextual sources – most not previously cited.

Armitage, John, Britannica *Book of the Year*. (Events of 1954), 1955 [Compendious official – imperious and imperial – version of that year – alphabetical.]

Biskind, Peter, *Seeing Is Believing: How Hollywood Taught Us to Stop Worrying and Love the Fifties*, 2001

Bond, Henry, *Lacan at the Scene*, 2009 [How to milk crime scene photos.]

Botham, Noel, *Margaret: The Last Real Princess*, 2002

Bowen, David, *Body of Evidence*, 2003

Bowlt, Eileen M, *Around Ruislip*, 2007 [The best of many such guides and local histories.]

Bronfen, Elisabeth, *Over Her Dead Body: Death, Femininity and the Aesthetic*, 1992

Campbell, Duncan, *Unsinkable Aircraft Carrier. American Military Power in Britain*, 1986

Castle, Charles, *Model Girl*, 1977

Cross, Tom, *Artists and Bohemians*, 1992 [Chelsea Arts Ball and much else about the Chelsea arts scene.]

Freeman, Iris, *Lord Denning: A Life*, 1993

Duke, Simon, *US Defence Bases in the UK*, 1985

Eisler, Benita, *Private Lives. Men and Women of the Fifties*, 1986

Esquire, *Etiquette. A guide to Business, Sports and Social Etiquette by the Editors of Esquire Magazine*, 1954 [Makes a companion to Ryan, below.]

Farson, Daniel, *Soho in the Fifties*, 1987

Furneaux, Rupert, *Famous Criminal Cases* [of 1954], 1955

Garland, Rodney, *The Heart in Exile*, 1961 [Atmospheric fiction depicting the gay London club scene in the fifties. Rodney Garland was the pseudonym of Hungarian émigré Adam Martin de Hedegus. His book became an underground best-seller in the UK and USA.]

Goodman, Jonathan and Pringle, Patrick, *The Trial of Ruth Ellis*, 1974

Goodman, Jonathan, (Ed), *The Art of Murder*, 1990. [Chapter on the 1954 William Hepper case.]

Gorer, Geoffrey, *Exploring English Character*, 1955 [One of the best sources for the mindset of the British 1950s.]

Hanson, Michele, *What the Grown-Ups Were Doing*, 2012 [Memoir of Ruislip in the 1950s.]

Holland, Steve, *The Mushroom Jungle*, 1993 [Post-war pulp fiction.]

Holland, Steve, *The Trials of Hank Janson*, 2004

Hornsey, Richard, *The Spiv and the Architect*, 2010 [Queer Studies explorations of post-war London.]

Hudson, Roger, and Blundell, Joe, *Covent Garden, Trafalgar Square and the Strand*, 1996

Hutchins, Chris, and Midgley, Dominic, *Goldsmith. Money, Women and Power*, 1998

Irving, Clive, *Scandal '63: A Study of the Profumo Affair*, 1963

Ivanov, Yevgeny, *The Naked Spy*, 1992

Keeler, Christine, *The Truth at Last* 2001.

Knightly, Phillip, and Kennedy, Caroline, *An Affair of State: The Profumo Case and the Framing of Stephen Ward*, 1987

Kynaston, David, *A World to Build. Austerity Britain 1945-48* [Precursor to his other overviews of the 1950s discussed in the text.]

Lake, Frances, *Daily Mail Ideal Home Book, 1953-54*, 1954 [Everyday dreams of homely modernity.]

Mander, Raymond, & Mitchenson, Joe, *Revue*, 1971 [The world of Michael Whittaker's Auntie Mabel.]

Marling, Karal Ann, *As Seen on TV: Visual Culture of Everyday Life in the 1950s*, 1996

Measham, DC, *Fourteen: Autobiography of an Age Group*, 1965 [Also referenced in the text – a unique source: children writing in their own terms about their experiences in the 1950s. The tone is different to adult memoirs. Childhood and schooldays are vital to understanding British culture. Brits are obsessed with schooldays and schools – Eton College or Hogwarts School of Witchcraft and Wizardry.]

Mort, Frank, *Capital Affairs. London and the Making of the Permissive Society*, 2010. [Frank has a heavy hand but some of his stories are good.]

Morton, James, *A Calendar of Killing*, 1997 [Which started the rift between Reg Hargrave and June Sweetzer. "It came to a head after I left a copy of the book, *A Calendar of Killing*, by James Morton (1997) – by accident [?] – at her mother's [Mrs Sweetzer's] house. I'd put a marker in the page about Jean Townsend's case. Later on, I couldn't find the damn thing, and had no idea what I'd done with it. And it wasn't until a year later when June came over again and – rather acidly – said to me, "Oh, I think this is yours..."]

Parker, Eileen, *Step Aside for Royalty*, 1982

"Petronius," *London Unexpurgated*, 1969

Pressley, Alison, *The Best of Times, Growing up in Britain in the 1950s*, 1999. [A scrapbook with snippets of several caustic memories belying the cute images.]

Raymond, Derek, *The Crust on Its Uppers*, 1962 [Novel, tagline: "Chelsea bohemia meets the underworld."]

Richardson, John, *Covent Garden Past*, 1995

Richardson, Nigel, *Dog Days in Soho*, 2000

Richardson, Paul, (Ed), T*he 1950s. Britain in Pictures*, 2008 [Clean-cut clichés, reminiscent of *Picture Post*.]

Reynolds, David, *Rich Relations. The American Occupation of Britain, 1942-1945*, 1995

Ryan, Mildred Graves, and Phillips, Velma, *Clothes For You*, 1954 [Meticulous account of style and etiquette for women.]

Shellard, Dominic, *British Theatre in the 1950s*, 2000

Sprengler, Christine Anne, *Screening Nostalgia: The American Fifties in British Visual Culture*, PhD (University of London), 2004

Thompson, Douglas, *The Hustlers*, 2007

Thumim, Janet (Ed), *Small Screens, Big Ideas. Television in the 1950's*, 2002

Thurlow, David, *Profumo. The Hate Factor*, 1992

Underwood, Peter, *Danny La Rue. Life's a Drag*, 1975 [Supplements LaRue's autobiography – cited in the text – good detail on Bermans, pp128-133.]

Willetts, Paul, *North Soho 999*, 2007

INDEX

Italic numbers are for appearances in images or captions. Numbers with an n after them are for references in footnotes.

Strange Attractor Press 2019